19.45

||||| IIII DØ850747

The Illness Narratives

THE
ILLNESS
NARRATIVES

Suffering, Healing, and
the Human Condition

ARTHUR KLEINMAN, M.D.

Basic Books, Inc., Publishers

NEW YORK

Library of Congress Cataloging-in-Publication Data

Kleinman, Arthur. m , 1941–
  The illness narratives.

  Bibliography: p. 269.
  Includes index.
  1. Chronic diseases—Psychological aspects. I. Title.
[DNLM: 1. Chronic Disease—psychology. 2. Chronic
Disease—therapy. WT 500 K64i]
RC108.K57 1988   616′.001′9   87–47772
ISBN 0–465–03202–8

To those who suffer chronic illness; to those who share the experience of disability as members of the family and social circle; and to the professionals who care for them.

The solid meaning of life is always the same eternal thing—the marriage, namely of some unhabitual ideal, however special, with some fidelity, courage and endurance, with some man's or woman's pains.

—WILLIAM JAMES
Talks to Teachers

Mortality, I take it, is the central fact of practical existence; death is the central fact of life.

—MICHAEL OAKESHOTT
Experience and Its Modes

If you miss being understood by laymen, and fail to put your hearers in this condition, you will miss reality.

—HIPPOCRATES
Ancient Medicine

Contents

Preface

During the early 1960s, in my second and third years at medical school, I encountered several patients whose powerful experiences of illness, at either pole of the course of life, fixed my interest on the intimate and manifold ways by which illness comes to affect our lives.

The first patient was a pathetic seven-year-old girl who had been badly burned over most of her body. She had to undergo a daily ordeal of a whirlpool bath during which the burnt flesh was tweez-ered away from her raw, open wounds. This experience was horri-bly painful to her. She screamed and moaned and begged the medi-cal team, whose efforts she stubbornly fought off, not to hurt her anymore. My job as a neophyte clinical student was to hold her uninjured hand, as much to reassure and calm her as to enable the surgical resident to quickly pull away the dead, infected tissue in the pool of swirling water, which rapidly turned pinkish, then bloody red. Clumsily, with a beginner's uncertainty of how to proceed, I tried to distract this little patient from her traumatic daily confron-tation with terrible pain. I tried talking to her about her home, her family, her school—almost anything that might draw her vigilant attention away from her suffering. I could barely tolerate the daily horror: her screams, dead tissue floating in the blood-stained water, the peeling flesh, the oozing wounds, the battles over cleaning and bandaging. Then one day, I made contact. At wit's end, angered at my own ignorance and impotence, uncertain what to do besides clutching the small hand, and in despair over her unrelenting an-guish, I found myself asking her to tell me how she tolerated it, what the feeling was like of being so badly burned and having to experience the awful surgical ritual, day after day after day. She stopped, quite surprised, and looked at me from a face so disfigured it was difficult to read the expression; then, in terms direct and simple, she told me. While she spoke, she grasped my hand harder and neither screamed nor fought off the surgeon or the nurse. Each day from then on, her trust established, she tried to give me a feeling of what she was experiencing. By the time my training took me off this rehabilitation unit, the little burned patient seemed noticeably better able to tolerate the debridement. But whatever effect I had had on her, her effect on me was greater. She taught me a grand lesson in patient care: that it is possible to talk with patients, even those who are most distressed, about the actual experience of illness, and that witnessing and helping to order that experience can be of therapeutic value.

The other memorable patient from my medical school days was an elderly woman who suffered chronic cardiovascular effects of the syphilis she had acquired from a serviceman in World War I. I saw her as an outpatient. Through months of conversations she gave me a poignant sense of what it was like to bear the stigma of syphilis; she showed me how it affected her relations with her family and the men she met, leaving her shunned and isolated. Each week she would detail for me the tragic personal experiences that had resulted from her diagnosis years before. Over time I realized that there were two sets of long-term problems: the insidious medical complications of the course of her chronic syphilis and the life trajectory that her illness had marked and inexorably shaped. I recognized, furthermore, that my medical training systematically educated me about the former but tended to discount and in certain ways even blind me to the latter. This patient, like her much younger counterpart, edified me about the difference between the patient's experience of illness and the doctor's attention to disease—a key distinction I will develop in the course of this book.

Over the past two decades, my interest in how chronic illness is lived and responded to by real people has led me to conduct clinical and ethnographic studies of the experience of illness among patients in China and North America. These studies have been published in technical articles and in books written for an audience of academic specialists. My clinical work, again centered on the psychological and social aspects of chronic medical illness, also has been described for a fairly narrow professional readership. My aim in this book is altogether different. I write here to explain to patients, their families, and their practitioners what I have learned from a career passionately devoted to this interest. I write because I wish to popularize a technical literature that would be of great practical value for those who must live with, make sense of, and care for chronic illness. Indeed, I will argue that the study of the experience of illness has something fundamental to teach each of us about the human condition, with its universal suffering and death.

Nothing so concentrates experience and clarifies the central conditions of living as serious illness. The study of the process by which meaning is created in illness brings us into the everyday reality of individuals like ourselves, who must deal with the exigent life circumstances created by suffering, disability, difficult loss, and the threat of death. Yes, chronic illness teaches us about death; the process of mourning for losses is as central to growing old as it is to healing. Illness narratives edify us about how life problems are created, controlled, made meaningful. They also tell us about the way cultural values and social relations shape how we perceive and monitor our bodies, label and categorize bodily symptoms, interpret complaints in the particular context of our life situation; we express our distress through bodily idioms that are both peculiar to distinctive cultural worlds and constrained by our shared human condition.

We can envision in chronic illness and its therapy a symbolic bridge that connects body, self, and society. This network interconnects physiological processes, meanings, and relationships so that our social world is linked recursively to our inner experience. Here we are privileged to discover powers within and between us that can either amplify suffering and disability or dampen symptoms and therefore contribute to care.

This book is written as well for my fellow practitioners, colleagues in the care of the chronically ill. It is clinically useful to learn how to interpret the patient's and family's perspective on illness. Indeed, the interpretation of narratives of illness experience, I will argue, is a core task in the work of doctoring, although the skill has atrophied in biomedical training. That message is the same theme I wish to bring before laymen: illness has meaning; and to understand how it obtains meaning is to understand something fundamental about illness, about care, and perhaps about life generally. Moreover, an interpretation of illness is something that patients, families, and practitioners need to undertake together. For there is a dialectic at the heart of healing that brings the care giver into the uncertain, fearful world of pain and disability and that reciprocally introduces patient and family into the equally uncertain world of therapeutic actions. That dialectic both enhances the therapy and makes of it and the illness a rare opportunity for moral education. One unintended outcome of the modern transformation of the medical care system is that it does just about everything to drive the practitioner's attention away from the experience of illness. The system thereby contributes importantly to the alienation of the chronically ill from their professional care givers and, paradoxically, to the relinquishment by the practitioner of that aspect of the healer's art that is most ancient, most powerful, and most existentially rewarding.

The organization of this book aims to further the purposes outlined in the preceding paragraphs. Two introductory chapters set out an analytical grid to assess the meanings of illness. The next eleven chapters provide detailed accounts of particular illness experiences of chronically ill patients whom I have either studied in clinical research or treated. Each chapter highlights a different aspect of illness meanings. The last three chapters switch the interpretive emphasis from patients and families to healers. They are intended as a guide for caring for the chronically ill and as a program for altering the education of medical students and postgraduate trainees so as to improve such care. While there is much to admire and recommend in current medical practice, the care of chronic illness is not one of the great success stories of contemporary medicine. The provocative title of the final chapter is intended to suggest that when we take as our starting point the meanings of illness experiences, then our very understanding of medicine is challenged.

A note on the use of quotations from interviews with patients and physicians is in order. In chapters 3 through 14, I make extensive use of such quotations. Approximately half of these statements are direct transcriptions of audio tapes that I used to record clinical and research interviews. The other half were written down, in my own system of speed writing, during the interviews. My written notes do not capture pauses, changes in voice pitch and tone, or "ah," "well," and other speech sounds. They also do not show when one voice interrupts another. Because my chief concern is the ease of reading the transcripts, I have for the most part removed intrusive elements of speech from the transcriptions of audio tapes as well, except where they seemed important to the person's meaning. This book is written for a broad audience, not a small group of experts. The speech quoted in this book, then, has been altered—perhaps tightened and simplified is more exact—but in only this and one other way. To protect the anonymity of patients and practitioners, I have removed or changed certain information that might identify them. When I have made such changes, I have drawn on information from patients with similar problems to make the alteration valid in the light of the experiences of the patient group as a whole.

—Arthur Kleinman, M.D.
Cambridge, Massachusetts
Winter 1986–87

Acknowledgments

I wrote this book in large part during a sabbatical leave from Harvard in 1986. I wish to express my deep appreciation to those individuals and institutions who made it possible to free this time so that I could devote it entirely to writing: Leon Eisenberg, chairman of the Department of Social Medicine, Harvard Medical School; Stanley Tambiah, then chairman of the Department of Anthropology, Harvard University; Myron Belfer, chairman of the Department of Psychiatry, Cambridge Hospital; Daniel Tosteson, dean of the Harvard Medical School; and A. Michael Spence, dean of the Faculty of Arts and Sciences, Harvard University. Grants from the Rockefeller Foundation, the National Science Foundation, the Social Science Research Council, and the Committee on Scholarly Collaboration with the People's Republic of China of the National Academy of Sciences underwrote much of my research with patients with chronic pain and other chronic illnesses in Boston and China. Several of the descriptions of patients with chronic illness were written under the useful discipline of having to assemble teaching materials for students in the Patient/Doctor Seminars of Harvard Medical School's brave New Pathway in Medical Education, and the vignettes benefited from the critical comments of students and fellow instructors. A decade of teaching residents in primary care and psychiatry at the Cambridge Hospital and the University of Washington Hospital sharpened my understanding of the problems chronic illness creates for practitioners. Through supervision of postdoctoral and predoctoral fellows in a National Institute of Mental Health–funded research training program in clinically applied anthropology, I widened my appreciation of the ethnographic contexts of care. Researching and especially caring for patients with chronic illness (and their families) taught me most of what I have written in these pages. It is an honor for me to express my indebtedness to these patients and their families.

Special insight on the subject of this book came from my own experience of chronic illness (asthma) and the care I received from two master clinicians, Gabriel Smilkstein and Charles Hatem.

I thank Professor Francis Zimmerman and Mme. S. B. Lamy for providing my family and me with just the right conditions to foster a successful sabbatical in France.

My thanks go to three editors at Basic Books: to Steve Fraser for his sensitive reading of the original manuscript, to Nola Healy Lynch for her fine copy editing, and to Paul Golob for shepherding the book through the production process.

I have had the good fortune of working in the past few years with a marvelously effective assistant, Joan Gillespie. Her practical labors for this volume have been prodigious, but I wish to thank her most for her loyalty and the warmth she has brought to our work setting.

I had felt for some years ready to write for a wider audience of educated readers, yet doing so proved to be more difficult than I had imagined. As in so many other areas, Joan Kleinman kept me from giving up or giving in.

The Illness Narratives

1

The Meaning of Symptoms and Disorders

Whatever is real has a meaning.
—Michael Oakeshott
([1933] 1978, 58)

For many Americans the meaning of disease is the mechanism that defines it; even in cancer the meaning is often that we do not yet know the mechanism. To some, however, the meaning of cancer may transcend the mechanism and the ultimate ability of medicine to understand it. For such individuals the meaning of cancer may lie in the evils of capitalism, of unhindered technical progress, or perhaps in failures of individual will. We live in a complex and fragmented world and create a variety of frameworks for our several ailments. But two key elements remain fundamental: one is faith in medicine's existing or potential insights, another, personal accountability.
—Charles E. Rosenberg
(1986, 34)

Illness and Disease

When I use the word *illness* in this book, I shall mean something fundamentally different from what I mean when I write *disease*. By invoking the term illness, I mean to conjure up the innately human experience of symptoms and suffering. Illness refers to how the sick person and the members of the family or wider social network perceive, live with, and respond to symptoms and disability.* Illness

*In this volume I use the terms *sick person* and *patient* interchangeably. But in fact the former conveys a more accurate sense of my point of view than the latter. Individuals who are

is the lived experience of monitoring bodily processes such as respiratory wheezes, abdominal cramps, stuffed sinuses, or painful joints. Illness involves the appraisal of those processes as expectable, serious, or requiring treatment. The illness experience includes categorizing and explaining, in common-sense ways accessible to all lay persons in the social group, the forms of distress caused by those pathophysiological processes. And when we speak of illness, we must include the patient's judgments about how best to cope with the distress and with the practical problems in daily living it creates. Illness behavior consists of initiating treatment (for example, changing diet and activities, eating special foods, resting, engaging in exercise, taking over-the-counter medication or on-hand prescription drugs) and deciding when to seek care from professionals or alternative practitioners.

Illness problems are the principal difficulties that symptoms and disability create in our lives. For example, we may be unable to walk up our stairs to our bedroom. Or we may experience distracting low back pain while we sit at work. Headaches may make it impossible to focus on homework assignments or housework, leading to failure and frustration. Or there may be impotence that leads to divorce. We may feel great anger because no one can see our pain and therefore objectively determine that our disability is real. As a result, we sense that our complaints are not believed, and we experience frustrating pressure to prove we are in constant pain. We may become demoralized and lose our hope of getting better, or we may be depressed by our fear of death or of becoming an invalid. We grieve over lost health, altered body image, and dangerously declining self-esteem. Or we feel shame because of disfigurement. All these are illness problems.

---

chronically ill spend much more time in the roles of sick family member, sick worker, sick self than in the role of patient, which is so redolent with the sights and smells of the clinic and which leaves an afterimage of a compliant, passive object of medical care. I wish to place stress on the sick person as the subject, the active agent of care, since in fact most treatment in chronic illness is self-treatment and most decisions are made by the sick person and family, not by health care professionals. *Sick person* also sounds more appropriate for the model of care I will advance. Care for chronic illness is (or should be) more like a negotiation among therapeutic allies than actions the physician takes on behalf of a patient. The patient and the practitioner bear reciprocal responsibilities, a point I will develop in chapter 15, where I describe a model of care. In spite of these good reasons, it sounds excessively artificial to avoid the term *patient*; hence I use the two terms interchangeably with the same meaning: more person, less patient.

Local cultural orientations (the patterned ways that we have learned to think about and act in our life worlds and that replicate the social structure of those worlds) organize our conventional common sense about how to understand and treat illness; thus we can say of illness experience that it is always culturally shaped. Paradoxical as it sounds, then, there are normal ways of being ill (ways that our society regards as appropriate) as well as anomalous ways. But conventional expectations about illness are altered through negotiations in different social situations and in particular webs of relationships. Expectations about how to behave when ill also differ owing to our unique individual biographies. So we can also say of illness experience that it is always distinctive.

Illness complaints are what patients and their families bring to the practitioner. Indeed, locally shared illness idioms create a common ground for patient and practitioner to understand each other in their initial encounter. For the practitioner, too, has been socialized into a particular collective experience of illness. Disease, however, is what the practitioner creates in the recasting of illness in terms of theories of disorder. Disease is what practitioners have been trained to see through the theoretical lenses of their particular form of practice. That is to say, the practitioner reconfigures the patient's and family's illness problems as narrow technical issues, disease problems. The patient may suffer pain that interferes with work and may lead to unemployment; self-absorption in a strict diet and severe gastrointestinal discomfort may intensify the stresses of school; or the fear of dying brought on by a heart attack may lead to social withdrawal and even divorce. Yet, in other cases, the physician diagnoses and treats elevated blood sugar that requires increased insulin, pain of uncertain origin that calls for diagnostic testing, or major depressive disorder that needs treatment with antidepressants. The healer—whether a neurosurgeon or a family doctor, a chiropractor or the latest breed of psychotherapist—interprets the health problem within a particular nomenclature and taxonomy, a disease nosology, that creates a new diagnostic entity, an "it"—the disease.

Disease is the problem from the practitioner's perspective. In the narrow biological terms of the biomedical model, this means that disease is reconfigured *only* as an alteration in biological structure or functioning. When chest pain can be reduced to a treatable acute lobar pneumonia, this biological reductionism is an enormous success. When chest pain is reduced to chronic coronary artery disease for which calcium blockers and nitroglycerine are prescribed, while the patient's fear, the family's frustration, the job conflict, the sexual impotence, and the financial crisis go undiagnosed and unaddressed, it is a failure. In the broader biopsychosocial model now making headway in primary care, disease is construed as the embodiment of the symbolic network linking body, self, and society (see Engel 1977). In the biomedical model the disease is an occluded coronary artery; in the biopsychosocial model it is a dynamic dialectic between cardiovascular processes (hypertension or coronary artery insufficiency), psychological states (panic or demoralization), and environmental situations (a midlife crisis, a failing marriage, the death of a parent from the same disorder). In the practitioner's act of recasting illness as disease, something essential to the experience of chronic illness is lost; it is not legitimated as a subject for clinical concern, nor does it receive an intervention. Treatment assessed solely through the rhetoric of improvement in disease processes may confound the patient's (and family's) assessments of care in the rhetoric of illness problems. Hence, at the heart of clinical care for the chronically ill—those who cannot be cured but must continue to live with illness—there is a potential (and, in many cases, actual) source of conflict.

To complete the picture, I shall introduce a third term, *sickness,* and define it as the understanding of a disorder in its generic sense across a population in relation to macrosocial (economic, political, institutional) forces. Thus, when we talk of the relationship of tuberculosis to poverty and malnutrition that places certain populations at higher risk for the disorder, we are invoking tuberculosis as sickness; similarly, when we discuss the contribution of the tobacco industry and their political supporters to the epidemiological burden of lung cancer in North America, we are describing the sickness cancer. Not just researchers but patients, families, and healers, too, may extrapolate from illness to sickness, adding another wrinkle to the experience of disorder, seeing it as a reflection of political oppression, economic deprivation, and other social sources of human misery.

Illnesses obviously vary in outcome. Some are brief, minimally disruptive of our life activities. Some are more distressing; they take longer to run their course. And the ones we are concerned with in this book never entirely disappear. Moreover, these chronic illnesses also vary greatly. Some lead to such devastating loss of functioning that the patient is almost totally disabled. Some, while less disabling, may yet eventually exhaust the family's resources and require institutionalization. And others ultimately terminate the patient's life. Imagine, as examples, the adolescent quadriplegic whose very life requires assisted respiration and round-the-clock help with all routine bodily functions and daily activities; or the business executive whose asthma is known only to his wife and children, who greatly, though secretly, limits his recreational, parental, and conjugal activities; or the young woman demoralized by the disfiguring radical surgery that removed her sense of self-esteem along with breast cancer and by the numbing realization that the signs of metastasis are omens of her own demise. For the first case, the illness problems arise from the total, inescapable life situation organized around the constant threat to vital functions and the necessity for continuous treatment; for the second, they stem from inability to deal with the feeling of vulnerability and loss of control as well as from the futile attempt to maintain two separate worlds—one free of sickness (work), the other where sickness is legitimized (home); whereas for the third, they center on the meaning of disfigurement and the menace of untimely death.

Chronic illnesses tend to oscillate between periods of exacerbation, when symptoms worsen, to periods of quiescence, when disability is less disruptive. By now a very substantial body of findings indicates that psychological and social factors are often the determinants of the swing toward amplification. The former include disabling anxiety, giving up. The latter are deeply threatening life event changes, impaired social support, and oppressive relationships that contribute to a vicious cycle undermining psychophysiological homeostasis (Katon et al. 1982; Kleinman 1986). Alternatively, the swing toward damping (a kind of internal health-promoting system that has received less research attention) frequently seems to be associated with strengthened social supports, enhanced sense of self-efficacy, and rekindled aspiration.

Periods of alleviation also reveal attendant diminution in anxiety and depression. There are rising feelings of mastery, often due to acceptance of a paradigm of care that substitutes a pragmatic notion of illness maintenance and disability reduction for the myth of cure.

Of course, swings from amplification to damping, and vice versa, need not reflect psychosocial influence: often biological change is responsible. As a result, there is uncertainty over the reason for exacerbation or remission, which, regretably, encourages a corresponding tendency to dismiss even the obvious social-psychological push of the swing. The upshot is conjoint (practitioner/patient, family) denial that chronic disorder is so influenced—a fateful complicity that in my experience correlates with pessimism and passivity. Not surprisingly, the effect is to worsen outcome.

The Meanings of Illness

Illness has meaning, as the cases I have mentioned suggest, in several distinctive senses. Each type of meaning is worth examining. From an anthropological perspective and also a clinical one, illness is polysemic or multivocal; illness experiences and events usually radiate (or conceal) more than one meaning. Some meanings remain more potential than actual. Others become effective only over the long course of a chronic disorder. Yet others change as changes occur in situations and relations. As in so many areas of life, their very ambiguity often supplies illness meanings with relevance, inasmuch as they can be applied now this way, now that way to the problem at hand. Chronic illness is more than the sum of the many particular events that occur in an illness career; it is a reciprocal relationship between particular instance and chronic course. The trajectory of chronic illness assimilates to a life course, contributing so intimately to the development of a particular life that illness becomes inseparable from life history. Continuities as well as transformations, then, lead to the appreciation of the meanings of illness.

The appreciation of meanings is bound within a relationship: it belongs to the sick person's spouse, child, friend, or care giver, or to the patient himself. For this reason it is usually as much hedged in with ambiguities as are those relationships themselves. But in the long, oscillating course of chronic disorder, the sick, their relatives, and those who treat them become aware that the meanings communicated by illness can amplify or dampen symptoms, exaggerate or lessen disability, impede or facilitate treatment. For reasons I will review later, however, these understandings often remain unexamined, silent emblems of a covert reality that is usually dealt with either indirectly or not at all. Powerful emotions attach to these meanings, as do powerful interests.

Social reality is so organized that we do not routinely inquire into the meanings of illness any more than we regularly analyze the structure of our social world. Indeed, the everyday priority structure of medical training and of health care delivery, with its radically materialist pursuit of the biological mechanism of disease, precludes such inquiry. It turns the gaze of the clinician, along with the attention of patients and families, away from decoding the salient meanings of illness for them, which interferes with recognition of disturbing but potentially treatable problems in their life world. The biomedical system replaces this allegedly "soft," therefore devalued, psychosocial concern with meanings with the scientifically "hard," therefore overvalued, technical quest for the control of symptoms. This pernicious value transformation is a serious failing of modern medicine: it disables the healer and disempowers the chronically ill (see chapter 16). Biomedicine must be indicted of this failure in order to provoke serious interest in reform, because a powerful therapeutic alternative is at hand.

There is evidence to indicate that through examining the particular significances of a person's illness it is possible to break the vicious cycles that amplify distress. The interpretation of illness meanings can also contribute to the provision of more effective care. Through those interpretations the frustrating consequences of disability can be reduced. This key clinical task may even liberate sufferers and practitioners from the oppressive iron cage imposed by a too intensely morbid preoccupation with painful bodily processes and a too technically narrow and therefore dehumanizing vision of treatment, respectively. In chapter 15, I will set out a practical clinical method that practitioners can (and should) apply to provide more effective and humane care of chronically sick persons. This alternative therapeutic approach originates in the reconceptualization of medical care as (1) empathic witnessing of the existential experience of suffering and (2) practical coping with the major psychosocial crises that constitute the menacing chronicity of that experience. The work of the practitioner includes the sensitive solicitation of the patient's and the family's stories of the illness, the assembling of a mini-ethnography of the changing contexts of chronicity, informed negotiation with alternative lay perspectives on care, and what amounts to a brief medical psychotherapy for the multiple, ongoing threats and losses that make chronic illness so profoundly disruptive.

Not the least of the reasons for studying illness meanings, therefore, is that such an investigation can help the patient, the family, and also the practitioner: certainly not every time, perhaps not even routinely, but often enough to make a significant difference.

Symptom as Meaning

The first kind of illness meaning that we shall consider, appropriately enough, is the surface denotation of symptom qua symptom. This is the ostensive, conventional signification of the symptom (for example, back pain, palpitations, or wheezing) as disability or distress. There is a tendency to regard such self-evident significance as "natural." But what is natural depends on shared understandings in particular cultures and not infrequently diverges among different social groups. The meanings of symptoms are standardized "truths" in a local cultural system, inasmuch as the groups' categories are projected onto the world, then called natural because they are found there. That is to say, we take for granted local forms of common-sense knowledge—a lump in the breast could be cancer, when overheated be cautious of drinking something very cold, suntanned skin is a sign of health, to be thin is better than to be fat, a firm stool once a day is normal—and these contribute to our shared appreciation of what sickness is and what is meant when a person expresses the sickness experience through established patterns of gestures, facial expressions, and sounds or words.

As a result, when we talk of pain, for example, we are understood by those around us. Yet even surface significances can be fairly subtle. In each culture and historical period there are different ways to talk about, say, headaches. And these differences make a difference in the way the members of the sick person's circle respond to him or her. Think of the many ways to complain of headache in North American society: "My head hurts," "My head really hurts," "My head is pounding," "I'm having a migraine," "It's only a tension headache," "I feel a fullness and heavy feeling in my temples," "It feels like a ring of pain is constricting my forehead," "My sinuses ache," "My scalp is tingling," "When I move my head I feel dizzy, as if a veil were passing before my eyes." Each expression shades and colors the bald term "headache." In the lifetime course of chronic headaches, key words take on special significance to the sufferer and family that no eavesdropper could interpret. We differ as individuals in how effective we are in the use of these conventional illness idioms and special terms. Some are more skillful in the rhetorical deployment of these potentially powerful words to influence the behavior of others in the desire to receive support, to keep others at a distance, to obtain time alone, to convey anger, to conceal shame, and so forth.

Implicit in the first-level meaning of symptoms are accepted forms of knowledge about the body, the self, and their relationship to each other and to the more intimate aspects of our life worlds. For members of Western societies the body is a discrete entity, a thing, an "it," machinelike and objective, separate from thought and emotion. For members of many non-Western societies, the body is an open system linking social relations to the self, a vital balance between interrelated elements in a holistic cosmos. Emotion and cognition are integrated into bodily processes. The body-self is not a secularized private domain of the individual person but an organic part of a sacred, sociocentric world, a communication system involving exchanges with others (including the divine).

For example, among traditionally oriented Chinese, the body is regarded as a microcosm in symbolic resonance with the social and even planetary macrocosm (Porkert 1974). The body's *qi* (vital energy) is thought to be in harmony with that flowing in the environment. *Yin/yang* constituents of the body-self are in complementary opposition and also are in interaction with *yin/yang* constituents of the group and nature. Emotion correlates intimately with bodily constituents, which in turn correlate closely with the weather, the time, the physical setting, and the sociopolitical order. Conceptions of illness are based on this integrated, dialectical vision.

In India the body-self is held to be permeable to substances and symbols in social interactions (Daniel 1984). Health is a balance among the body's humors and the constituents of the outer world, mediated by diet and a hierarchy of social relations tightly organized around a systematic categorization of the world in terms of purity and pollution. A child is polluted by the touch of a menstruating mother because menstrual blood can enter the porous body (Shweder 1985), just as food received from someone in a lower caste gets incorporated into the body and pollutes it from within. The body is also permeable to supernatural and mystical forces.

Among the Navaho, the body is in perfect aesthetic and moral harmony with the physical landscape of the Navaho world (Sandner 1979; Witherspoon 1975). Body symbolizes landscape, and landscape body. A similar idea is found among the Chinese (Unschuld 1985) and many other societies. In these cultures bodily complaints are also moral problems: they are icons of disharmonies in social relationships and in the cultural ethos. Reading the Hippocratic medical texts suggests that, although some of the conceptions are quite different, a similarly integrative, dialectical view of body, self, and world was found in ancient Western society.

Meaning of a social kind is stamped into bodily processes and experiences, sometimes literally so, as, for example, when ritual circumcision and other forms of mutilation (subincision, tatooing, clitoridectomy, amputation of finger joints, scarification) mark life transitions and group and personal identity. Among Australian aboriginals a person's totem is embroidered into the skin through ritual scarification; the person receives a skin name that identifies his social group and personal status (Warner 1958; Munn 1973). Social experience is embodied in the way we feel and experience our bodily states and appear to others (Turner 1985). The tightly corseted female body in an earlier era in Europe constituted as much as expressed a particular vision of women and their role in society. The association in many societies of femaleness with the left side of the body—which also frequently symbolizes pollution, darkness, dampness, sinister motives, and a host of other negative oppositions to the male (right) side of the body—informs bodily experience as much as social categories with the moral meaning of gender (Needham 1973). The great concern in North American culture with unblemished skin surface, deodorized, youthful bodies, sexualized body shapes and gestures is part of a diffused capitalist system of commercialized symbolic meanings, which, like all cultural systems, orients the person to body and self experiences and to the priorities and expectations of the group. Indeed, through these embodied values social control is internalized and political ideology materializes as corporeal feelings and physiological needs. To understand how symptoms and illnesses have meaning, therefore, we first must understand normative conceptions of the body in relation to the self and world. These integral aspects of local social systems inform how we feel, how we perceive mundane bodily processes, and how we interpret those feelings and processes.

We do not discover our bodies and inner worlds *de novo*. All humans learn methods to monitor bodily processes and rhetorical idioms (verbal and nonverbal) to communicate bodily states, including states of illness. There are distinctive styles of eating, washing, laughing, crying, and performing routine bodily functions (spitting, coughing, urinating, defecating, menstruating, and so forth). And these styles of normal activities influence illness idioms (Nichter 1982). We learn how to identify and react to pain, how to label and communicate dysfunction. The idioms we learn are often the same channels used to communicate troubles of any kind. Chest discomfort may signal anxiety or angina, pneumonia or bereavement. Tension headaches may express a number of states: from exhaustion, chronic inflammation of the cervical spine, or the distress of an acute upper respiratory infection or of worsening diabetes to the misery that results from job loss, an oppressive work situation, or a systematically demoralizing marital relationship. Not infrequently, a bodily idiom will express several of these forms of distress simultaneously. Where a physiological stress reaction or a chronic medical disease provide the particular biological substrate, there is a specific channel of established complaints (including weakness, shortness of breath, chest discomfort, and abdominal pain) that can be amplified to express distress of various kinds. Hence, at the very core of complaints is a tight integration between physiological, psychological, and social meanings (Kleinman 1986).

Illness idioms crystallize out of the dynamic dialectic between bodily processes and cultural categories, between experience and meaning. Among New Guinea natives in the Sepik region, illness is indicated by the sick person's dramatic withdrawal (Lewis 1975). He shows the intensity of the felt experience by covering the body with ashes and dirt, refusing food, and remaining isolated. In some cultures illness idioms may be more gregarious and mundane, and in others they may be embodied as stoical silence. In some communities in India, for example, illness is expressed in the special tropes of that society's core hierarchical relationship between purity and pollution, which determines to whom one shows symptoms and from whom one accepts food and medicine. For the traditional Brahmin mother who is menstruating, the fear of polluting her son, even when he is ill, may prevent her from touching him and cause her to warn him not to come too near (Shweder 1985). In India as well as many other societies, illness behavior and care are demonstrated in the pattern of food sharing and diet (Nichter 1982). Diet is adjusted to right putative humoral imbalances. Special foods and indigenous medicines may be shared among individuals whose kinship or friendship ties bring them together into a lay therapy management team responsible for the patient's treatment (Janzen 1978). In small-scale, preliterate societies—for example, the Inuit of Alaska and the Kaluli of the New Guinea highlands—illness is expressed in the system of balanced reciprocity among members of the group that is the central structural principle of each of these societies (Briggs 1970; Schieffelin 1985). This system defines who shall do what for whom in return for who has done (or should have done) what for whom in order that in the future who will do what for whom.

In North American society we, too, possess these conventionalized understandings of the body, these customary configurations of self and symptoms. But given the marked pluralism of North American life styles; ethnic and religious backgrounds; and educational, occupational, and economic statuses, we must distinguish between popular cultural meanings that are shared and those that are restricted to particular subgroups. As a result, it is more sensible to speak of local systems of knowledge and relationships that inform how we regard symptoms; these may differ substantially from each other. Within these local systems shared meanings will be negotiated among individuals of unequal power who attempt to persuade others of the intensity of their distress and of the need for access to more resources. Members of such local systems may seek to deny the implications of an obvious abnormality, or they may try to enlist significant others in the quest for care. Obviously, individuals differ in their rhetorical skills in deploying idioms of distress (Beeman 1985).

Lay understandings of illness influence verbal as well as nonverbal communication. There may well be enough universality in facial expressions, body movements, and vocalizations of distress for members of other communities to know that we are experiencing some kind of trouble (Ekman 1980). But there are subtleties as well that indicate our past experiences, chief current concerns, and practical ways of coping with the problem. These particularities are so much a part of local assumptions that they are opaque for those to whom our shared life ways are foreign. Moreover, these distinctive idioms feed back to influence the experience of distress (Good 1977; Kleinman and Kleinman 1985; Rosaldo 1980).

I hear you say your headache is a migraine, or a tension headache owing to too much "stress," or that it is "beastly," "awful," "pounding," "throbbing," "boring," "aching," "exploding," "blinding," "depressing," "killing," and I interpret something of that experience and how you feel and want me to feel about it. (You also interpret your own language of complaining and my response to you, which will affect your symptoms.) It is a testament to the subtlety of culture that we share such a wide array of understandings of surface meanings of symptom terms. (Nigerian psychiatric patients, for example, frequently complain of a feeling like ants are crawling in their heads, a complaint that is specific to their culture [Ebigbo 1982].) I may no longer explicitly understand the Galenic system of hot and cold bodily states and the humoral balance and imbalance it connotes in Western folk culture, but I get your point that you have a "cold" and therefore want something "hot" to drink and feel the need to dress warmly to protect your "cold" from "the cold." Our understanding is based on a grand cultural convention that would make "feed a cold, starve a fever" incomprehensible to someone without this shared local knowledge (Helman 1978).

Yet there is obviously also great uncertainty at this outer level of signification. I am not entirely sure what you mean when you say your "head is splitting," because I feel I do not know you well enough to make full sense of your experience. Are you generally stoical, hysterical, hypochondriacal, manipulative? Understanding who you are influences how I interpret your complaints. The relationship we have will inform how I respond to your complaint of headache. That relationship includes a history of how I have responded to you in the past (and you to me), along with our mutual understanding of the current situation; in the case of chronic illness, it includes as well the pattern of response and situation that has already been established over hundreds of complaints. My interpretation of your communication of distress is organized by the pattern of our daily interactions in times of sickness. Indeed, the language of your complaints has become a part of the language of our relationship. Hence, even the superficial significance of symptoms qua symptoms is embedded in the meanings and relationships that organize our day-to-day world, including how in interaction we recreate our selves. This makes of even superficial symptoms a rich metaphoric system available for many kinds of communication.

A corollary to the meaning of symptoms is the semiotics of diagnosis. For the practitioner, the patient's complaints (symptoms of illness) must be translated into the *signs* of disease. (For example, the patient's chest pain becomes angina—a sign of coronary artery disease—for the physician.) Diagnosis is a thoroughly semiotic activity: an analysis of one symbol system followed by its translation into another. Complaints are also interpreted as syndromes—clusters of symptoms which run together over time—that indicate through their relationship a discrete disorder. Clinicians sleuth for pathognomonic signs—the observable, telltale clues to secret pathology—that establish a specific disease. This interpretive bias to clinical diagnosis means that the patient–physician interaction is organized as an interrogation (Mishler 1985). What is important is not what the patient thinks but what he or she says. Since 80 percent of diagnoses in primary care result from the history alone, the anamnesis (the account the physician assembles from the patient's story) is crucial (see Hampton et al. 1975). That tale of complaints becomes the text that is to be decoded by the practitioner cum diagnostician. Practitioners, however, are not trained to be self-reflective interpreters of distinctive systems of meaning. They are turned out of medical schools as naive realists, like Dashiell Hammett's Sam Spade, who are led to believe that symptoms are clues to disease, evidence of a "natural" process, a physical entity to be discovered or uncovered. They are rarely taught that biological processes are known only through socially constructed categories that constrain experience as much as does disordered physiology; this is a way of thinking that fits better with the secure wisdom of physical science than with the nervous skepticism of the medical profession.

The upshot is that practitioners, trained to think of "real" disease entities, with natural histories and precise outcomes, find chronic illness messy and threatening. They have been taught to regard with suspicion patients' illness narratives and causal beliefs. The form of those narratives and explanations may indicate a morbid process; the content may lead them astray. The way of the specialist diagnostician, which is not to credit the patient's subjective account until it can be quantified and therefore rendered more "objective," can make a shambles of the care of the chronically ill. Predictably, the chronically ill become problem patients in care, and they reciprocally experience their care as a problem in the health care system. Illness experience is not legitimated by the biomedical specialist, for whom it obscures the traces of morbid physiological change; yet for the care giver of the chronically ill who would be an effective healer, it is the very stuff of care, "a symbol that stands for itself" (Wagner 1986). Legitimating the patient's illness experience—authorizing that experience, auditing it empathically—is a key task in the care of the chronically ill, but one that is particularly difficult to do with the regularity and consistency and sheer perseverance that chronicity necessitates. The interpretation of symptoms in the longitudinal course of illness is the interpretation of a changing system of meanings which are embodied in lived experience and which can be

understood through the acquisition of what amounts to an ethnographic appreciation of their context of relationships, the nature of
their referents, and the history of how they are experienced.

Cultural Significance as Meaning

Illness has meaning in a second sense, insofar as particular symptoms and disorders are marked with cultural salience in different
epochs and societies. These special symptoms and illness categories
bring particularly powerful cultural significance with them, so to
speak, often of a stigmatizing kind. Few North Americans have ever
seen or heard of a case of leprosy, yet so fearsome is the mythology
surrounding this category of disorder in the collective consciousness
of the West that equally few would be likely to react without
abhorrence or terrible fright if told that they or a close acquaintance
were suffering from leprosy. No wonder the horrific name of this
illness has been changed to the innocuous "Hansen's disease."

In the late Middle Ages, the Black Death (bubonic plague)
depopulated the European continent by an astounding three-
fourths. In so doing, the Black Death became a symbol of evil and
terror. It came to signify several things: the wrath of God, man's
fallen state of sin and suffering, and death as transcendence of the
immortal soul (Bynum 1985; Gottfried 1983). Whatever particular
religious meaning the Black Death had for a community was overwhelmed by the immensely powerful practical meaning the term
held for the afflicted and their families. The application of this
illness label placed home and neighborhood under the isolation of
quarantine and made the inhabitants doomed outcasts who posed
the gravest dangers to society. That the word *plague* radiates hardly
any significance today is an illustration of the process of transformation of meaning that Foucault (1966)—using the example of
insanity in the West—showed can substantially change the nature
of the culturally salient mark certain illnesses impress on the
afflicted. The disappearance of plague epidemics must have contributed powerfully to this transformation.

In the Gilded Age of late nineteenth-century America, the vaporous paralyses of hysteria, neurasthenic weakness, and neurotic angst due to crises of personal confidence over career and family responsibilities were specially salient disorders regarded as products of the age. They spoke of a widespread middle-class malaise associated with the very rapid pace of social change that was transforming a North American society anchored in eighteenth-century ideals and rural or small town life styles into the twentieth-century culture of industrial capitalism (Drinka 1984). There was great concern with the effect of this massive societal transformation on individuals, usually bourgeois and upper-class men and women, whose symptoms were viewed ambivalently as the price that members of society had to pay for their world to become fully modern.

Let us take another example of culturally marked illness: witchcraft. Accusations of witchcraft in the early New England Puritan world congealed many of the core fears of the time, including threats of deviance, egocentricity, antisocial behavior, and sexuality. It represented an obsession with the control of jealousy and envy, and with explaining the presence of misfortune and maleficence in a world ruled by a stern but just God. In twentieth-century tribal societies in Africa, witchcraft symbolizes a similar concern with the sources of jealousy, envy, and misfortune, though here the emphasis is on human rather than Satanic evil. In the African setting, witchcraft also conveys fears regarding threats to procreativity and village unity (Turner 1967; Janzen 1978). In both societies witchcraft became a major explanatory model of malignant illnesses that were random and unpredictable, like witchcraft itself; it offered, furthermore, a magical means to exert control over seemingly unjust suffering and untimely death.

In Chinese society over the millenia, severe mental illness—labeled insanity, *fengbing*—held particular salience (Lin and Lin 1982). Even today insanity places stigma not just on the sick person but on the entire family. A marriage go-between traditionally asked if insanity was present among members of the family; if it was, she ruled the family out as a suitable source of spouses—a catastrophe in the family-centered Chinese social system. Families of schizophrenic and manic-depressive patients in present-day China and Taiwan, and even among the traditionally oriented Chinese in the

United States, still experience such great shame and other negative effects of stigma. It is often preferable to the members of this familistic culture that the patient remain institutionalized or live apart from home. The diagnosis of mental illness among Chinese is so threatening that the euphemism "neurasthenia" continues to flourish in China in the 1980s, long after its vogue in the West and other non-Western societies; the term provides a legitimate physical disease label as a cloak to disguise psychiatric problems that remain illegitimate and unacceptable. In 1980 and 1983 my wife and I conducted research in China (Kleinman 1982, 1986; Kleinman and Kleinman 1985) which disclosed that neurasthenia conveys other tacit problems as well, especially serious political, work, and family crises that have given rise to demoralization and alienation. One of the neurasthenia cases from our research in China will be described in chapter 6 to illustrate the cultural meanings of illness. The Chinese example offers a remarkable comparison with neurasthenia in late nineteenth and early twentieth century North America and Europe. For although this quintessential biopsychosocial problem crystallizes certain meanings unique to each society, there are also many instances when the social iconography of neurasthenia as *sickness* communicates identical meanings.

Perhaps the disorders of our own period in the West that carry the most powerful symbolic loading are cancer, heart disease, and the new venereal epidemics—herpes and acquired immune deficiency syndrome (AIDS). The first—still a highly malignant, seemingly randomly occurring, largely uncontrollable problem—is a direct threat to major values of late twentieth-century American society. The specific values I have in mind include the transformation of chaotic human problems into closed-ended practical issues manageable by technological means rather than into open-ended questions concerned with moral ends. Cancer is an unsettling reminder of the obdurate grain of unpredictability and uncertainty and injustice—value questions, all—in the human condition. Cancer forces us to confront our lack of control over our own or others' death. Cancer points up our failure to explain and master much in our world. Perhaps most fundamentally, cancer symbolizes our need to make moral sense of "Why me?" that scientific explanations cannot provide. Cancer is also freighted with meanings of the risks of invisible pollutants, such as ionizing radiation and even the chemical constituents of the very foods we eat. These menacing meanings meld ancient fears of contamination with the great modern threat of man-made catastrophes that poison the environment with toxic wastes. They disclose our inability to control the effects of technology. The popular view of anticancer drugs as poisons extends the imagery of risk from causes to treatments and seems to implicate biomedical technology as part of this danger.

Contrary to earlier assumptions, the more we have learned, the more threatening our environment has become. Heart disease, like cancer, seems to implicate our very way of life: what we choose to eat, what we like to do. It points to the frenetic pace of an economy predicated on ever more rapid technological change and its accompaniment, disordered physiology. It speaks to us of the risks of our personality style (in fact, that narcissistic personality precisely crafted to be most successful in the capitalist system). Heart disease invokes the ubiquitous tension in our lives, the breakdown of intimate social bonds, and the loss both of leisure and of sustained physical activity in our workaday world (Lasch 1979; Helman 1987).

The society-wide response to each problem also tells us much about the value structure of American society. We manage as medical problems the symptoms resulting from the social sources of distress and disease. We blame the victim in the ideology of personal life-style change. We avoid the hard, value-laden questions that underlie public health concern with cigarette smoking, exposure to carcinogens, promiscuous sexual practices, and what is euphemistically called unavoidable stress (what Taussig [1986] calls the "nervous" system of modern society). Both cancer and heart disease intensify our awareness of the dangers of our times and of the man-made sources of much misery. But the governmental response is meant to obfuscate this vision of sickness as meaning something is wrong with the social order and to replace (medicalize) it with narrowly technical questions. Is there a better mirror of what we are about?

Like cancer and heart disease, we can say of genital herpes and AIDS that these disorders bring particular cultural meaning to the person (Brandt 1984). As in the cases of syphilis and gonorrhea before them, herpes and AIDS brand the victim with the painful (and in the case of the latter, deadly) stigmata of venereal sin. At the same time, the response to these diseases suggests that the dominant, commercialized sexual imagery of postindustrial capitalist society hides a double standard of both amoral promiscuity on behalf of individual rights and consumer values and highly moral, if archly hypocritical, condemnation of the venereal results. For each of these disorders meaning arrives with a vengeance together with the diagnosis: "She's got breast cancer and may die!" "I've got coronary artery disease and can't work any longer!" "Her boyfriend has herpes and infected her without warning her!" "Can you imagine, that fellow down the street has AIDS. You know what that means!" Each statement encases the patient in a visible exoskelton of powerfully peculiar meanings that the patient must deal with, as must those of us who are around the patient. These meanings include the fear of a lingering and untimely death, the threat of disfiguring treatment with the concomitant loss of body- and self-image, the stigma of self-earned illness, discrimination against homosexuals, and so forth. That exoskeleton is the carapace of culturally marked illness, a dominant societal symbol that, once applied to a person, spoils radically that individual's identity and is not easily removed.

Less solemn cultural meaning is exemplified by the lay perspective on hypertension in North America. Blumhagen's (1980) research describes the beliefs about hypertension held by a largely middle-class, college-educated clinic population in Seattle. The lay model takes the essence of hypertension to be too much tension, not necessarily high blood pressure, which is what the term denotes in biomedical usage. Blumhagen shows that the lay interpretation of hypertension as an illness is a North American folk model that helps explain the high rate of noncompliance with the medical drug regimens that characterize this disorder. Noncompliance is held by physicians to be a major obstacle to the effective management of hypertension. When patients feel "hyper-tense" they believe they are suffering the disorder and they take the medication. When they do not feel tense, they deny that they have hypertension and don't take the medicine. Here the illness model is the obverse of the disease model. The object of therapy is to control the blood pressure on a daily basis, independent of stress or tension. This folk model, with its important implications for care, appears widespread in North American society in spite of health education campaigns in clinics and in the media. Its persistence is a measure of the staying power of cultural meanings.

It is not just the labels of disorders that are value laden. Symptoms, too, can carry cultural significance. For example, in the ancient Chinese medical texts, "headaches," "dizziness," and "weakness" receive special attention; the same symptoms are highlighted by patients and physicians in clinical settings in modern China (Kleinman 1986). Benveniste (1945), in an early and still provocative account of the relationship of symptoms to the tripartite social division of ancient Indo-European society, notes that wounds, blindness, and a weakness-exhaustion-debility complex of complaints have held special salience in Western society and have been associated with military, priestly, and agricultural functions, respectively. The epidemic of chronic pain complaints in North America suggests that pain has peculiar present-day significance and seemingly has usurped the cachet of exhaustion-weakness complaints of neurasthenia. Perhaps North American culture's ideology of personal freedom and the pursuit of happiness has come to mean for many guaranteed freedom from the suffering of pain. This meaning clashes strikingly with the expectation in much of the nonindustrialized world that pain is an expectable component of living and must be endured in silence.

It is not just that certain symptoms are given particular attention in certain cultural and historical settings, but that the meanings of all symptoms, as I have already noted, are dependent on local knowledge about the body and its pathologies. Hence, weakness in local Chinese communities connotes loss of vital energy (*qi*), a central theme in traditional Chinese ethno-medical theories. Excessive loss of semen, through masturbation or an overly active conjugal sex life, has always generated marked anxiety among Chinese because semen contains *jing,* or the essence of *qi,* which in turn is lost when semen is lost. This makes semen loss a potentially life-threatening illness in Chinese medical theory. Because of this set of beliefs, tradition-oriented Chinese adolescents and young adults are particularly fearful of the consequences of nocturnal emissions and other forms of semen loss; their view stands in striking contrast with that of their counterparts in the present-day West, where it would seem to be positively valued. In South Asia, where Ayurvedic medical theory holds that both men *and* women contain semen, leucorrhea carries the same fearful connotation for women. That female semen loss is impossible in biomedical theory illustrates the great semantic gap between illness and disease.

Other culturally particular symptoms described in the anthropological and cross-cultural psychiatric literature include "fright" leading to "soul loss" in Mexico and in various Asian societies, "nerves" in North and South America, fear that the penis is shrinking among Southeast Asians, and startle-related copying and echoing behavior (*latah*) affecting Malays. There exists a large assortment of so-called culture-bound complaints (see Simons and Hughes 1985).

It is a sign of the marked pluralism of North American society that symptoms hold special significance not just in the society as a whole but also in the distinctive life worlds shaped by class, ethnicity, age, and gender. Menopausal complaints are a preoccupation of white, middle-class women in midlife. But women of most other cultures pass through the menopause with few serious complaints and no conception of this life transition as an illness (Kaufert and Gilbert 1986; McKinlay and McKinlay 1985). Yet menopausal complaints are highlighted by the media and the medical profession for economic reasons. They have entered the popular North American culture as a marker of the feared transition to old age and asexuality in a society commercially centered on the cult of youth and sexual attraction. Similarly, premenstrual tension is a symptom constellation unheard of in much of the world and among members of traditional ethnic groups in the United States; but it is increasingly commonplace in white, middle-class North America. Non-Western practitioners regard premenstrual syndrome as yet another example of the unwillingness of middle-class Westerners to endure any pain or suffering, no matter how limited and expectable. Perhaps its cultural significance lies in the strong ambivalence associated with traditional procreative functions and femininity among women in Western society. Rural blacks and poor whites in Appalachia complain of "high blood," "sugar," "fallin' out," "nerves," and other ailments that hold little, if any, significance in the urban Northeast and that define this population as much as does their dialect (Nations et al. 1985). Complaints of "soul loss" (*susto*) among working-class Mexican-Americans in Los Angeles, spirit possession among Puerto Ricans in New York, voodoo among Haitian immigrants in Boston, "airs" (*aires*) and hot/cold imbalance among working-class Cubans in Miami, and evil eye among recent refugees from Latin America serve a similar function. They mark ethnic, class, and recent immigration statuses. They should signal to health professionals major cultural differences that require sensitive evaluation. All too frequently, however, they stimulate traditional ethnic stereotypes that may exert a mischievous influence on care.

Culturally salient illness meanings disclose change as well as continuity over time and place. The meaning of a lump in the breast is no longer limited to wealthier and better educated women in North America, and the potential physiological significance of coughing and wheezing among smokers is much better appreciated now than in the past. Alternatively, the bloody sputum, hectic flush, and elegant pallor so well known to readers of nineteenth-century Western literature as signs of tuberculosis have lost their significance as a cohesive, popular cultural category. The significance of each of these disorders will hold a meaning different for Ethiopians than for Bostonians. Where acute disorder, starvation, and epidemic infectious disease are rampant it is unlikely that the symptoms of chronic conditions will hold as powerful a place in the local collective consciousness as they do in societies that have passed through the epidemiological transition to chronic disorder as the chief source of morbidity and mortality.

Baldness and impotence among middle-aged men, acne and short stature among adolescent males, obesity and eating preoccupation (bulimia and anorexia) among adolescent and young adult women, and cosmetic concerns among the elderly are culturally marked conditions that express the narcissistic preoccupation of modern Western society. Agoraphobia (fear of leaving the house) has been said to express through its symptom of houseboundedness the Western woman's ambivalence about the choice between having a working career and being a housewife (Littlewood and Lipsedge 1987). At present, the dementia of Alzheimer's disease captures popular attention in North America as an unacceptable index of the final assault of aging on the autonomy of the person. Relabeling alcoholism as an illness and child abuse as a symptom of family pathology are further examples of the widespread process of medicalization in Western societies, whereby problems previously labeled and managed as moral, religious, or criminal are redefined as disorder and dealt with through therapeutic technology. These problems open a window on Western society, showing its chief cultural concerns and conflicts.

To recapitulate our main argument, cultural meanings mark the sick person, stamping him or her with significance often unwanted and neither easily warded off nor coped with. The mark may be either stigma or social death. Whichever, the meaning is inescapable, although it may be ambiguous and although its consequences can be significantly modified by the affected person's place in the local cultural system. People vary in the resources available to them to resist or rework the cultural meanings of illness. Those meanings present a problem to patient, family, and practitioner every bit as difficult as the lesion itself.

A final aspect of this type of illness meaning deserves mention. The cultural meanings of illness shape suffering as a distinctive moral or spiritual form of distress. Whether suffering is cast as the ritual enactment of despair, as paradigmatic moral exemplars of how pain and loss should be borne (as in the case of Job), or as the ultimately existential human dilemma of being alone in a meaningless world, local cultural systems provide both the theoretical framework of myth and the established script for ritual behavior that transform an individual's affliction into a sanctioned symbolic form for the group.

The German phenomenologist Plessner (1970) makes the cultural point about suffering this way. Illness in modern Europe or the United States, he avows, brings the sick person to the recognition of a fundamental aspect of the divided nature of the human condition in the West: namely, that each of us *is* his or her body and *has* (experiences) a body. In this formulation, the sick person is the sick body and also recognizes that he or she has a sick body that is distinct from self and that the person observes as if it were someone else. As a result, the sick both are their illness and are distanced, even alienated, from the illness. T. S. Eliot may have had this in mind when he spoke of the "dissociation of sensibility" (cited in Rycroft 1986, 284) The modern Western cultural orientation contributes to our experience of suffering precisely through this reciprocal relationship between the actual experience qua experience and how each of us relates to that experience as an observing self. We might say that culture fills the space between the immediate embodiment of sickness as physiological process and its mediated (therefore meaning-laden) experience as human phenomenon—for example, as an alienated part of body-self, as a vehicle for transcendence, or as a source of embarrassment or grief. Illness takes on meaning as suffering because of the way this relationship between body and self is mediated by cultural symbols of a religious, moral, or spiritual kind. Inasmuch as the Western experience of the body-self dichotomy has throughout this century been exported to the rest of the world as a psychological component of modernization, perhaps the division of experience and meaning will become, at least for those most strongly influenced by Western values, universal in illness around the globe.

Let us restate the issue in sociological terms. Following Schutz (1968) we can view the individual in society as acting in the world by taking up a common-sense perspective on daily life events. The perspective comes from a local cultural system as the accepted way of conceiving (and thereby replicating) social reality. We create, not just discover, meaning in experiences through the process of meeting practical resistances in the real world, obstacles owing to the unequal distribution of available resources or the unpredictability and uncontrollability of life problems, for example. When we meet up with the resistance offered by profound life experience—the death of a child or parent or spouse, the loss of a job or home, serious illness, substantial disability—we are shocked out of our common-sensical perspective on the world (Keyes 1985). We are then in a transitional situation in which we must adopt some other perspective on our experience. We may take up a moral perspective to explain and control disturbing ethical aspects of our troubles, or a religious perspective to make sense of and seek to transcend misfortune, or, increasingly, a medical one to cope with our distress. In traditional societies, shared moral and religious perspectives on the experience of life crises anchor anxieties in established social insti-

tutions of control, binding threat in webs of ultimate meaning. In
the fragmented, pluralistic modern world, anxiety increasingly is
free floating and requires personal processes of creating idiosyncratic meaning to supplant the shared moral and religious significance that guided our ancestors on how to suffer (see Obeyesekere
1985). Lacking generally agreed-upon authorization for how to interpret misfortune, there is a definite tendency in the contemporary
world to medicalize such problems and therewith to turn to the
cultural authority of the health professions and science for an answer to our predicaments. Taking on a medical or scientific perspective, however, doesn't help us to deal with the problem of suffering:
in contemporary biomedicine and the other helping professions
there is no teleological perspective on illness that can address the
components of suffering relating to problems of bafflement, order,
and evil, which appear to be intrinsic to the human condition.
Instead, the modern medical bureaucracy and the helping professions that work within it, as we have seen, are oriented to treat
suffering as a problem of mechanical breakdown requiring a technical fix. They arrange for therapeutic manipulation of disease problems in place of meaningful moral (or spiritual) response to illness
problems.

Clinical and behavioral science research also possess no category
to describe suffering, no routine way of recording this most thickly
human dimension of patients' and families' stories of experiencing
illness. Symptom scales and survey questionnaires and behavioral
checklists quantify functional impairment and disability, rendering
quality of life fungible. Yet about suffering they are silent. The
thinned-out image of patients and families that perforce must
emerge from such research is scientifically replicable but ontologi-
cally invalid; it has statistical, not epistemological, significance; it is
a dangerous distortion. But to evaluate suffering requires more than
the addition of a few questions to a self-report form or a standardized interview; it can only emerge from an entirely different way of
obtaining valid information from illness narratives. Ethnography,
biography, history, psychotherapy—these are the appropriate research methods to create knowledge about the personal world of
suffering. These methods enable us to grasp, behind the simple
sounds of bodily pain and psychiatric symptoms, the complex inner

language of hurt, desperation, and moral pain (and also triumph) of living an illness. The authenticity of the quest for such human knowledge makes us stand in awe because of some resonant sensibility deep within. What is the metric in biomedical and behavioral research for these existential qualities? And lacking such understanding, can the professional knowledge that medical science creates be at all adequate for the needs of patients, their families, and the practitioner?

The problem of illness as suffering raises two fundamental questions for the sick person and the social group: Why me? (the question of bafflement), and What can be done? (the question of order and control). Whereas virtually all healing perspectives across cultures, like religious and moral perspectives, orient sick persons and their circle to the problem of bafflement, the narrow biomedical model eschews this aspect of suffering much as it turns its back on illness (as opposed to disease). Clinicians struggle, therefore, to transcend the limits of biomedicine so as to respond to personal and group bafflement by broadening their professional framework to include other models—such as the biopsychosocial or psychosomatic models—or by joining their patients through adapting either a common-sensical moral view or a more particular religious perspective. The difficulties of importing value systems into the patient–doctor relationship to fill a moral lacuna cannot be overemphasized. For these can and frequently do create even more conflicts than they resolve. The practitioner's values may not be the patient's. A narrowly particularistic moral or religious perspective may alienate, not aid, the family. But what is the alternative?

Consider a situation in which a moral or religious view is shared, forming the basis for the group's response to suffering. The value orientations of Buddhism and medieval Christian theology make of suffering not a wholly disvalued experience to be managed or negotiated, but an occasion for the work of cultural processes to transcend pain and dying. In fourteenth-century Europe, as already noted, when the Black Death depopulated the continent to an unequaled degree, the problem of suffering, articulated as both the question of meaning and the question of control, was a fundamental crisis for society. Society responded by reasserting the core religious and moral meanings that were threatened by the highly malignant epidemic, as well as by applying those few social and technical controls available at the time. In our own time, the threat of man-made catastrophe raises similar questions of suffering; yet the societal response is almost entirely limited to rational-technical manipulations aimed at controlling practical problems, with scant attention to their deeper significance. Indeed, one reason for lay misinterpretations of the scientific discourse on risk is the tendency of laymen to reinterpret, in qualitative, absolute, personalized (non-random) terms, the scientists' quantitative, bell-shaped curves of the random distribution of risks in the population. That is to say, questions of the cultural significance of risk as bafflement come to the fore in spite of professional (and societal) attempts to expunge meaning and value from the equation of care. Suffering is not easily put aside by biomedical science; it remains central to the experience of illness, a core tension in clinical care.

2

The Personal and Social Meanings of Illness

Unscientific utterances can, and indeed usually do, have double meanings, implied meanings, unintended meanings, and can hint and insinuate, and may indeed mean the opposite of what they apparently mean, especially if they are said in a certain tone of voice.

—CHARLES RYCROFT
(1986, 272)

In successfully identifying and understanding what someone else is doing we always move towards placing a particular episode in the context of a set of narrative histories, histories both of the individuals concerned and of the settings in which they act and suffer.

—ALASTAIR MACINTYRE
(1981, 197)

Life World as Meaning

Illness has meaning in a third sense, a sense so central to understanding chronic illness that I will spend much of the rest of this book elaborating and illustrating it and expanding on its therapeutic implications. For in the context of chronic disorder, the illness becomes embodied in a particular life trajectory, environed in a concrete life world. Acting like a sponge, illness soaks up personal and social significance from the world of the sick person. Unlike cultural meanings of illness that carry significance *to* the sick person, this third, intimate type of meaning transfers vital significance from the person's life to the illness experience.

A flareup in the heart disease of an elderly business executive in North American society can become a part of his bereavement for the wife who died six months earlier. This illness incorporates his worsening alcohol abuse and his bitter conflict with his children over control of the family business. It assimilates his fear of dying and guilt over being a lapsed believer, along with his lifelong psychological conflict stemming from fears of passive dependence and of being controlled by others—fears that took origin from a demoralizing relationship with a brutally authoritarian father. Having become an integral element of the illness experience, those fears have recrudesced under the threat of serious incapacity and the undisguised aim of his children to persuade him to enter a nursing home. They are also intensified by his powerful need near the close of life to make sense of key losses by working out the denouement of the narrative of his life's course. The detailed empirical and symbolic particularities of this life trajectory, like those of every other, create a unique texture of meaning—external layers written over internal ones to form a palimpsest—for each person's experience of chronic illness.

This third type of illness meaning is best illustrated with case examples. I will present on the following pages a brief vignette to illustrate the web of meaning that links illness experience to life world. Here the meanings relate to a worsening course and difficult complications of illness at certain critical points in the life course. The central meaning is loss, a common significance of chronic disorder. Care becomes an opportunity to grieve. In the chapters that follow, the cases, which are described at greater length, principally illustrate this third type of illness meaning, though because they are cases from real life they include other types, too. But I take personal and interpersonal meanings to be clinically the most important ones. In fact, it is only in the detailed context of a lengthy case description that we fully appreciate the personal and social meanings of illness. This truncated vignette can offer only a superficial glimpse of how illness absorbs and intensifies life meanings while creating circumstances for which new interpretations are needed.

THE CASE OF ALICE ALCOTT

Alice Alcott is a forty-six-year-old white Protestant female from New Hampshire with a history of juvenile onset diabetes mellitus compounded by cardiovascular complications.* She was referred by her attending surgeon for psychiatric evaluation during recovery from the amputation of her leg below the knee due to a gangrenous ulcer on the left foot; she was tearful and sad to a degree that her physicians and family felt was out of keeping with her prior experiences with the effects of her chronic disorder.

Mrs. Alcott has been married for twenty-three years to a banker in a small New Hampshire town. Three generations of her family have been born and raised in this town. Alice herself was born in the town and attended the local schools. At age ten she developed diabetes, was treated by the town's only medical group, and was hospitalized frequently in the small local hospital. She married a childhood boyfriend, raised two children (Andrew, now twenty, and Christine, seventeen), and became a leading citizen and director of the local public library, historical society, and birding club.

Between the ages of ten and eighteen, she was hospitalized at least once each year for problems related to control of her diabetes. These hospitalizations included two for diabetic coma and several for hypoglycemia owing to exogenous insulin; she has by now had to use the drug for more than thirty-five years.

From the time she went away to college at age eighteen until the birth of her first child when she was twenty-six, Alice had no further hospitalizations. She learned to manage her own disorder on a daily basis, which is in keeping with her independent personality and family tradition. Although Mrs. Alcott was told that pregnancy could make her diabetes worse, and she did experience considerable difficulty with both pregnancies, she delivered two normal babies.

At age thirty Mrs. Alcott experienced some visual problems, and her local physician diagnosed diabetic retinopathy. Over the years she has been treated for this condition at the Massachusetts Eye and Ear Infirmary in Boston, most recently with laser photocoagulation therapy. While her vision has worsened, she is able to read, drive, and carry out almost all other daily activities. At age forty Mrs. Alcott developed a gangrenous toe on her left foot, and the toe was amputated. When she was forty-two another toe was amputated.

---

*All the cases described in these pages have fictitious names to protect their real identity. I have also changed place names, geographical areas, and certain additional details to assure anonymity and confidentiality. Otherwise, the case histories are described as I elicited them either in clinical interviews or in research encounters in patients' homes as well as in clinical settings.

Two and one-half years ago she began to experience pain in both feet when walking fast. Her physician diagnosed intermittent claudication (pain in the legs with exercise because of circulatory insufficiency). With a program of exercise training, relaxation, and progressively longer walks, Mrs. Alcott was able to control this problem. Twelve months before our first meeting, Mrs. Alcott developed chest pain (angina) when walking fairly briskly or climbing stairs. At first she denied the significance and nature of the problem, even though her eighty-year-old mother had developed angina three years before. But her progressive disability became so noticeable to family and friends that Mrs. Alcott felt obliged to visit her physician. She underwent an electrocardiogram (EKG) and treadmill test, which documented coronary artery insufficiency. Mrs. Alcott rejected the recommendation that she have coronary arteriography. She did accept a calcium blocker and nitroglycerine tablets. The former led to substantial side effects of fatigue and weakness.

For the first time in the course of caring for this patient over twenty years, her physician found her irritable and depressed. Her husband, children, and parents corroborated his assessment.

Six months before her initial psychiatric evaluation, Mrs. Alcott developed an ulcer on her left ankle. She had had a similar episode before, caused by compromised venous circulation, and her ulcer had responded well to conservative medical management. On this occasion, however, the ulcer rapidly deteriorated, and osteomyelitis (infection in the bone) was diagnosed by X-ray. The decision to amputate was made only with great reluctance and much anger by the patient, and following a trial of a high-dose intravenous antibiotic.

When I first interviewed Alice Alcott, she was sitting up in her hospital bed looking out her window fixedly, with tightly pursed lips and a mixture of anger and sadness in her expression. She had refused physical therapy, and she had requested that her husband, children, parents, and two sisters not visit her for several days. When her local physician had called to speak to her she had refused to answer the telephone. On morning work rounds her attending surgeon had found her silently crying. She refused to discuss her sadness with the attending surgeon or house staff. She became irascible when her nurses and physical therapist confronted her with the implications of her withdrawal and noncompliance. As a result, the request for psychiatric assessment was made and I found myself entering Alice Alcott's room—and soon thereafter, her world.

At first she refused to speak to me. But no sooner had she angrily dismissed the concerns that led to my visit than she apologized and admitted she needed help.

> It's the final loss. I can't take it anymore. This is too much for me, for anyone. I want to give up. I don't want to try anymore. What's the use? I've contended with this thing since I was a child. It's been one darn thing after another. All losses. What I could eat. What I could do. Diet, insulin, doctors, hospitals, then my eyesight, my walking, my heart, now my leg. What's left to give up?

It was apparent that Mrs. Alcott was grieving her many losses. I would later learn that she was inwardly preparing herself to deal with what she regarded as her final loss, her death, which she thought would not be far off. It was not death that she feared, she would tell me, but the seemingly relentless march toward becoming an invalid. Loss of her leg forced the realization that she was now partially dependent and that one day she would be more completely so.

Alice Alcott, a fifth-generation American, had grown up in a middle-class business family of tough, stoical, dour Yankees. Her ancestors were yeoman farmers from Yorkshire, England, who had settled several small valleys in southern New Hampshire. Her Calvinist cultural background emphasized values of rugged individualism, self-reliance, industry, perseverance, and moral strength. When she was sick as a child, her grandparents told her it was good to endure suffering because it tested and tempered one's character. When she felt self-pity for being the only child with diabetes in her elementary school, her parents and grandparents chided her for being weak and not meeting God's test.

In spite of her diabetes and the frequent hospitalizations, Alice participated actively in high school activities, including sports. During her college years, her diabetes was so well controlled that Alice at times fantasized that she was no longer chronically ill. When they married, she and her husband did not think about what problems or restrictions diabetes would create in their lives. Although she was urged by her physician to consider not having children, Alice Alcott rejected the idea outright. She had successfully coped with her illness, she could do so again. Both pregnancies caused problems with the management of her diabetes, but Alice accepted the difficulty willingly. However, she and her husband agreed to limit their family to two children. Later in life, Alice would remark that this was one of her first significant losses; they had wanted a big family.

In her late twenties and thirties Alice did not let her disease significantly affect her child-rearing plans. She also lived a life of extraordinary energy in community service and as a librarian. The Alcotts were active birders with great interest in the outdoors; they camped, climbed, hiked, and went canoeing and white-water rafting with little attention to Alice's condition.

All of this began to change with the effects of the diabetic retinopathy. Her visual problems were substantial enough to interfere with library work. Eventually she gave up her job and took up the largely honorary position of director of the library committee. Characteristically, Alice denied her symptoms and did not seek medical help until her retinopathy was advanced. Her ophthalmologist and primary care physician admonished her for this behavior and pointed out that the retinopathy would have been easier to treat and less disabling had it been diagnosed earlier.

When Alice was forty a gangrenous toe resulted from another delay in seeking care. Alice had treated the infected toe on her own, as she was accustomed to treating herself with insulin and doing her own blood- and urine-sugar tests. The loss of the toe came as a shock. Alice said that she had had the ominous feeling that this was the beginning of more serious problems. The intermittent claudication was an even more substantial blow. She had felt at first that her outdoor activities, active lifestyle, and work would end. But as with so many other of the problems that had arisen, this, too, seemed to come under control.

Then the angina started. Terrified by the implications of this problem, Alice responded with even more substantial denial than she had used to deal with the earlier complications of the diabetes. Alice experienced pain as she shopped, visited the library, and went out with friends and family. It became obvious to many in her town that something was seriously wrong. Her husband, children, and parents had to work hard to force Alice to admit that she had to see the doctor.

"By that time I couldn't face up to it anymore. I didn't want Dr. Torres to tell me that my diabetes had reached my heart. I didn't want to know."

Alice did not take the doctor's news well; she began to feel hopeless and demoralized.

How was I going to live with this limitation? What a burden I would be on my family and friends. I feared becoming the town invalid. I was terribly guilty. I had felt all along that my illness had interfered with my relationship to my children. I never had enough time to give them. I was more preoccupied with myself than with their problems. I was in the hospital at critical times for them. Now I would be nothing but a burden. As far as my husband goes, the guilt was worse. After the chest pain, I feared having sexual relations. We became celibate. The claudication, the angina, they interfered with the things we loved: long walks in the country, birding, climbing, sports. I had to become self-centered in order to control my condition. I felt like a survivor—all I was good for was hanging on. . . .

The calcium blockers at first made things worse. The side effects of weakness and exhaustion frightened Alice Alcott even more than the chest pain.

That was when I began to see how terrible it would be to be incapacitated—to give up even the semblance of my independence, my control, my role in the family and in the community. What a relief to learn it was the side effect of the medication. The dosage was reduced, and either the side effects lessened or I learned to control them. Anyway, I had fought my way back once more. I was getting back to myself. I was able to be a wife and mother again, albeit with plenty of guilt and self-doubts. And then this ankle. It was the last straw. Not another problem. Not another loss. I felt like I couldn't go on. About the only things left to go were my kidneys, and when they did I felt it was all over for me. I began to feel really helpless, and lost my sense of worth. I was shattered and broken. How much more could I deal with before I gave up?

When she had experienced the angina, Alice had also begun to feel considerable anger. She felt she had done all the things she was supposed to do for her diabetes (carefully regulating her diet, taking insulin daily, testing blood and urine sugar since childhood). She had avoided the hypertension that other diabetic patients she knew had developed. She worked hard to control her risk factors, and still it had done no good.

"I was tremendously angry. Angry at the doctors, at myself, at the diabetes. Angry even at God. Why was He doing this to me?"

The loss of the foot, coming so close on the other problems, seemed overwhelming. Mrs. Alcott became demoralized; as she put it:

I was ready to give up. I felt as if I were grieving for my lost health and life itself. Death might be better. Certainly being very dependent on others, being an invalid, looked bad, very bad. I had run out of alternatives. I felt I might just as well wallow in my own misery.

From a psychiatric standpoint Alice Alcott was deeply distressed and depressed in response to her chronic illness, but although she was desperate, her state did not warrant the clinical diagnosis of major depressive disorder or any other serious psychiatric syndrome. Her problem was not a mental disease but a reaction, in large part (it seemed to me) justified by her suffering and disablement. I saw her periodically over the next few years, whenever she was in Boston. Her emotional state improved as she became more effective in dealing with her amputation. Eventually she got back to many of the activities that made up her world. She is a remarkably resilient woman with great adaptive strengths and a marvelous support system. Early in psychotherapy, our sessions centered on grief for her multiple losses. But as her spirits lifted, she returned to her characteristic denial. The last few times we met, she would discuss her children's problems, her parents' problems, anything but her own.

I choose to remember Alice Alcott by a statement she made at our third or fourth meeting in the hospital room. Her words have left a powerful mark on my work with the chronically ill:

Time is running out for me, doctor. For others there is hope of cure. But for me this disease can never go away. The complications get more severe. The losses are greater. Soon, if not now, there will come a time when those losses are so great I will not want to bounce back. I have lost all confidence in my body. My disease has taken over. If not now, then next week, next month, next year—things will be worse again. In the meantime, what is there for me: no left foot, a bad heart, poor circulation even to my good leg, failing vision. Parents I can't take care of, children for whom I am unavailable. A husband as exhausted and despondent as I am. Myself, doctor, facing the long downhill road. Perhaps speaking to you will help me now, but can it change that road? No! I will do my best again to fight back.

I will try to get on top of this thing. Yet in the long run, I will go down that road myself. Neither you nor anyone else can prevent it, or control it, or understand it for me. Can you give me the courage I need?

For Alice Alcott, a stoical style of expressing illness problems (especially serious ones), a characteristic use of denial, and a crescendo of symptoms that are specially serious for her illustrate the first layer of illness meanings. Her diabetes has no special cultural cachet in present-day North America. But she confided that her friends seemed to regard diabetes as a relatively minor problem when compared to other chronic disorders, one they thought would not lead to significant disability. This erroneous view angered her because she knew diabetes to be very serious and found that others' misconceptions were burdensome and needed to be responded to. At the third level of illness meanings, Alice Alcott was absorbed by many losses: she grieved for the loss of a body part, physical function, body- and self-image, and way of life; she also experienced bereavement in anticipation of her own demise. The psychotherapeutic treatment she received involved the work of grieving; in my experience, psychotherapy for the chronically medically ill is often a kind of mourning. But clinical actions to remoralize patients may follow other paths. The practitioner helps patients (and their families) to gain control over fear and to come to terms with their overwhelming anger at functional limitation. He or she helps the patient to restore confidence in body and self. The work of the healer is also to educate sick persons to escape both excessive feelings of guilt over failures in life activities and jealousy toward others who are free of serious disorder. Finally, the practitioner will help the patient to prepare for death.

UNDERSTANDING THE PATIENT'S INNER WORLD

For analytical purposes, I will canvass the third type of illness meaning, illustrated by the case of Alice Alcott, beginning with the private, inner world of personal experience and thereafter moving outward through the webs of interpersonal significance that bind a person to the social world. Yet I do not want to distort the interconnections between affect, cognition, and local social system that make of each life a seamless whole: social structure is an integral part of inner experience, and fantasies and emotions are equally integral to the very stuff of the social world.

Much of the most original work of twentieth-century psychiatrists and psychologists who have studied either medical disorders or the inner world of the person has emerged from investigations of the peculiar personal significance of chronic illness. Freud devoted his prodigious critical skills to this problem, which, after all, in the guise of hysteria was the founding clinical problem for psychoanalysis. Among his followers, Paul Shilder, Franz Alexander, Felix Deutsch, Michael Balint, and Georg Groddeck were as intrigued as the master himself by the workings of the symbolic continuum between psyche and soma, which each could see held rich therapeutic implications for a thoroughly psychosomatic approach to medicine.

To begin with, symptoms were interpreted by the early analysts as symbols indexing deeply personal significations: sexual conflicts, issues in dependency and passivity, drives to control and dominate. At times these meanings were held to cause the symptoms with which they were associated, through a process of psychosomatic transduction that materialized psychic conflicts as somatic complaints. Such symptoms were thought to be a symbolic expression of core unconscious themes in the repressed neurotic conflict of the patient's psychic life. Although the model proved to be a useful explanation of the classical symptoms of hysterical conversion (conversion disorder), it was shown not to apply to most psychosomatic or chronic medical conditions (Lipowski 1968, 1969). Indeed, there has not been empirical support for the association of particular symptoms either with particular personality types or with particular neurotic conflicts. To the contrary, the same psychological problems seem either to be nonspecifically associated with the entire gamut of psychosomatic and chronic medical problems or not to be related at all to such problems.

The narrowly psychoanalytic approach to the interpretation of illness meanings has become an extremely difficult path to follow, a tortuous lane, which, for all its fascination and promise, leads to the dead end of speculation and an absence of research.

In some cases of classical conversion, however, the unaccepted meanings of inner psychic conflict can quite literally be seen to materialize as symptom symbols, the disappearance of which can be brought about by the deeply felt expression or symbolic manipulation of the unconscious conflict. Hence the original insight into the problem continues to intrigue and provoke. For example, I once evaluated a patient with acute paralysis of the legs (paraplegia), which his neurologist suspected was conversion because the neurological examination revealed no clear-cut pathology; the patient had previously been in good physical health. During our interview the patient, a vulnerable man in his late twenties who was quite obviously in the throes of a major neurotic conflict, revealed that he was deadlocked in a no-win battle with his father. The father insisted that the patient take over the family business and adamantly refused to consider his son's poignant request that he be allowed to pursue a career as a painter and sculptor. The patient broke down into tears as he recounted his father's overbearing, insensitive attitude and his own fear that his father would force him to renounce his dreams. After lamenting that his father regarded his artistic interests as silly and unmanly and had always criticized his son for being "effete and effeminate," the patient began to rehash a lifetime of frustrating interactions with this family autocrat who had terrorized the patient since childhood.

"I never have been able to stan, stan, stand up on my own two feet before my, my, my father," he stuttered. Moments later, almost as suddenly as it had come on, his paralysis began to disappear. Over the course of a half hour it was entirely gone, leaving no physical consequences.

The symbolic meaning in this case was not terribly complex or original: the patient's paralysis of the legs expressed graphically the his childlike helplessness in not being able to resist his father's dominance and choose an autonomous career in keeping with his own adult self-image. How paralyses like this are actually caused and what mediating psychophysiological processes in catharsis and abreaction are responsible for their resolution constitute a great mystery at the heart of psychosomatic medicine. Nonetheless, enough is known about conversion symptoms to describe them as the literal embodiment of conflicted meanings, somatic symbols that have psychological and social uses. Here the paralysis of muscle covertly expresses the patient's paralysis of will, while the resulting disability has the practical effect of legitimately preventing the patient from doing what his father demands but what for him is unacceptable. The problem with psychoanalytic interpretations is that their creators are dissatisfied with this level of analysis and reach for "deeper" meanings for which there is usually little clinical or scientific justification. A single-minded quest for psychoanalytic reality can dehumanize the patient every bit as much as the numbing reductionism of an obsessively biomedical investigation.

Symptom onset in this case, and in many similar ones treated by psychiatrists, is interpreted in the context of the special meanings within which the illness is embedded. Symptom and context can be interpreted as symbol and text. The latter extends and clarifies the significance of the former; the former crystallizes the latent possibilities of the latter. The text is laden with potential meanings, but in the symptom-symbol only one or a few become effective. There is, of course, both sufficient redundancy in the living symbolism of the symptoms and density of meanings in the life text and enough uncertainty and ambiguity in their interpretation to make this aspect of clinical work more like literary criticism or anthropological analysis of a ritual in an alien society than like the interpretation of a laboratory test or a microscopic slide of a tumor. And yet there is also something similar in the interpretive process of these human actions of reconfiguring illness as disease, especially as they are affected by the exigent context of illness and the therapeutic mandate to intervene to relieve suffering, that makes each of these clinical behaviors diverge from the methods of physical science. Perhaps I am describing what it is in the nature of illness behavior (for, after all, patient and family are actively engaged in interpretation, too) and the tasks of doctoring that suggests both are closer to the human sciences, where the work of interpretation is now seen to be a fundamental activity.

Although the contribution of bodily symbols, as illustrated by the case of hysterical paralysis, is not significant, nor need be so, in most cases of chronic illness, health professionals have become accustomed in cases like Alice Alcott's to examining (usually intuitively and casually) how the personal domain of passions and inner turmoil worsen the illness experience. Freud's great contribution here was to authorize the interpretation of the biography of the patient

and the interpersonal context of disorder as an appropriate component of the practitioner's craft. For Freud and his followers, events
in the kitchen, the office, the schoolroom all were necessary to
interpret the text of illness fully. This vision continues to attract
numbers of psychiatrists, psychologists, primary care physicians,
nurses, social workers, and other members of the helping professions to construct a new language of general health care that ad-
dresses the deeply private significance of illness.

When the patient under examination disrobes to expose a body
covered with the ugly scars of eczema or with the raw, red, flaking
plaques of psoriasis, the practitioner should recognize that shame,
hurt, anger, despair, or other constellations of feelings probably are
present. As key ingredients of the illness experience, these feelings
are likely to affect the patient's life experiences in general, the illness
per se, and the response to care. The role of the health professional
is not so much to ferret out the innermost secrets (which can easily
lend itself to a dangerous kind of voyeurism) as it is to assist the
chronically ill and those around them to come to terms with—that
is, accept, master, or change—those personal significances that can
be shown to be operating in their lives and in their care. I take this
to constitute the essence of what is now called empowering patients.

Explanation and Emotion as Meaning

Alice Alcott's case is an example of yet another kind of illness
meaning, the struggle of sick persons, their families, and practitioners to fashion serviceable explanations of the various aspects of
illness and treatment. Roughly speaking, these explanatory accounts seem to respond to any or all of the following questions:
What is the cause of the disorder? Why did it have its onset precisely when it did? What does the illness do to my body? What
course is it following now, and what course can I expect it to follow
in the future? What is the source of improvements and exacerbations? How can I control the illness, its exacerbations, and its consequences? What are the principal effects the illness has had on my

(our) life? What do I most fear about this illness? What treatment do I wish to receive? What do I expect of the treatment? What effects of the treatment do I fear? Although I have stated the questions in the terms of the sick person, these are also the concerns of the family. When practitioners engage patients' views of illness, they, too, must respond to these concerns.

These questions are not asked simply to obtain information. They are deeply felt. The facial expression, tone of voice, posture, body movements, gait, and, especially, the eyes expose the emotional turmoil that is so much a part of the long-term experience of chronic illness. The manner in which difficult sentiments—anger, despair, guilt, worry—are expressed and dealt with also reveals how the sick person and the family are handling the illness. For affective turbulence is not so much a reaction to the chronic problem as an expectable part of being chronically ill. Such turbulence, furthermore, is an expression of a physiological dialectic that can produce or result from major alterations in the illness. Change in chronic illness is almost never inconsequential. The chronically ill live at the margins. Even a modest change can be the difference between acceptable, if frustrating, quiescence, and an eruption of symptoms distressing enough to yield a condition that is unacceptable and, not infrequently, dangerous.

Chronic illness behavior can mask a mood with a dissimulating smile or a stiff upper lip; on the other side, it can be as limpid as a gush of tears or a bloody curse of frustration. It has been said of Mozart's music that even where all seems quiet and under control it is best regarded as a formal Italian garden built on the side of an active volcano. The undercurrent of chronic illness is like the volcano: it does not go away. It menaces. It erupts. It is out of control. One damned thing follows another. Confronting crises is only one part of the total picture. The rest is coming to grips with the mundaneness of worries over whether one can negotiate a curb, tolerate flowers without wheezing, make it to a bathroom quickly enough, eat breakfast without vomiting, keep the level of back pain low enough to get through the workday, sleep through the night, attempt sexual intercourse, make plans for a vacation, or just plain face up to the myriad of difficulties that make life feel burdened, uncomfortable, and all too often desperate. It has always seemed to me that there is a kind of quiet heroism that comes from meeting these problems and the sentiments they provoke, of getting through each day, of living through the long course with grace and spirit and even humor; sick persons and their families understand the courage, even if most others do not.

Chronic illness also means the loss of confidence in one's health and normal bodily processes. The asthmatic can no longer count on unobstructed breathing or a quick end to a fit of coughing. The epileptic lives under the very point of the sword of Damocles, uncertain when a fit will come. The sufferer of chronic sinusitis goes from partially blocked nasal passages on one side to some obstruction on both sides, then to completely stopped up passages with fullness, pounding in the ears, and mouth breathing—which interferes with sleep and causes air swallowing and its effects (gas, abdominal cramps). The sick person intervenes with nasal inhalers or oral decongestants. The former are transiently useful, but over time have less effect and may produce rebound sinus congestion. The latter may produce abdominal discomfort and lethargy, and they may worsen asthma. All of this endured, calculated, worried over, so as to avoid the next episode of illness. Each time the cycle of symptoms begins, the sufferer loses faith in the dependability and adaptability of basic bodily processes that the rest of us rely on as part of our general sense of well-being. This loss of confidence becomes grim expectation of the worst, and, in some, demoralization and hopelessness.

A closely related feeling, illustrated by our case vignette, is grief and wretchedness over loss of health, a mourning for the bodily foundation of daily behavior and self-confidence. The fidelity of our bodies is so basic that we never think of it—it is the certain grounds of our daily experience. Chronic illness is a betrayal of that fundamental trust. We feel under siege: untrusting, resentful of uncertainty, lost. Life becomes a working out of sentiments that follow closely from this corporeal betrayal: confusion, shock, anger, jealousy, despair.

Physiological aspects of chronic illness shape explanatory models and the meanings they encapsulate. Helman (1985) shows that the explanations given by asthma and ulcerative colitis patients are different in large measure owing to the experience of two distinctive kinds of pathological change: acute threat to vital processes and chronic discomfit, respectively. Meaning and physiological experience intertwine so that dread and self-defeating self-concept cascade, provoking physiological processes already poised and conditioned to tumble. From there the vicious cycle can commence with symbol or symptom. The worst outcome is giving up, which registers in the explanatory account of patients as an inveterate, unappeasable, inexorable expectation of decline.

Patients and families are coping with a day-by-day course that encompasses many individual episodes and events. There are serious consequences, some avoidable, others not. There are spells of improvement and periods of worsening (at times understandably, at other times inexplicably, linked). And there are threats to daily activities, special occasions, career, relationships, and, perhaps most distressingly, self-esteem. The treatment of chronic illness brings added difficulties. Expenses are substantial. Enormous blocks of time are spent traveling to and from clinics, sitting and standing in doctors' offices, undergoing laboratory tests, lying in hospital beds, waiting. Time is also dissipated prodigally in special treatment regimens that can interfere significantly with diet, life style, recreation, and the otherwise taken for granted activities of daily living. Symptoms must be explained to receptionists, nurses, and different doctors. The same questions are answered over and over again. The patient must wait for the pharmacist or doctor or insurance company to call. All are exhausting. They create frustration, irritability, and not infrequently a low-grade rebelliousness that periodically explodes into open revolt. There are also disturbing and unpredictable side effects of medications. Risky tests and new interventions have iatrogenic consequences. Many chronically ill persons experiment with health foods, acupuncture, self-hypnosis, and the whole gamut of alternative therapists who, on the one hand, like the snake-oil salesmen of old, live off the inefficacy of available orthodox cures, yet, on the other hand, give hope and sometimes help. Self-treatment, lay advice, and doctor shopping are routine. So are problems in therapeutic relationships with practitioners who often are as frustrated and impotent feeling as patients. Moreover, this panoply of activities takes up the interest and energy of the social network too, so that, with time, frustrating resentment and exasperation spread to others. And behind the frenetic activity and worry and uncertainty looms the threat of awful complications and untimely death.

For the chronically ill, details are all. To cope with chronic illness means to routinely scan minute bodily processes. Attention is vigilantly focused, sometimes hour by hour, to the specifics of circumstances and events that could be potential sources of worsening. There is the daily quest for control of the known provoking agents. Enervating decisions must be made about when to initiate or terminate an activity, when to move from baseline medication to second-level drugs, and when to seek professional help. And all this occurs in the context of active lives that are filled with the same pressures, threats, vagaries, and exultations that make of normal living such a "blooming, buzzing confusion" (James [1890] 1981, 462). Is it any wonder that exhaustion is one of the common shared experiences of chronic illness?

There are hundreds of varieties of chronic illness. Several chronic illnesses per person are the norm among the frail elderly, those over seventy-five years of age. Most individuals over sixty experience at least one chronic disorder. And chronic illness is also common in the other stages of the life cycle. Thus, we are discussing an immense burden of morbidity, present in all societies. Through the personal and economic costs of distress and disability chronic illness leaves no unit of society unaffected. The chronically ill, if not you or I, are our parents, grandparents, children, siblings, aunts and uncles, friends, neighbors, co-workers, or clients. With such a ubiquitous problem, one can only marvel at the societal devices of denial that keep this normative aspect of life so well hidden. Images of widespread chronic illness are not what capitalist or socialist ideologies want to represent to their members as the states try to encourage consumption or mobilize enthusiasm for governmental campaigns. The imagery of infirmity and disorder provokes moral questions that most social systems prefer not to encourage. In the current age, where image making is the essence of politics, no regime wants to expose these realities lest they threaten the naive optimism they seek to maintain in the population.

To try to deal with the difficulties I have reviewed, questions about cause and effects and effective ways of managing illness must arise. The answers to these questions come not only from the sick person but from anyone in the social network, the media, or the orthodox and alternative therapeutic systems. These explanatory accounts are essential for the more immediate tactics of tacking through the rough seas of chronic illness; moreover, the long-term strategies for assessing the deeper, more powerful currents that influence the chronic course of disorder also require continuous surveillance and information gathering. Thus, the chronically ill are somewhat like revisionist historians, refiguring past events in light of recent changes. (They are, unfortunately, also frequently condemned to repeat history even when they learn from it.) Interpreting what has happened and why and prognosticating what might happen make of the present a constant, self-reflective grappling with illness meanings. Does this event portend a break in the dike of therapeutic and preventive defenses? Did that experience mean I can no longer rely on this coping strategy? Will that upcoming circumstance provoke an exacerbation, as it did a year ago, or pass by unnoticed, as it did two years ago?

The chronically ill become interpreters of good and bad omens. They are archivists researching a disorganized file of past experiences. They are diarists recording the minute ingredients of current difficulties and triumphs. They are cartographers mapping old and new territories. And they are critics of the artifacts of disease (color of sputum, softness of stool, intensity of knee pain, size and form of skin lesions). There is in this persistent reexamination the opportunity for considerable self-knowledge. But—as with all of us— denial and illusion are ready at hand to assure that life events are not so threatening and supports seem more durable. Myth making, a universal human quality, reassures us that resources conform to our desires rather than to actual descriptions. In short, self-deception makes chronic illness tolerable. Who can say that illusion and myth are not useful to maintain optimism, which itself may improve physiological performance (Hahn and Kleinman 1982; Tiger 1980)? The point I am making is that the meanings of chronic illness are created by the sick person and his or her circle to make over a wild, disordered *natural* occurrence into a more or less domesticated, mythologized, ritually controlled, therefore *cultural* experience.

Patients' explanatory models of chronic illness open up practical behavioral options in its treatment; they also enable sick persons to order, communicate, and thereby symbolically control symptoms. One of the core tasks in the effective clinical care of the chronically ill—one whose value it is all too easy to underrate—is to affirm the patient's experience of illness as constituted by lay explanatory models and to negotiate, using the specific terms of those models, an acceptable therapeutic approach. Another core clinical task is the empathetic interpretation of a life story that makes over the illness into the subject matter of a biography. Here the clinician listens to the sick individual's personal myth, a story that gives shape to an illness so as to distance an otherwise fearsome reality. The clinician attends to the patient's and family's summation of life's trials. Their narrative highlights core life themes—for example, injustice, courage, personal victory against the odds—for whose prosecution the details of illness supply evidence.

Thus, patients order their experience of illness—what it means to them and to significant others—as personal narratives. The illness narrative is a story the patient tells, and significant others retell, to give coherence to the distinctive events and long-term course of suffering. The plot lines, core metaphors, and rhetorical devices that structure the illness narrative are drawn from cultural and personal models for arranging experiences in meaningful ways and for effectively communicating those meanings. Over the long course of chronic disorder, these model texts shape and even create experience. The personal narrative does not merely reflect illness experience, but rather it contributes to the experience of symptoms and suffering. To fully appreciate the sick person's and the family's experience, the clinician must first piece together the illness narrative as it emerges from the patient's and the family's complaints and explanatory models; then he or she must interpret it in light of the different modes of illness meanings—symptom symbols, culturally salient illnesses, personal and social contexts.

Illness story making and telling are particularly prevalent among the elderly. They frequently weave illness experience into the apparently seamless plot of their life stories, whose denouement they are constantly revising. In the terminal phase of life, looking backward constitutes much of the present. That gaze back over life's difficult treks is as fundamental to this ultimate stage of the life cycle as dream making is in adolescence and young adulthood. Things remembered are tidied up, put in their proper place, rethought, and, equally important, retold, in what can be regarded as a story rapidly approaching its end: the tale of the aged. Constructing a coherent account with an appropriate conclusion is a final bereavement for all that is left behind and for oneself.

Illnesses, like other misfortunes, occupy an edifying place in this tale as exemplary difficulties and determinant forces, something that was formidable, now to be smiled over. Illness, assimilated to a life story, helps the elderly patient illustrate life's high and low points. The very same process of narratization that is central to the psychobiological transformation of this developmental phase, not very surprisingly then, is an integral component of the elderly patient's response to illness, past and present. Telling this tale is of great significance. It establishes a kind of final expertise to authorize the giving of advice and to reaffirm bonds with the young and with those survivors who will carry on the account after a person's death. For the care giver what is important is to witness a life story, to validate its interpretation, and to affirm its value.

Most of us figure out our own thoughts by speaking them to the persons whose reactions are as important as our own. Something like this happens as the elderly rehearse with us their stories, though with the cognitive losses of advanced aging the former dialogues more and more become soliloquies. Few of the tragedies at life's end are as rending to the clinician as that of the frail elderly patient who has no one to tell the life story to. Indeed, becoming a surrogate for those who should be present to listen may be one of the practitioner's finest roles in the care of the aged.

Restrospective narratization is also frequent in situations where an illness had a catastrophic end, or when such an end has narrowly been avoided. In these instances, the narrative may hold a moral purpose; it acts something like the recitation of myth in a ritual that reaffirms core cultural values under siege and reintegrates social relations whose structural tensions have been intensified. Illness narrative, again like the ritual use of myth, gives shape and finality to a loss (cf. Turner 1967). The story of a sickness may even function as a political commentary, pointing a finger of condemnation at perceived injustice and the personal experience of oppression

(Taussig 1980). For these reasons, retrospective narratization can readily be shown to distort the actual happenings (the history) of the illness experience, since its raison d'être is not fidelity to historical circumstances but rather significance and validity in the creation of a life story.

A more ominous kind of retrospective narratization occurs in the tendentious reworking of an account of illness and treatment to fit the line of argument of a disability suit or malpractice litigation. There is a reciprocal activity in the physician's recording of the case, where disease episodes are at times reconstructed with an eye on peer review and official examination of the record; the account may serve to protect the practitioner from bureaucratic criticism and legal sanction. In an era of epidemic medical-legal suits with unprecedented peer review pressures, we can expect this aspect of illness meanings to take on increasingly menacing personal and public significance. Of course, retrospective narratization by the practitioner often serves functions reciprocal to those described for lay persons: cautionary tale, moral exemplar, final reckoning of a patient's life, and so forth. Inasmuch as all practitioners need to believe in their own professional competence, which comes under acute assault in the unpredictable, poorly controlled course of chronic disorder, the health professional's creation of a narrative may function as a kind of second guessing that protects against feelings of inadequacy and even failure.

There is an analogue of the patient's and family's explanatory models of illness in what the clinician *interprets* for the illness behavior of a particular patient with a particular disorder in a particular situation at a particular time. Clinicians (and researchers, too) come to recognize not only the disease. They also see the personal significances and social uses of chronic illness. But physicians' visions are not panoramic. Rather they focus upon different elements in their explanatory accounts: the person, the setting, the illness, or an aspect of the illness behavior. Every journeyman clinician knows that chronic illness is overdetermined and conveys several and often many meanings: not this or that, but this and that—and that. How does the clinician decide in a given case which meanings are primary and which secondary? The process of selective interpretation reflects the interests of the observer-professional and the intended uses of the interpretations for the care of a chronically ill patient. This practical therapeutic orientation constrains the interpretation as much as do the interests of the patient and family. I will disclose this process in the illness accounts that are described in chapter 7, and in the two concluding chapters I expand on this topic as part of my consideration of the relationship of illness meanings to the work of the practitioner. Here I simply wish to point out that personal (countertransference) and professional (disease) interests of the clinician strongly influence the illness interpretation. The clinical account, in turn, is perhaps better regarded as the active creation of illness meanings in a dialogue with the subject than as the resultant of passive observation of them in the patient as an object.

That is to say, illness has particular meanings for practitioners who listen to a patient's account of illness in light of their own special interests (therapeutic, scientific, professional, financial, personal). Even before the physician entifies an elusive illness into a precise disease, the very ways of auditing the illness account influence the giving of the account and its interpretation. Patients are usually aware of the demands of different settings—home, public clinic, private office, disability agency, courtroom—and how these help cast the story in a certain form. Similarly, health professionals, when they stop to think about it (and in the exigency of the clinical day most do not), recognize that how they listen to these accounts constrains the telling and the hearing. The busy surgeon in an emergency unit, the obstetrician on hospital rounds, the internist in a union or industry clinic, the psychiatrist in a state hospital ward or in a private office, the exhausted intern, the professor out to make a point about bioethics—all attend differently. The way they nod their head, fidget, or look at the patient influences how the patient tells the illness story. Moreover, the priorities of the practitioner lead to selective attention to the patient's account, so that some aspects are carefully listened for and heard (sometimes when they are not spoken), while other things that are said—and even repeated—are literally not heard. The physician's training also encourages the dangerous fallacy of over-literal interpretation of accounts best understood metaphorically.

I regard these phenomena as the way *clinical reality*—the definition of the problem at hand and the awareness of the others' expectations about how to act therapeutically—is constructed differently by different health professionals interacting with different patients in different settings. Financial issues, the ubiquitous bottom line in a capitalist society, loom large as a not-so-hidden interest in clinical encounters and not infrequently distort clinical communication and practice. Clinicians (and researchers, too) need to unpack their own interpretive schemes, which are portmanteaus filled with personal and cultural biases. They also must rethink the versions of the clinical world they create. They must be certain where therapeutic interests are being altered by concerns of theory validation, research publication, or just plain making a living and advancing a professional career. The professional biases that underwrite invidious stereotypes of certain categories of chronic patients (for example, as "crocks" or "trolls" or "your typical pain patient") are another example. These human interests need to be the subject of ongoing self-reflective sorting by the interpreters of patient accounts to be sure that the interpretations they render are not tendentious delegitimations of the illness experience, obstacles to effective care. This is a simply enormous problem in clinical practice and research with chronic patients that has not been adequately addressed.

At this fourth level of illness meanings, Alice Alcott's physicians did not want to hear or see her demoralization. Denial is most often a social act. They were deeply threatened by her tacit explanatory model that the course of her illness would lead relentlessly downhill (an expectation they came to share silently). Alice Alcott stopped short of giving up, and she adapted once again to a serious loss. She has insight into her own tendency to give up and its dangerous implications. And her practitioners came to terms with their own feelings of frustrating impotence. Dr. Torres, a Hispanic-American physician, learned to change his ethnic biases about New England Yankees, namely, that they are cold and insensitive. He eventually saw Alice as neither of these. He came to recognize that his stereotype was a means of avoiding his own grieving for her condition. As the consulting psychiatrist, I had to overcome both my tendency to insist on diagnosing a treatable psychiatric disease (that is, major depressive disorder), in spite of evidence to the contrary, and my desire to place Alice on antidepressant pharmacologic agents that would, I fantasized, lead to a cure.

Remoralization in the progressively incapacitating downhill phase of illness derives, I believe, not from a particular technique but from the combination of many clinical acts. I have emphasized empathic witnessing. That is the existential commitment to be with the sick person and to facilitate his or her building of an illness narrative that will make sense of and give value to the experience. But the practitioner also struggles to model courage and to see it in others. Doctors also sanction suffering by drawing on irony, paradox, humor, and what wisdom they have acquired—including the knowledge of when to stop. This I take to be the moral core of doctoring and of the experience of illness. The commoditization of the healer–sick person relationship as an economic transaction cannot quantify this aspect of the relationship, which, as a shared virtue, is not captured by a cost/benefit equation or financial bottom line. It is rather the healer's gift as well as that of the patient.

William James, addressing the distinguished audiences assembled in Edinburgh for his 1896 Gifford lectures, which would become his still-influential masterpiece, *The Varieties of Religious Experience,* spoke of two kinds of practical personal perspectives on experience, which—with a sensitivity to the problem of suffering and also to his audiences' likely stereotypes of Europeans as sophisticates and Americans as innocents—he aptly characterized the once and twice born. The once born James took to be native optimists who tended to see everyday life and religion on the surface: hopeful, positive, well-ordered, progressive. The twice born, in contrast, were more pessimistic. They tended to focus on the darker underside of experience. The twice born were absorbed by questions of social injustice and personal pain.

The experience of chronic illness often converts the once born into the twice born. As the Soviet dissident and now émigré poet Irina Ratushinskaya (1987, 19), meditating on her own hard-won wisdom, ironically puts it in one of her poems about her brutal prison experience:

> Such a gift can happen only once,
> Perhaps one needs it only once.

The moral lesson illness teaches is that there are undesired and undeserved pains that must be lived through, that beneath the façade of bland optimism regarding the natural order of things, there is a deeper apprehension of a dark, hurtful stream of negative events and troubles. Change, caprice, and chaos, experienced in the body, challenge what order we are led to believe—need to believe—exists. Disability and death force us to reconsider our lives and our world. The possibility for human transformation, immanent or transcendent, sometimes begins with this disconcerting vision. Literalists about behavior and its sources may thus acquire a more textured, figurative, self-reflective vision of the world. The rational calculus that is supposed to make "supply and demand" the hardheaded wisdom of economic man will seem to mystify what is at stake in self-knowledge for man the afflicted. For the seriously ill, insight can be the result of an often grim, though occasionally luminous, lived wisdom of the body in pain and the mind troubled. For family members and practitioners, moral insight can emerge from the felt experience of sympathy and empathy. It is this particular sense that I take to be the inner moral meaning of chronic illness and care.

These four kinds of illness meanings, and the variety of subtypes I have traced out in these pages, are not meant to be exhaustive. There are surely other types. But I believe that I have covered the most important varieties. My intention has been to set out a theoretical grid that we can use to analyze actual cases of chronic illness and thereby generalize from the issues outlined in these first chapters. In the human context of illness, experience is created out of the dialectic between cultural category and personal signification on the one side, and the brute materiality of disordered biological processes on the other. The recurrent effect of narrative on physiology, and of pathology on story, is the source of the shape and weight of lived experience. That felt world combines feeling, thought, and bodily process into a single vital structure underlying continuity and change in illness. Coming to terms with this human dialectic transforms our understanding of the difficult life problems that issue from chronic illness and of how they are best treated; it also alters our appreciation of what medicine and health care are all about. I turn now to detailed descriptions of the illness experiences of actual patients with distinctive illness problems.

3

The Vulnerability of Pain and the Pain of Vulnerability

For the person in pain, so incontestably and unnegotiably present is it that "having pain" may come to be thought of as the most vibrant example of what it is to "have certainty," while for the other person it is so elusive that "hearing about pain" may exist as the primary model of what it is "to have doubt." Thus pain comes unsharably into our midst as at once that which cannot be denied and that which cannot be confirmed.

—Elaine Scarry
(1985, 4)

. . . I am bound
Upon a wheel of fire that mine own tears
Do scald like molten lead.

—William Shakespeare
King Lear (IV.vii.46–48)

Chronic pain is a major public health concern in North American society (Osterweis et al. 1987). Whether in the form of disabling chronic lower back pain or severe migraine headaches or in the somewhat less common types affecting neck, face, chest, abdomen, arms and legs, or the whole body, chronic pain syndromes are an increasingly common source of disability in our time (Stone 1984). Paradoxically, the medical profession is dangerous for chronic pain patients. Medical care fosters addiction to narcotic analgesic drugs, polypharmacy (the use of multiple drugs) with medications that exert serious side effects, overuse of expensive and risky tests, unnecessary surgery that can produce serious damage, and obstacles to leaving the disabled role. The disability system contributes as well by its active disincentives for the patient to undertake rehabilitation and to return to work. Both systems create anger and frustration for patients and families (Katon et al. 1982; Turner and Chapman 1982).

If there is a single experience shared by virtually all chronic pain patients it is that at some point those around them—chiefly practitioners, but also at times family members—come to question the authenticity of the patient's experience of pain. This response contributes powerfully to patients' dissatisfaction with the professional treatment system and to their search for alternatives. Chronic pain discloses that the training and methods of health professionals appear to prevent them from effectively caring for the chronically ill. Reciprocally, chronic pain patients are the bête noire of many health professionals, who come to find them excessively demanding, hostile, and undermining of care. A duet of escalating antagonism ensues, much to the detriment of the protagonists.

Chronic pain involves one of the most common processes in the human experience of illness worldwide, a process I will refer to by the inelegant but revealing name *somatization*. Somatization is the communication of personal and interpersonal problems in a physical idiom of distress and a pattern of behavior that emphasizes the seeking of medical help. Somatization is a sociophysiological continuum of experience: at one end are cases in which patients complain of bodily ailments in the absence of any pathological bodily processes—either as a conscious act (malingering, which is unusual and easy to detect) or as an unconscious expression of life problems (so-called conversion, which is more common); at the other end are cases in which patients who are experiencing the disordered physiology of medical or psychiatric disease amplify beyond explainable levels their symptoms and the impairment in functioning those symptoms create, usually without being aware of their exaggeration. In the latter category of patients, which is by far the largest, three types of influences intensify the illness experience and promote overutilization of health care services. These are social (particularly family and work) conditions that encourage expressions of distress, cultural idioms of misery that use a language of bodily complaints to represent personal and interpersonal problems, and individual psychological characteristics (often anxiety, depression, or personality disorders).

In its minor form, somatization is something each of us encounters in daily life. When we are under considerable stress, our autonomic nervous system, neuroendocrine axis, and limbic system of the brain are aroused. As a result, there are changes in our physiology, including increased pulse and breathing rates, difficulty sleeping, dizziness, tingling and numbness in hands and feet, ringing in the ears, headaches, abdominal discomfort, constipation or diarrhea, frequent urination, dry mouth and throat, difficulty swallowing, dyspepsia, tightness in the chest, and change in menstrual patterns, among a wide assortment of symptoms of stress. Not everyone experiences all of these complaints. For some there may be one or two that are most troubling, for others a wider range. Under stress, moreover, we scan our bodily processes more frequently and with greater attention to bodily change. We also fix with anxious concern on such change as a sign of a potentially serious health problem. Could that slight pressure in my chest be a sign of a heart condition? Are the cramps I feel in my lower abdomen serious? Should I take something for this headache? Is the blood on the toilet paper due to hemorrhoids? Should I go see my physician about this problem?

All of us, of course, are experiencing bodily sensations all the time. Most of the time we pay little attention to this twinge or that cramp. But when we are experiencing stressful events in our lives, when these events have disturbed our equilibrium and make us feel anxious or frightened, when symptoms carry potentially important cultural meaning (for example, could blood in the stool be an early sign of colon cancer?), or when symptoms are of special personal significance (such as slight congestion for an asthmatic or a muscle spasm in the back for a patient with degenerative disc disease of the spine), rather than normalize them we vigilantly attend to them. In the very process of worrying over them, we amplify the experience of the symptoms and take some action. We may avoid certain situations (stay home from school or work, break a date, cancel a trip), change our diet or pattern of exercise, take medicine, visit a practitioner. Social activities and problems, then, get transformed, either in or out of awareness, into bodily experience. When our personality type is such that we exaggerate the significance of stress or anxiously ruminate about our bodily processes, then amplification of physical symptoms is enhanced. Our cognitive style, affective state, and verbal and nonverbal forms of communication contribute to the effect.

Where stress occurs over a prolonged period or where a chronic medical or psychiatric disorder is present, as I have noted in the preceding chapters, existing pathology may be exaggerated by the meanings of situations and relationships, or by institutional constraints such as disability claims. But such somatization also stems from our prior experience of the symptoms and our current anticipatory fears of, and need to control, symptom exacerbation. That is to say, somatization occurs routinely to patients with asthma, heart disease, arthritis, diabetes, and chronic pain syndromes, as does its opposite, minimization and denial of symptoms. The experience of chronic illness provides personal training in both ways of responding to symptoms. Physicians contribute to somatization in several ways: they may help to confirm the patients' suspicions that there is something worth worrying about; or they may medicalize personal or interpersonal problems, during the process coming to disregard the stress that provoked the complaints while focusing only on the complaints themselves. Families, too, often contribute to somatization by untoward patterns of responding to, and therefore inadvertently encouraging, certain forms of complaints.

In cases of chronic pain, as we shall soon see, the problem is magnified. For chronic pain syndromes are almost by definition conditions in which the degree of pathology does not seem to explain the severity of perceived pain or the limitations in bodily functioning the pain produces. In this setting the pain patient feels pressure to convince self and others that the pain is real—hence the unwillingness of many pain patients to accept psychosocial explanations that appear to deny that their pain is founded in a "real" bodily experience deserving of somatic remedies and a legitimate medical sick role.

With this as an introduction, we are prepared to examine the lives of pain patients for examples of the different meanings of chronic pain and to consider the reciprocal influence of meanings (cultural, personal, situational) on pain and pain on meanings. Over the past fifteen years I have treated or studied more than two thousand patients with chronic pain syndromes. From these case records I have selected three lives that illustrate certain of the illness meanings and somatization experiences we have discussed. I will of course highlight similarities, but more important are the differences in the lives. For it is my contention that chronic illness, though it creates undeniable similarities owing to shared problems and though it sharpens recognition of certain uniformities in the human condition, is as distinctive as the lived experience of different individuals. Because in the end it *is* the lived experience of different individuals. The first case vignette is an illustration of pain as a way of life. As Emily Dickinson (herself a pain patient) wrote:

> Pain—has an Element of Blank—
> It cannot recollect
> When it began—or if there were
> A time when it was not—
>
> It has no Future—but itself—
> Its Infinite realms contain
> Its Past—enlightened to perceive
> New Periods—of Pain.
>
> (from Johnson 1970, 323–24)

The reader should be aware that the emphasis in each of these lives of pain patients is on their experience as revealed by my interpretation of their narratives. I do not spend much time on their treatment, nor do I recommend in this context a specific course of therapy. It is not my purpose in chapters 3 through 5 to advance a particular therapeutic paradigm. I do that explicitly in chapter 15, when we will revisit certain of these cases to see what could be done to relieve their suffering and lessen their disability.

The Vulnerable Police Lieutenant

My first impression of Howard Harris was of vulnerability. This six foot–seven inch, broad-shouldered, craggy-faced man in his late fifties, with thinning light brown hair and electric green eyes, has a rigid posture controlling a tentative, mincing gait. Howie—as he is ubiquitously known in the small city in Delaware where he is a police lieutenant—conveys his disability without saying a word, almost in pantomime. In one hand he carries everywhere with him a white cushion shaped for his lower spine. His other hand touches the back of each piece of solid furniture as if he wanted to be sure which could be relied on to support him in the event that his back were to give way and he were suddenly to fall. That same hand, when he sits, tends to stroke the back of nearby chairs, making an observer think that he is comparing the stability of their spines with that of his own.

Howie sits bolt upright, both feet on the floor about one foot apart, his lower back and upper torso rigid. Every few minutes he grimaces, and every twenty to thirty minutes he stands up stiffly and gently moves his spine from side to side while firmly gripping the back of the chair he has previously judged to be the steadiest. Periodically, the furrows of his grimace deepen, his mouth opens into a near perfect oval, and his eyes fill with tears, as he endures a jolt of pain. Watching him, you feel he is doing all he can to keep from yelling and—once you learn the image in his mind—literally falling apart. After a few seconds his hand carefully touches his lower back and begins to gently rub the muscles and the spine. There is a constant alertness to his gaze, a hypervigilance that bespeaks his expectation that nothing about his back can be taken for granted and that defensive strategies to reduce the pain and its effects are best employed before the pain strikes anew. Howie acts as if his spine could give way at any moment, which is wholly in keeping with his profound fear that should he fail to protect his fragile back it could "break."

"That's how I feel, like it could break, and I would fall to the ground in terrible pain. My back would split into pieces and wouldn't hold together anymore, and the pain would be unbearable." This is what he told me at the first of the meetings we had as part of a research project on chronic pain.

Howie Harris has gone through almost every available orthodox and alternative treatment for his chronic lower back pain during the twenty years that it has, as he puts it, "screwed up my life." He has seen dozens of physicians of almost every variety: orthopedists, neurosurgeons, neurologists, anesthesiologists cum pain experts, internists, family physicians, rehabilitation experts. He has also visited members of many of the other health professions that surround pain clinics: nurse practitioners, physical therapists, acupuncturists, medical hypnotists, and experts in biofeedback, meditation, behavioral medicine, massage, and hydrotherapy. He has attended pain clinics, pain classes, and pain groups; he has read medical as well as self-help books on the back. Lieutenant Harris has had four major surgical procedures on his spine and, in spite of feeling that the pain became much worse after each, is fearfully contemplating a fifth. "The fusion, you see, wasn't good. My back's unstable. I kind of picture it as the spine being split apart. What I need is a kind of glue to hold the pieces together." He has also taken, by his reckoning, almost fifty pain medications, including powerful narcotics, to several of which he became addicted. There have been other serious side effects of these drugs: most notably, anemia and allergic rashes. Howie Harris now receives weekly nerve blocks, and he formerly wore an electrical stimulator to block the transmission of pain through the spinal cord. He also wore various braces and corsets in the past. He sleeps in a special bed, sits in a specially designed chair, and spends thirty to forty minutes each day doing exercises, "postural strengthening" movements, and meditation. In addition to biomedical professionals he has consulted several chiropractors, health food advisers, a polarity therapist, a fundamentalist minister who does charismatic healing, and an expert in Korean martial arts. During the two years of our interviews, Howie consulted several psychologists, a psychiatrist, and a practitioner of traditional Chinese medicine. He has also employed a great variety of self-treatments and therapies recommended by family members, friends, and co-workers, including heat, ice packs, liniment rubs, mustard plasters, herbal poultices, tonics, special foods and diet, orthopedic shoes, rest, and activity, to mention just a few.

Some degree of pain is present every day, but it greatly increases from time to time, forcing him to take to bed, sometimes to scream into his pillow. The words he most commonly uses to express his pain are "radiating," "burning," "a stiffness in the exact center of my back," "a jolt of pain tearing through the nerves and muscles." Reading through the list of adjectives provided by the McGill Pain Questionnaire, a standard checklist used to assess the quality, degree, and pattern of pain, Howie circles "pulsing, flashing, stabbing, sharp, gnawing, burning, hot, stinging, tender, exhausted, fearful, punishing, annoying, tearing, nagging" to characterize the pain and the way it makes him feel. At its worst the pain is "horrible," much worse than the severest toothache, headache, or stomachache he has experienced. Sudden movement, lifting, and walking can make the pain worse. Of all the treatments he has undertaken, only ice packs, rest, and medication make the pain less intense, though nothing makes it completely disappear. A limited amount of pain (3 to 4 on a scale of 10) nags his back all day. More severe pain comes in clusters lasting days or weeks. Such clusters occur at most several times each month and at least once every few months. "Extreme pain," which Howie mentions with his deepest grimace, his eyes dilated, tearful and intensely focused in front of him in an expression approaching horror, lasts only a few hours and occurs very infrequently. Yet it is so terrible that he confided in me once it would be better to be dead than have to experience it again— although he immediately added, "And I'm a born-again Christian and would never consider suicide." It reduces him to the state of a cringing, terrified survivor feeling utterly helpless and devastated, barely able to hold on.

Pain comes with movement, either during or after. Reaching for something in the kitchen, bending over to pick up a small garbage bag, twisting to lift up the receiver of the telephone, leaning the wrong way when driving the car, helping his wife lift a bag of groceries, stretching his spine while showering, tripping over an unevenness in the floor of the police station, being thrown about in a speeding squad car, bending the wrong way at his desk to grab a file, even doing the therapeutic exercises—all can trigger a flash of pain that radiates downward and upward from the small of his back. Not knowing which of these frequent jolts will actually escalate into a cluster, Howie responds to each as if it could be an early omen, the pathognomonic feeling that begins another cycle of intense hurt. Indeed, Howie doesn't respond so much as anticipate. He waits for the pain. He seeks out its earliest sensation. He attempts to "catch it early," "keep it from developing," "prevent it from getting worse."

Howie Harris was once a bruising lineman on the local high

school football team, a former building contractor accustomed to regularly lifting a hundred-pound load and walking with it up a long work ramp, a one-time bouncer and champion arm wrestler in a neighborhood tavern, a decorated Korean War veteran, a cop who prided himself on being "tough as nails." He has been transformed by his illness.

It changed me. I've become fearful, afraid of injuring my back. I never thought about, worried about getting hurt. But now all I think about is that damn pain. I don't want it to get worse. I can't tolerate it. I'm afraid of it. Yeah, me, I'm afraid of it. I'll be honest with ya, I haven't told anyone else, doc, I think it's turning me into a coward.

Often Howie cannot tell what has worsened the pain, but retrospectively he pieces together an image of what probably happened. Pain, to his way of thinking, can be a residue of a very stressful day at work, of doing more than he should around the house, of giving in to the urge to throw a ball with his sons, of not being constantly on guard, prepared to defend his vulnerable spine. Pain is most likely to bother him at home: when he is with his family, before leaving for or after coming back from an outing, upon returning from work, or while thinking about how he is going to make it through the next workday.

Pain leads to withdrawal, to isolation. He goes into his room, locks the door, closes the drapes, turns off the light, and lies on the bed; he tries to rest, to find a position that "reduces the tension of the muscles," with an ice pack against his back to "cool the hot, burning nerves." During such an episode he cannot talk to others or the pain worsens; he cannot tolerate noise, light, or "pressure." He can't even tolerate his own thoughts:

I just want it to be blank, dark, no thoughts. Then slowly I begin to feel things ease up, the tension lessens. I feel the muscles relax and the pain decreases gradually, but I now know it will be better. That's maybe when I feel most relieved. I can relax. I can feel it improve. But sometimes it can take hours or days to reach that point, that moment when I feel the pain lessen, at first very slightly, then more and more.

The pain began before Howie Harris joined his hometown police force, when he was assisting in the building of a church in a distant

town. The project had fallen behind schedule, and Howie felt under
pressure to keep up the pace of work. A problem occurred involving
a heavy piece of equipment. Rather than wait for help and delay
work further, Howie attempted to lift it himself.

I lifted it all right, but something seemed to snap. Then I was on the ground in
agony. All the X-rays and tests showed nothing—except muscle spasm. But I know
something bad had happened right there in the center. I knew, I knew even though
it seemed to get better real quickly. Before then I was a different man. I was big
and strong, could do just about anything I felt. Afterwards I knew something had
broken. I had really hurt myself. I would have to be careful of my back, protect
it. I never felt vulnerable before that: not in the tavern, not in the army, not in
work. A few weeks later I was throwing a ball to my small son and I turned I guess
too quickly and, wow, I felt that bolt of pain right there in the small of my back.
I knew then it wouldn't be the same. I had to try to learn what I could and couldn't
do. Now there isn't much I can do.

After leaving the building site because of fear of reinjuring his
back, and not having a disability leave, Howie jumped at an opportunity to join the police department. The pay was lower, but he felt
that he could do the job with a smaller chance of reinjuring his back
and that the job offered more security for the future. At the time
of the initial injury, Howie was under some pressure in his family
life. His wife had just given birth to twins and felt overwhelmed in
caring for them, an older son, and her infirm aunt (who had recently
moved in with them after a debilitating stroke). Against her wishes,
Howie had left home to manage the distant construction project. He
had felt guilty about leaving her in such a difficult situation, and the
guilt worsened when the project was delayed. "We had always had
a communication problem. I never said very much generally. And
I didn't talk the job decision over with her. I just did it; it involved
a lot of money, and I just went and did it."

Over the years, in spite of the worsening pain, Howie Harris
moved up the ranks of the small police department until, as lieutenant, he was second in command. He thinks he might have made it
to captain if he hadn't frequently missed days because of the pain
and the surgeries. But surprisingly he does not feel frustrated by his
career experience.

"I'm not even a high school graduate, see. I really shouldn't be lieutenant. I'm over
my head and I know it. I can barely keep up with the paperwork. I don't really want

the responsibility. I don't want any more pressure. With my back as it is, I've got all I can do to complete a day's work. I'm worried if I miss much more work—since my injury, you know, ain't service-connected—they will put me on early retirement. With a kid in graduate school and the twins in college, we can't afford to live on a pension.

Even a disability pension, which would be more lucrative than a retirement pension, and which a number of policemen in his department have received, would be a significant financial burden for the Harris family.

Work is a serious strain not only because of the pain but also because Howie Harris feels caught between a blustering, ineffective boss and a force that, while overall a good one, contains several incompetent members.

It's all politics. The boss is totally unqualified. He just knows how to get in people's way, bellow, and make a real hash of things. He got the job because of who he knew. . . . But he messes up so often, is so little help and, you know, he's got an absolutely impossible personality: a complete egotist, always wants it his way, can't say no. He treats me like dirt. He treats everyone that way. But some days it's really, you know, the last straw. He gets me furious and frustrated. And I've got to watch my back. What am I doing getting upset?

Howie Harris's view of work has changed over the years. When he started out in the police force he strived to be an outstanding policeman. Now he thinks of himself as a survivor, trying to hold on without missing too many days of work and without making any serious mistakes. *Vulnerable* is a word he applies to his job as well as his back. There is the possibility that owing to financial and manpower constraints, which seem tighter each year, he could be pensioned off on early retirement. Howie Harris's view is brutally frank: "I've got to hold on as long as I can. Each day is a success for me, but it won't mean anything if I lose my job before the kids make it through school. Even after that, what would I do without this job? Who would hire me at my age with my back?"

The work situation is one he feels he can just barely manage. "I get by. The boys know about the back and cover for me when it's real bad. I'm not supposed to be in a desk job, but that's what I have made it. And most of the patrolmen are excellent. They help me make a go." He organizes the workday so as to minimize the strain on his back. Because the pain is worse in the late afternoon, he has arranged to begin his work early and leave early. He delegates to his assistant work that is physically difficult to perform. The paperwork is cumbersome, and he feels the limitations of his education. He thinks that he is working to capacity. At home, whenever he is not consumed with his pain he is consumed with the job. He thinks about the physical problems that he can't handle; he prepares himself to endure the pressures of the next workday; he fights to control his increasing anger at his boss; and he worries either about covering up his limitations or about what will happen when they are finally obvious to all, especially his superiors.

His wife puts the matter starkly:

There are two Howies at home. One worries about the pain, the other about the work. He is totally absorbed by these two things. There is none of him left over for the family, for having a good time, simply for laughing. It seems like years since we laughed together. Look at him! Look at his face, his eyes. You can see it, too.

That comment sums up a family life that has become deeply distressed. Ellen, Howie's wife of thirty-five years, is a tall, attractive, assertive woman with tinted blond hair, who dominates the conversation when they are together and has a sharp tongue and tendency to say what she feels at the moment. For the first decade of their married life, she was a housewife barely able to manage with a frequently absent husband, demanding small children, and a dependent aunt. Under the pressure she became depressed and threatened divorce; but then she pulled herself together. "As Howie got worse, I got better. I went back to school, finished my degree, and got myself a job, a good job. I gave up on Howie. I wasn't going to wait for him to ask me out. I'd never get out of the house. I started going out on my own with my friends."

Ellen is bitter about her husband's illness.

It's miserable, it's ruined our family life. He has no time for the kids. Couldn't stand the noise. Couldn't play sports with them. Couldn't even go on family picnics or vacations. And he isn't much better with me, though we communicate better now. He stays by himself. I know he's in pain. But every day? Can it always be that bad? I think he is part of the problem. He's a bit of a hypochondriac. Once he starts worrying about the pain, he can't get off it. We have no personal life. We haven't had sexual relations for years because of his back. Finally I've lost interest. I feel sad for him. He was so different when we were young. But I feel sad for me, too, and for the kids. I hate to say it, but he knows it's true: they haven't had a father. All right, I'm bitter about it. So would you, if you were in my shoes.

Ellen also fears that Howie will lose his job, but her fear seems to stem from a reason different from his. She feels he would be impossible if he were home all the time. The work distracts him, gets him out of the house, and gives him something besides pain to manage and talk about. Howie recognizes this, too: "What would I do? The pain would be worse. If I were home all day, I'd think of it all day. I do when I'm home now. The work is interesting and I like it and it takes my mind off my body, at least for a while."

Howie's three children resent their father. In recent years the children have increasingly expressed their frustration and anger to him. The oldest son says: "He's a ghost. We never see him. In his room, off to work, in his room. He never spends time with us. He seems like a stranger."

"I can't stomach hearing about the pain," complains one of the twins. "How do we know it's as serious as he says? I mean, I believe him but you can't see it. He isn't dying or anything like that."

Howie routinely confronts in others—family members, co-workers, physicians—a questioning attitude, a doubting that his pain is as bad as he says it is. "That's the worst thing about pain. You can't see it. You can't know what it's like unless, God help you, you suffer from it. I feel like people don't believe me at times, and it makes me mad, really mad. What the hell do they think I am, a malingerer?" The surgeries have had one clearly positive effect, in Howie's view. They have created icons of his travail, scars that he can show people, that he can touch to assure himself that there is something "physically wrong" with his back. After each of his surgeries, he felt that his family, fellow police officers, and doctors became more sympathetic. As he contemplates yet another major surgical procedure, this latent social function of surgery is a large part of the decision making, since his overall judgment about the surgeries is that they have made things worse.

Howard Harris is deeply pessimistic. Nothing, he believes, can cure his problem or even reverse any of the damage. The pain will slowly but ineluctably worsen. The evidence for this is that it takes longer to recover from each exacerbation and the baseline of every-day pain is higher. For each of the last several years he has missed more than one month of work. This year he has missed even more time. He sees no way to prevent things from worsening. He visits his doctors at least once a week to receive nerve blocks, injections of narcotic analgesics, prescriptions for the latest pain medicine, and neurological and orthopedic reassessment.

During the course of our interviews, he reported giving up prayer, because he felt it had had no effect. He does not believe his disability is a divine punishment or test. In one of his few moments of relaxation in over ten hours of interviews, he responded to my question about what role God played in his illness by offering a rare but weak smile, "He's got more important things to think about, and if he isn't, he should."

Like 50 percent of patients with chronic pain syndrome and also a significant number of the chronically medically ill in general, Howie Harris meets the official criteria for major depressive disorder. But his depressive mood represents demoralization from the life of pain more than anything else; and his sleep, appetite, and energy disturbance—and even his guilt, low self-esteem, and thoughts about death (all part of the official diagnostic criteria)—can be traced directly to his experience of severe pain. So it is difficult to know whether he truly is suffering a discrete psychiatric disorder or, more likely, is simply deeply distressed owing to his chronic medical problem. The fact that he has been treated by pain experts with therapeutic doses of antidepressants without any effect on the pain or demoralization makes this second possibility seem more reasonable. On the other hand, his family history, which includes depression and alcoholism in his father and paternal grand-father, places him at greater risk for this psychiatric disturbance. Still, Howie's illness account, like that of most pain patients, strongly suggests depression as a consequence, not a cause, of pain.

Howard Harris comes from a Dutch family. His father was a plumber who drank heavily, physically abused his wife, and divorced her when Howie was five years old. Howie has not been in contact with him since then. "I never really knew him. I heard bad things about him from my family, but I hardly remember being with him. I grew up with a sense of not having a father."

When Howie was nine, his mother remarried. He felt that from the first days of her second marriage she withdrew from him, becoming distant and cold. She went on to have two children with her second husband. Howie moved in with distant relatives at age twelve and lived with them until he joined the army at twenty. Over the years his ties to his mother weakened to the point that, although they live only a few miles apart, he has seen her only once the past year. He never developed a close relationship with his stepfather.

Howie describes himself as having been a strong and very independent person when he was young and as having slowly, under the pressure of the chronic pain, become dependent and weak. Howie Harris has always been quiet, reserved, dour. "We never spoke much in my family. Only when I was sick did I receive much attention." His mother suffered from frequent backaches. She would withdraw to her room for days at a time when the pain was severe. "She was an irritable mother generally, and when she was having pain, we knew she would scream at us if we got too close and bothered her. We learned to stay away." Howie also learned to pay careful attention to complaints of pain, to read them as signifying both physical and emotional states. But his mother did not reciprocate when his own pain began.

When I speak to her she tells me about *her* illnesses, *her* diabetes, *her* hypertension, *her* backaches, but never asks me about *mine*. She never came to see me when I was in the hospital. Not once! When I have seen her I have nothing to say. She still frightens me more than angers [me]. She's tough as nails. I guess I might as well be dead as far as she is concerned.

(It is intriguing that on several occasions Howie mistakenly referred to his mother as "my stepmother" and "my stepsister.")

His reserved personality contrasts with his wife's. "She's a real talker. She goes on and on. I used to tune her out, but I've learned to listen." When a major problem occurs, Ellen jumps right in, while Howie holds back. "But if she can't handle things quickly, which she usually does, she gets hysterical. I stay calm and work things out slowly. My judgment is better than hers. But later on I feel the effect in my back—the stress makes it worse afterwards." Ellen has increasingly come to dominate their relationship, though she has always played the central role in the family. (For example, in our interview together Howie routinely deferred to Ellen, although he looked very uncomfortable when she talked at length about him.) Howie knows that, like his sons, his wife sees him as weak and dislikes him for his weakness.

Among the aspects of his personality that have been transformed by the pain are his trust in others and his confidence in himself and his body. "It has been terrible for me. I know, even though I can't change it, I have become tense, self-conscious, and hopeless. I'm easily hurt and feel others don't respect me." Howie never used the term with me, but several times I felt he could have added the term *spineless*—that this image was part of how he regarded himself. For example, his wife has pushed him to go to school and get some kind of degree so that he can earn a promotion. Howie contends that although he would like to do these things, his back problem prevents him from studying. It is a transparent excuse even to him, and on one occasion he admitted that his back was not the only reason he did not seek promotion. As already noted, he feels overextended at work, at the frontier of his competence.

Wilber Mason, Howie Harris's former primary care physician, is deeply frustrated with Howie's care. He believes that his patient is a somatizer who amplifies his symptoms and disability. He finds Harris a problem patient who tries his patience and at times infuriates him.

He's pathetic. He's half his own problem. He's basically given up. What can I do? He comes to me in pain, I've got to give him something. I don't feel there is much we can do, really. I can't bear to see his name on the list of patients in my clinic. I think in the year I have seen him regularly he has never once said he was feeling better or smiled or been optimistic. This pain problem is getting him down and has clearly gotten to his family and is getting to me, too. I feel up against the wall. I've sent him to all the specialists and used all the latest drugs. I don't think we are any longer dealing with a disease; this pain has become his way of life.

Interpretation

The chief meanings of Howie Harris's pain are transparent, available for virtually anyone to see. Dominating them all is the sense of extreme vulnerability and the strict self-limitations he has placed on his life in order to prevent serious episodes and complications of the pain. Each twinge and cramp is carefully tracked. A minute change is observed assiduously, and so on, so that his entire life is his pain. The pain controls him.

The central mechanical image of a broken spine that literally could split apart undergirds his pain complaints and behaviors. If one knows this image and if one can understand how strongly Howie believes in it, then most of his illness behavior is explicable. But the weak spine and vulnerability to falling apart are also metaphors of another set of fears that relate to Howie's job, his marriage, his childhood experience of growing up with an absent father and emotionally distant mother, his personal fears of inadequacy, inefficacy, and dependence. The illness has taken on these meanings from Howie's life world. I don't know whether these meanings actually contributed to the onset of the pain, but they certainly influence the course of his pain. Whatever role, if any, his marital problems may have played in those early days of the pain, at present the pain behavior expresses those tensions just as clearly, if indirectly, as Ellen's cutting commentary on her husband.

The pain itself cannot be directly measured; but its effect on Howie's (and Ellen's and others') behavior can. For the patient and family this deeply frustrating, self-defeating cycle of problems is what is meant when they talk of the pain. Removing the pain would mean removing these hurtful experiences and despairing relationships. Chronic pain registers even in the expression and actions of Howie's former physician, who has been converted to a frustrating anger and hopelessness every bit as deep as that of the patient and the family. Where is the illness? In the back, all right. But what about its presence in Howie's sense of self, in his interpretation of his childhood, in his relationship with Ellen and his mother, in the reactions of his children, in his work setting, in his doctor? The pain is the central idiom of a network of communication and negotiation. In a sense, the network is in pain.

In books on pain or in professional conferences on chronic pain, most of the time is devoted to neurophysiology and physiological pathology, some to psychiatry, increasingly some to behavior. But after interviewing hundreds of persons who, like Howie, have pain infiltrating every aspect of their lives, I feel it is reasonable to ask,

Where in that book or that conference is chronic illness as a way of life? I am convinced that understanding the meanings of pain and tracing out the dynamics of somatization in the fullness of the life of pain patients will show all those who are willing to see (and patients, families, and practitioners have gone through so much that they often are not) that there is no such thing as *the* pain patient (or, for that matter, *the* patient with chronic illness of any type). The single-minded pursuit of a single ideal treatment for all but a few atypical cases can also be readily shown to be a dangerous myth. The patient's improvement requires changes in vicious cycles of meaning and experience that deeply affect (and are affected by) the patient's local social system.

What is needed is a kind of care radically different from that now routinely available. For Howie Harris that means treatment that would address simultaneously his behavioral impairment, the distress in his social relationships, and his demoralization and self-defeating personality pattern. Treatment should begin with the systematic evaluation of the psychosocial crises in his life experience. It should include therapeutic interventions directed at each of these major problems and integrated within a comprehensive clinical approach to pain. Such an approach would seek not merely to control the pain but especially to prevent the chronicity and disability. Even the demoralization and anger of Howie Harris's care givers, which contribute to ineffective care, should be described and dealt with in this comprehensive framework.

Indeed, I have come to believe that this life in pain and the others that follow teach us that our science as much as our clinical practice is at fault in the repeated failure to understand pain and its sources; we are unwilling to take the meanings of pain as seriously as we take its biology. There is a brute reality to those meanings, which are so visibly valid in Howie Harris's world that we can talk about them reliably and with precision. That is to say, the science of pain must include social science interpretations together with biomedical explanations. It must bring to bear knowledge of the economic, political, and social psychological sides of pain.

But it is also possible to ask more of the interpretation of illness meaning than it can provide, to make claims for social science that are dangerously utopian. Psychoanalysis and interpretive cultural

analysis often involve themselves in excessive speculation and un-
warranted assurance about hidden meanings. Perhaps as important
as the recognition of the different meanings of illness is the recognition of the limits of interpretation. Much more than I have ventured
can be read into the story of Howie Harris's pain, and doubtless
readers will do so. Is his pain linked to passive dependence created
by the absence of a close relationship with a paternal figure? Does
the pain relate to the vivid model of his mother's pain, which is the
only aspect of her life with which he symbolically expresses his
powerful need to identify? Does the fact that she attended to him
as a child only when he was sick and has paid scant attention to his
back pain mean that its persistence is an angry, desperate cry for
love? Or is his pain part of a self-defeating, passive, hostile communicative system in his marriage, which persists because it creates a
strange balance in a family system that would otherwise disinte-
grate?

All of us should ask of any interpretation, including these, Is it
valid? We should be willing to stop at that point where validity is
uncertain. Four kinds of validity are at stake here: correspondence
to reality, coherence, usefulness in the context of a person's problem, and aesthetic value. Each can take us in a different direction.
For the clinician the third is what counts. An interpretation is valid
if it is useful in the treatment of the patient to diminish disability
and suffering. For the researcher the others may be equally or even
more important. I have barely scratched the surface of the question
of meaning in this account of illness.

4

The Pain of Living

I think of the nestling fallen into the deep grass,
The turtle gasping in the dusty rubble of the highway,
The paralytic stunned in the tub, and the water rising,—
All things innocent, hapless, forsaken.

—THEODORE ROETHKE
(1982, 227)

There is no way of observing social cause and effect in a pure
environment, so a residue of indeterminacy obscures all causal
generalizations—not because the causal nexus itself remains uncertain (that is the case, too, with natural events) but because the
problem of identifying the elements to be included in that nexus
is inherently indeterminate.

—ROBERT HEILBRONER
(1986, 189)

If Howie Harris's story is life dominated by pain, Rudolph Kristiva's
is close to the opposite: pain dominated by life. Rudolph is a thirty-
eight-year-old white unmarried male, of Bulgarian-Jewish background, with chronic abdominal pain of fifteen years duration. He
works as an accounts clerk in the payroll office of a major West
Coast research organization. During almost three years of observation, Rudolph Kristiva experienced low-grade, persistent intestinal
pain that periodically would become severe and debilitating. He
also described bouts of pain in the shoulders and chest wall, as well
as dizziness, weakness, and constipation. The pain and related
symptoms do not cause him to miss many days from work, nor,
most of the time, do they interfere in a major way with his job or
personal life. They are rather, as we shall see, an additional source
of worry in a life devoted to fears and frustrations.

The onset of the pain was an episode of severe abdominal distress and weakness when Rudolph was a graduate student specializing in the society and politics of the Alsace region of France at a West Coast university. The initial medical workup was described as negative, meaning that no precise pathological cause could be detected. Rudolph was treated for the symptoms and in three weeks his symptoms ended. The next occurrence was one year later, during his anthropological field work in Alsace. This time the pain was more severe and lasted for over a month before it gradually improved. A series of gastrointestinal X-rays and other medical tests again failed to reveal a treatable cause, and treatment consisted of a bland diet and an analgesic.

Rudolph describes this period of his life as complex: though he greatly enjoyed living in French society and developed a circle of close friends, his field research was "in a rut." He felt extremely guilty about enjoying his social life while devoting so little time to his academic research. He held a good fellowship and lived better than he had in the United States, but he was bothered by a troubling doubt that he would get enough research completed to use in his dissertation. "I had a psychological block of some sort. I never got going on my own work, though I did have a wonderful experience." Rudolph's pain seemed to occur at the time of maximum ambivalence, prior to his resigning himself to an unsuccessful academic outcome.

The next bout of pain occurred six months later in San Francisco; this time the pain and accompanying weakness lasted for many months and was as intense as before. The medical evaluation disclosed diverticulitis, and Rudolph was placed on an appropriate medication. However, after having cleared up, persistent pain soon returned and continued at a low level for several years. "My personal life was in disarray for most of the period, with unemployment and marginal employment and general isolation and unhappiness." Work on the dissertation was "oppressive." "I could sniff demoralization all over the place. I felt it was an impossible task, like Sisyphus. I felt the dissertation was shit, and I was an academic charlatan."

After a long period of unemployment, Rudolph found work, first as a janitor, later as a clerk. All the while he lived with distant relatives (his immediate family lives on the East Coast), who gave him room, board, and emotional and sometimes financial support. The work deeply affected Rudolph:

> . . . lots and lots of unhappiness—downright despair. I played around with the dissertation, but in my spirit I had already left the world of academe, even the middle-class world. I was unable to find anything to do. A miserable, self-defeating way of living. Then I was in blue-collar jobs, and felt brutalized by the meaninglessness of the work, the hostility and even frank anti-Semitism. Since childhood I felt that I myself was sloppy, absent-minded, forgetful of details. My folks and teachers told me this, while complimenting me for "brilliance." I got the feeling I had no practical sense or skills and couldn't complete things on my own. The unemployment, the kind of jobs I found, and the way I was treated (like a dummy), all made me begin to think those negative things could be true. And sure enough, work on the dissertation proved it.

It is significant that the pain and weakness subsided only when Rudolph returned to Alsace for a lengthy trip to visit French friends. By 1982, after further experiences with unemployment alternating with unacceptable jobs, Rudolph finally found his current position as a low-level employee in the payroll office of a large research foundation. The pay isn't good and he dislikes his job, but at least, he observes, the setting is very similar to academia. Also, he has been able to rent his own apartment. Shortly after beginning this job, Rudolph suffered a brief recurrence of symptoms when he was assigned his present supervisor, a young man with whom he has a most trying relationship. "My work situation, while quite unsatisfactory, was not nearly as routinely horrible as in the previous period of pain." But over time a deteriorating and demoralizing pattern of harassment emerged in the office: "He wanted to fire me."

For all the hidden injuries to his pride and the uncertainty about his job future, the chief source of Rudolph's worries was "the increasing panic over AIDS." As a homosexual who had led a promiscuous sex life in France and the United States, Rudolph felt doomed to develop AIDS. His self-loathing over his academic inefficacy— more specifically the inability to finish his Ph.D.—and the low-status job is intensified by the homosexuality, "which I can't accept." The sense of panic has disappeared, but Rudolph still dreams that he will develop AIDS and then "descend even further to the very bottom of existence and die like a hunted animal."

The pain clearly gets worse when I am under greater stress at work or when I worry about this AIDS business, but there are longstanding problems that exacerbate it, too. When I begin to think about my self-contempt, the self-loathing over the homosexuality, over the failure to finish my doctorate, over the low-level job I'm in, over the lack of relationships, all these things make it worse. But really these other aspects of my life are a greater problem than the pain, which I can live with. Since early life I remember feeling something was wrong with me—always told I was gifted but never performing up to potential. I consider myself a failure. The pain is just another defeating situation, a weakness of character, something you've got to cover up because it detracts from the picture you want to put out.

The pain is not present every day. When it is present, it is worse in the late morning and early afternoon. It is a "pulling or stretching feeling, like something breaking. I visualize the intestine bumped and tubular, in spasms and sometimes as if white hot when the pain gets severe." On the pain questionnaire's list of adjectives, Rudolph circles the following descriptions of his pain: "quivering, bloating, cramping, wrenching, hot, heavy, tender, tearing, fearful, troublesome, nauseating." His medical treatment is an antipain medication. In spite of regarding his complaints as "low-level," Rudolph sees his physician almost weekly. He spends most of the time during his visits talking about the work stress and other problems in his life. Relaxing and being away from work and not thinking about it relieve his pain. Going to work makes it worse. On the weekend the pain is greatly reduced. During the three years of observation, Rudolph's pain cycled between bouts of moderate worsening and bouts of improvement, which coincided almost exactly with periods of worsening or improvement in work, family, and other life stresses. On one occasion, when an outbreak of articles on AIDS in the newspapers reflected hysteria over the unknown magnitude and rapidity of spread of the epidemic, Rudolph's pain became so severe that he had to visit an emergency room.

The Person

Rudolph Kristiva is a pale, nervous-looking man with a short, well-clipped red beard, thick eyebrows, a receding hairline that exposes a permanently furrowed, prominent brow, and darting eyes and fidgeting hands that never seem to stay still. Like his eyes and hands, his body tends to be in movement even when he sits: slouching, twisting, bobbing up and down, suddenly bolt upright. And like hands, eyes, and body, his mouth is in constant activity: smiling, pouting, sneering, stifling yawns or belches, but mostly talking rapidly and with great intensity. Dressed in light gray slacks that have become shiny with years of wear, a heavily wrinkled tan Harris tweed sport jacket, a battered but usually polished pair of cordovan dress shoes, and rather drab, wide ties that look like they date from the 1960s, Rudolph appears to be somewhere between an aging graduate student and an impoverished office worker who is fighting to keep up a semblance of gentility. But this image turns out, like so much else in Rudolph Kristiva's life, to be a disguise; under the surface lives a personality of great complexity with a marvelous imagination, a love of talk, and a savoring sense of words. Rudolph Kristiva possesses a biting, brilliant, and often scatologically funny wit. He abounds with infectious enthusiasms for ideas, causes, and especially people; he has a connoisseur's love of excellent French wines, Alsatian cuisine, and herbs from Provence, made all the richer by an inability to afford these luxuries. Perhaps most impressive is a passionate prodigality of self-reflections (the product, as he puts it, "of a lifetime of psychoanalysis—autodidactic, professional, and in my ethnic collective unconscious"), which range from luminous moral insights to brutally self-abnegating character dissections. Numerous psychiatrists and psychologists disagree about which professional taxon accurately describes this complicated and complicating personality. But all seem to have agreed that Rudolph has a longstanding and debilitating personality disorder. In the course of our interviews, I saw a strong obsessional and suspicious streak and personal quirks that must have infuriated his supervisor and put off new acquaintances. But my description hardly does justice to Rudolph's personality. He oscillates rapidly from blithe narcissism to sardonic self-contempt. He is often engaged in behaviors that seem classically passive-aggressive and that reiteratively and frustratingly defeat his aspirations. He draws on a seemingly bottomless well of anxiety, fears, and such profound demoralization that in listening one comes to share, even against one's better judgment, a sense of ultimate hopelessness. Rudolph describes himself as "nervous, weak, lonely, easily hurt, overly self-conscious, and chronically guilty." Although Rudolph experienced a "breakdown" in adolescence that was quickly resolved, there is no evidence, beyond the serious personality problem, of any other psychiatric disease.

Most notable, and in keeping with his personality disorder, is Rudolph Kristiva's feeling that he is a pariah: "I don't belong. I'm an outsider. I feel like I'm hiding from others. That people basically are not attracted to me. That I'm shit." This feeling dominates his sense of self. In spite of the many positive things he can (though usually doesn't) say about himself (for example, "I've got a good sense of humor; I like being with others; I'm a good talker, maybe not a serious intellectual, but a cultured thinker with a strong vocabulary; and I'm a hard worker, at least when I'm given something important to do"), Rudolph thinks of himself as an outcast with a spoiled identity. The pain fits into that self-caricature as yet another source of difference.

Rudolph Kristiva earned $13,000 in 1985. He lives in a pathetically small, single-room attic apartment in a somewhat seedy section of the city. The apartment contains a bed, four broken chairs, a very small desk, a secondhand stereo, a surprisingly large number of books, and a tiny kitchen area with a bathtub. The apartment is dirty and poorly cared for. The plaster on the ceiling is damp, and the walls are peeling. The windows are filthy and kept closed even in hot weather, which makes the room almost airless; yet when the windows are open, the room is exposed to the noisy street so that passers-by can be easily overheard and the roars of heavy machinery drown out all other sounds. It is as if he were actually living right on the street. There is about this unadorned and decidedly unattractive room—Rudolph Kristiva's world—such a pathetic feeling of being cramped and cornered that as a visitor I thought I had a palpable symbol of Rudolph's inner life. I felt initially a strong urge to run away as fast as I could from the room's oppressive and demoralizing effect. Yet once I had relaxed and become the beneficiary of Rudolph's sardonic humor and of his palpable relief to have significant human contact, I felt that I could not leave for several hours without casting Rudolph down the well of self-destructive despair that seemed to be present with us. Sometimes I felt as if our weekly, then monthly, then less frequent interviews were, if not Rudolph's major outlet for revealing

his humanity, then at least much more important to him than research interviews should be for respondents. Rudolph was terribly
lonely. His family was far away. Without good friends, with a
supervisor who either humiliated or terrorized him, with such a
desperate sense of barely holding on, what was warm and attractive in his personality was locked up, caged in by an oppressive
self-disgust that dominated his life. The pain was not a minor
theme, however; it had the quality of a distraction, a part of experience that broke into his isolation by proving that he was real.
And it brought him contact with the only caring human beings in
the city with whom he had developed a relationship: his nurses
and doctors, and now a pain researcher.

The Work Situation

Rudolph Kristiva's symptoms mediate his work experience. His
supervisor is a man who is much younger than he is and has less
education; he is threatened by Rudolph's academic background and
appetite for work. He regularly criticizes him, seemingly enjoying
putting Rudolph in his place as a déclassé, failed intellectual. He
controls what he works on, when he takes breaks, how fast he
works, and what happens to the work he produces. He has tried
harassing him in each of these spheres as part of what Rudolph
describes as a campaign (once overt, now tacit) to fire him. Although
his job is beneath his intellectual level and ambitions, it is all he has
at present; he has fought to keep it, going over his supervisor's head
to complain successfully about his tactics. "I feel like I can never
please him and that I have done something wrong. Now that I'm
older, I want job security. I've lost my earlier exalted career goals.
But he demeans me; I'd be enraged if I overheard most of the things
he says about me." By staying in the job he has increased his
self-loathing; or perhaps it is more accurate to say his job has become congruent with that terrible feeling.

   Nonetheless, Rudolph doesn't know what the future has in store.
"I feel in limbo, at a crossroads." He feels that if he were to lose the
job he would become overwhelmed. "I would prove to myself I can't

cope." But keeping the job increases his daily stress. "My boss puts me ill at ease on purpose. He doesn't want me. Each day is terribly unpleasant." This double bind is a constant source of tension, which he literally feels as pressure building in his intestines as the workday progresses. "Only at home can I release the pressure and relax." The act of defecating, which he does after he has returned home, has come to mean getting rid of the tension inside that has accumulated at work. The product of defecation is what he associates with all tension- and guilt-dominated activities.

Although his symptoms do not significantly affect his home life, that life is also a source of distress. He rarely has friends or family to his home. He eats alone almost every night and has hardly anyone with whom to talk. Rudolph reads, then listens to French tapes and folk music, and eventually falls asleep. Nonetheless, this situation is preferable to his work setting. He periodically works on the dissertation, but confesses: "Who am I kidding? It won't, it can't be completed."

Family Life

My life recapitulates my father's. He always feared I would be a failure like he regards himself; he's not, but I am. The lighting-fixture business he started has never gone anywhere. He blusters and thunders and is in emotional turmoil because he can't control his own sense of being ineffective. He has too high a sense of responsibility and standards, can't live up to them. That's true of us all. . . . He projects his own problem, lack of self-worth, on me. I am one more failure to him.

Rudolph describes his mother as a competent, hard-working woman who gets his father going and calms his volatile emotions. She has been a constant model of pain, especially headaches. Rudolph Kristiva loves his parents and five sisters. "They are all I've got. I can't talk to them about my illness, they get too upset." The homosexuality is a taboo topic, though Rudolph believes his father knows.

He would view it as his fault, one more source of failure. . . . I was always treated as if different, I got the feeling I didn't belong, had something wrong in me, couldn't live up to the expectations. . . . My father keeps his arthritis and chronic constipation silent; he covers them over. So was I, too, to do the same with my problems.

The Personal Experience of Illness

There is cloying pathos, but also edifying irony, in Rudolph Kristiva's perception of his illness experience as well as in his view of his life in general. He is redolent of chronic futility, exasperation, disappointment, humiliation, shame, being beaten down by life, being stuck with few options—feelings that he experiences in many aspects of his life and of which illness is only one part. But Rudolph Kristiva is aware of his own contribution to these feelings, and he is not slow to laugh at himself. He also has insight into the experience of other patients with his medical problems.

I am like lots of pain patients I have met: we make high demands; our performance is unimpressive; we get down on ourselves, frustrated, disappointed, because we are perfectionists. We worry too easily; we are too easily hurt by life, maybe because we feel too deeply and get so disappointed and desperate. Or maybe it is we who have an accurate view of life. That life is painful, demoralizing, terrorizing. At any rate, medicine doesn't do much for us. Why do we keep going back? I don't know, perhaps pain is our way of asking for help, for protection, for someone stronger and bigger to take care of us.

When I'm in a bad mood I see my life as a failure. I have no close friends, a terrible job. I can hardly make it economically, am far away from family members—and when I get close I don't fit in. I am spiritually dissatisfied, too. But when I'm feeling better I can see some strengths, too: I'm close to my sisters. Surviving itself is a kind of success. I've made some acts of kindness and generosity. I have a strong if corrosive intellect. My biggest successes I guess are the remission of the diverticulitis (knock on wood!), having my own apartment and being on my own, surviving even if powerless, seeing that things are generally less bad. But I have also recapitulated my father's problems. I have no confidence in myself, and that alternates with a kind of phony excessive overconfidence. I have a psychological block with my writing and with my homosexuality. If the economy becomes worse I easily could become unemployed. The pain? Why, it's just one more aspect of life, my life. It makes me worry—I could get worse, get cancer—but these are no worse worries than I have about my job, my social life, AIDS, etc.

Interpretation

All the meanings of illness are present in this case description. Kristiva's pain opens a window on his world and discloses a wealth of personal and interpersonal significances. Furthermore, his symptoms have special meaning for him, as we see in his image of the source of his abdominal symptoms and in his view of pressure building up in his intestines owing to job problems that can't be expressed at work. AIDS holds powerful cultural meanings in Western society, and its social construction as the latest and most deadly venereal scourge, as a modern plague, is something we have all read about in the newspapers and magazines and seen on television. That cultural significance is a dark fear in the mind of Rudolph Kristiva, as it is throughout the homosexual community and increasingly in the rest of society. Finally, Rudolph Kristiva's personal explanatory model of his illness includes his self-reflective interpretations of the place of pain in his life and even an account of his beliefs about the psychological characteristics of chronic pain patients that cause or result from their illness. This insight seems to me as good as that of many students of this subject, yet one will not find patient's insights such as this included in clinical and research reports on chronic pain. It is also easy to see how the chronic personality disorder that has dogged Rudolph's life has strongly colored his experience of illness and contributed, together with work and other social problems, to exacerbations.

I find an anthropological interpretation of Rudolph Kristiva's illness as an exemplar of the sources of chronic pain in North American culture particularly useful. Kristiva is one of the losers in American society. He hasn't made it. And indeed he has moved down the ladder of employment and income from his parents' middle-class, if fragilely so, status, to a proletarian existence. Doubtless his psychological problems have contributed to this fallen social status, but that fall in turn has exposed Rudolph Kristiva to the forces of exploitation that abound especially in the lower reaches of the capitalist system and that, as Lu Xun, a great Chinese writer of short stories on human misery, has written, "eat" people (1981, 4). The powerless in society are at greater risk for stresses they can't control, supports they can't mobilize, illnesses of almost all kinds, and death (Berkman 1981; Black 1980; Cohen and Syme 1985; Mechanic 1986). Our economic and social system places pressures on all of us, but for the powerless the local social system does not (or cannot) deflect the impact or reduce the effect of those pressures on the person. Unemployment, underemployment, and defeating work situations contribute to vicious cycles in which those with the least access to local resources are exposed to ever greater financial pressure, as well as to oppressively unjust relationships about which they can do little. These local environments generate or exacerbate feelings of hopelessness and lead to the generalization of such feelings from a specific problem to the entirety of a person's life, creating distress, demoralization, and despair (Brown and Harris 1978). Chronic pain syndromes, originating in the biology of injury and disease, are worsened and prolonged by these vicious cycles of misery (Osterweis et al. 1987). Clearly, preexisting psychological problems and mental illness may perpetuate these cycles, though psychiatric conditions can also result from them. Rudolph Kristiva's life is caught up in such a cycle.

In our work in China we found the same phenomenon in the lives of the powerless in a socialist society (Kleinman 1986). And my reading of the cross-cultural literature leads me to believe that we are talking about a universal aspect of the human predicament. The case we have described suggests that there are psychiatric, public health, and social work interventions that could reduce the force of local cycles, and perhaps even break them, even if it takes accompanying social change to do so. In this respect, perhaps what is most unfortunate in Rudolph Kristiva's situation is his morbid passivity, his predilection to blame himself rather than to operate more effectively on his local social situation, and his neurotic propensity to recreate the preconditions contributing to his own distress. Nonetheless, Rudolph Kristiva's pain points to something more general at the heart of modern life, something that for increasing numbers of people is a cause of alienation and makes a contribution to chronic illness. This something rotten at the core, this pain of living, deserves to be the subject of medical and social science research just as much as the problems to which it contributes.

Two themes from Rudolph Kristiva's case require further discussion. The scatological metaphor, so frequent in his usage, is also his father's favorite idiom of distress. His homosexuality and abdominal distress, too, are encompassed by this semantic network. Perhaps we should view this linkage as a particular instance of a symbolic stench mediating his social world and physiology. If so, this complex of sign-object interpretation is impressive both for its thoroughly negative significance and for its multiple channels of communication (words, sights, smells, sounds, abdominal sensations, defacatory routine). Until we discover ways to correlate symbol and self, sound and physiology, the senses and sensibility, we will never understand this connection, let alone be able to reverse its dire direction.

There is also the matter of Kristiva's Jewish ethnicity. Rudolph sometimes seemed to me to be a Woody Allen creation, a caricature of archetypal Jewish traits. But there are deeper strata below this superficial Semitism. Rudolph Kristiva's Ph.D. field research concerned the Nazis in Alsace. He was onto something that the Alsatians did not want him to delve into too deeply. As a Jew in a French-German domain with a long history of Judaism and anti-Semitism, the home of Dreyfus and therefore symbol of France's own divided history of anti-Semitism and philo-Semitism, Kristiva started out with a courageous line of inquiry into who had become Alsatian Nazis and what role they had played in occupied France and after the war. He couldn't get all the archival material he wanted. There was foot-dragging, lost files, long delays, unwillingness to be interviewed. And he was told to avoid upsetting a fragile balance. In the end Rudolph capitulated. His enjoyment of the life style was at the expense of what should have been his effort at uncovering the murderers of his fellow Jews and even some of his extended family. He should have dug deep, and instead he stayed at the surface of things. If there is a single theme that characterizes the Jewish consciousness in modern times it is a profound distrust of surface reality combined with a passionate desire to uncover hidden motives and meanings. Marx, Freud, Kafka, Lévi-Strauss, and the thousands of others who have enriched modern intellectual life were explorers of this hidden zone, where fear and hate so murderously commingle. Rudolph Kristiva never did what he believes he should have done for his people, for all of us. And here his personal guilt, in his own view, merges with the existential guilt of those who looked on passively and did nothing while the cattle cars filled with people departed into the night.

A text has meaning through what it has to say, but also through the wider context of associations it opens for the reader, who brings to it a set of interpretive needs and contexts. Is a life any different? Can this be a useful analogy for the patient–doctor relationship, and for the subject–researcher nexus, too? The researcher in this case is also a Jew. I had once visited Alsace, moreover, one sunny, chaotic summer during my college years, and had enjoyed myself as Rudolph had. While there I paid no attention to the history of Alsace during the 1940s, only a decade earlier, until one day, while walking on the lovely canals outside a small Alsatian town, I was caught in a sudden thunderstorm. As the rain started, I ran for a copse of trees. So hard was I running to get out of the downpour that I ran smack into a tall, rusted wrought-iron gate, which swung open with the force of my weight. As I passed through, I realized that there was a Star of David above me. I literally ran into a marble monument, against which I leaned to catch my breath and duck my head from the rain. I was in a cemetery, a Jewish cemetery. The monument was to the family Rubin. I recall eleven names. You could tell who were the grandparents, who were their children, who the little grandchildren by the different dates of birth. The date of death was the same for all the Rubins. Slowly, beginning in my chest, I felt a wave of feeling rise up, terrible and intense. A huge question and, simultaneously, its awful answer came to mind. I had pierced a shiny surface and come to see its dark interior. I relived this indwelling scene of inauthenticity while Rudolph Kristiva told me of his failure as a moral witness, as a guilt-ridden searcher after a small part of the large truth of his peoples', our peoples', holocaust. You may call it countertransference if you wish. I prefer Rudolph's term, "moral witness." The story of the witnesses of pain—family, practitioners, researchers—is integral to the life in pain.

Most patients with chronic illness, like the rest of us, live quietly and unremarkably in the daily struggle of living. Our pains, like our joys, are small, interior, simple. There is no great moment to the illness or the life. Yet illness, together with other forms of misery, sometimes brings a kind of passion and knowledge of the human condition, giving an edge to life. And for some patients with chronic illness pain and suffering have more to do with life—and specifically with that aspect of life which is dark and terrible and, therefore, denied—than with a disease process. Perhaps the healer and the family, like the historian of human misery, must allow themselves to hear—within the symptoms and behind the illness, especially for the complaints of those of us who are most ordinary—the wail.

5

Chronic Pain:
The Frustrations of Desire

Pain wanders through my bones like a lost fire;
What burns me now? Desire, desire, desire.
—Theodore Roethke
(1982, 246)

Knowledge and intention are integral parts of the social universe,
so that all behavior carries a volitional element, however submerged this may normally be.
—Robert Heilbroner
(1986, 193)

Pain and Freedom

Antigone Paget is a fifty-seven-year-old painter who has had
chronic pain in her upper back and neck for the past eight and
one-half years.* She is a tense, vulnerable-appearing woman: tall,
frail, with fine white skin, a tightly drawn facial expression, and
deeply incised crow's feet by both eyes; she looks ten years older
than she is. Mrs. Paget walks stiffly and frequently maneuvers her
neck from side to side as if she were working out stiffness or a

---

*This case is an amalgam of the experiences and stories of several chronic patients, which
were so similar that I thought it appropriate to present them as one. I have given this patient
the pseudonym Antigone for two reasons: first, because of the eponymous irony of a real
protagonist (Mrs. Paget) who is not able to choose and thereby worsens her own and perhaps
others' pain, and a mythic protagonist (Sophocles's Antigone) whose choice is too decisively
final and thereby ushers in a train of tragic consequences for herself and others. Second, I
wanted to suggest, following Erik Erikson's (1958) treatment of Martin Luther, that the
solution to a personal question may express and perhaps also help resolve a cultural dilemma.

cramp. Occasionally, a grimace passes across her face—fleetingly, without sound or comment from her. I first interviewed her on a very cold, damp winter's day. But in spite of the numbing cold, she politely but firmly insisted that I turn off the heater in my office because she was concerned that the current of warming air might expose her neck to a draft, thereby worsening her pain.

The pain is continuous, with episodes of worsening; pain-free periods last at most an hour. Mrs. Paget describes the pain as "pulsing, boring, sharp, hot, aching, tight, nagging, punishing." Daily muscle spasms complicate the pain. They make the pain much worse over a period of minutes, with very slow relief over a period of hours. Codeine and various analgesic and anti-inflammatory agents have had little success. The pain is exquisitely sensitive to drafts, extended movements of her arms, and physical activities such as sports or heavy exercise. In the morning the pain is mild, but by midafternoon it is more severe. Because of the pain, Mrs. Paget feels troubled, frightened about the future, blocked in getting things done, and blue; she has lost a sense of "pleasure or interest in things." The pain also exacerbates longstanding difficulties in making decisions. At its onset, it worsened the hot flashes of her menopause. Now it contributes to a constant sense of tension. And it leaves Mrs. Paget weak, exhausted by the end of the day.

Antigone Paget's pain is the result of an automobile accident. The day before Christmas in 1975 she had driven with a friend an hour from her home in Chicago to shop for holiday presents, and they were returning on a major highway.

I guess I was thinking about the past, the problems I was having, and wondering what to do in the future. Christmas made all the family problems seem more real. All of a sudden, a car pulled sharply in front of us. Its rear tire had blown out. My friend had to swerve quickly to avoid hitting him, and we skidded on the ice, throwing my friend's car first against the guard rail, then spinning it around into the oncoming traffic. I don't know how we managed not to get hit head on. My friend was all right, but my body was wrenched around. I had a badly bruised shoulder. But I was in a state of shock and didn't feel or think I was hurt. I guess I realized I could so easily have been killed, and just being alive seemed good. The pain started gradually the next day and got worse and worse over the weeks. First I felt a creeping feeling in the back. Then by the end of the month I got the full thing, the pain I have now. Only it was much worse that first year. I think my body was thrown against the shoulder seatbelt with a lot of force. Thrown in different directions, abruptly.

Mrs. Paget pictures the source of her pain as

a big lump—red and hot—of muscles, nerves, tendons bunched together in my upper back. Feels as if everything has been ripped after being pulled in different directions; a lot of stretching has happened. The pain feels like it comes from tightness, tension. The pain shoots up into my neck, which feels stiff sometimes and other times vulnerable, weak, like it could break off.

I hope it will gradually improve. But I fear it will get worse and worse with severe arthritis and deterioration. It already limits my physical activities and affects my work, but I feel it could extremely hurt what I do. I'm discouraged it hasn't gone away. No, that's not the right word: I'm terribly disappointed and very frustrated.

Repeated medical workups documented soft tissue injury and muscle spasms with trigger points, but no evidence of serious skeletal or neurological system damage. Psychiatric evaluation showed that indeed Antigone Paget had a low-grade, chronic depression, the onset of which occurred in the first year following the accident; her condition has been punctuated by several bouts of major depressive and panic disorders lasting for a few months and responding to a combination of antidepressant medications and short-term psychotherapy. Complicating the depression and panic have been periods of generalized anxiety. Prior to the accident she had no experience of mental illness, although she describes herself as having always been an anxious person who from childhood has suffered from various vague physical complaints—complaints thought by her physicians to have been psychosomatic. As a child she suffered rheumatic heart disease, which left her with a low-grade heart murmur but neither symptoms nor clinical evidence of current heart disease.

When I'm in stressful relations things tighten up an awful lot in my neck. There is a pulling feeling. I picture this one place—fibers coming together into a ball— where there is a lot of pulling. It feels like two long cords are being pulled. I see them as red, hot threads, lots of them. In my painting if I'm not careful colors run together, form a blob, and ruin the painting. I see it like that.

The pain is made worse at key points of her workday. She can work only two hours or so in her studio. When she works under pressure to finish a painting or hang it, she feels her neck stiffen and she has to stop for the day.

The major meaning of the pain for Mrs. Paget was expressed to me only after I had interviewed her several times over an eighteen-month period; finally we had developed a relationship of trust that permitted her to tell me about how the pain related to other problems in her life.

It controls me. It's limiting. I can only go so far and then the pain stops me. Whenever I have to do something really physical or deal with a stressful situation, the pain increases terrifically. I've had to stop thinking about decisions I need to make in my marriage and relax and get the pain under control. Can't deal with my financial and career needs when the pain is bad.

It is very difficult for me to be independent and not give in. Financially because I am not secure, it makes the whole process more difficult. I don't have the sense I can be completely independent. Also, the guilt I feel at breaking up the family. Other side is to be free, in charge of my own life. Right now things are in the balance. I'm feeling somewhat depressed.

You know what I think? The stiff neck is a kind of symbol, an icon of what I need to become: tough, stiff-necked. The weak, vulnerable neck—it's the opposite. That is what I am, or fear I am. Stiff-necked or weak-necked? Is it the result of the pain, or is the pain merely the vehicle to express this tension at the center of my life? I don't mean the pain is unreal. But being there, it comes to carry, to express this meaning. I would go on with the metaphor. Have you seen the great Renaissance and medieval paintings of Christ hanging there limp on the cross? Head down, neck under such great stress, arms out. That's the position, when I stop to look at what I've done in my painting, that places the pressure on my neck and brings out the pain the worst.

Crucified! I presume that is the meaning of this last image. Not by the pain, as she says, but with pain as a symbol of something else. That something else emerges luminously when we learn about the rest of Antigone Paget's life. But first, the theme that she expresses is worthy of emphasis. This is the struggle to be independent, tough, and in charge of her own life, not dominated by the pain or whatever else it signifies. She has a strong sense of being oppressed and an equally strong need to stand up and, as she put it at another time, "free myself from the bonds that have shackled me all my life. Yes, freedom is what this conflict is about."

The problems in her life that Mrs. Paget associates with this theme begin with the history of her family and childhood. A fifth-generation Norwegian-American, Mrs. Paget is the scion of strongly independent, familistic Protestant immigrants who settled in northern Minnesota. Her ancestors—both distant and recent—were skilled laborers; Antigone was the first to attend college and one of the first to leave the tight enclave of her rural home. Her grandmother, who favored her, often told her that because she was a woman, life would be grim and thankless.

Her ancestors were religious, stubborn, slow to change. Her father, a trainman, had always wanted to be a lawyer; but since he was only a high school graduate, the family mythology held that he had to settle for worrying excessively over the health and personal problems of his family: Antigone and her older and younger brothers and sisters. "He made a great issue when we had symptoms. It wasn't so much that he supervised our treatment, but he became anxious, even frightened about the possible consequences." The family ethos was generally strict, distant, and "tense." But when the children were sick the tension became even greater.

There also were lots of restrictions on our activities to prevent us from getting sick or being injured. We didn't travel far, stayed in at night, and when there was lightning, storms, and the like we had to be in the protection of the home. I wasn't allowed to have a boyfriend, or to go to friends' homes for the evening. It's funny. It all sounds so oppressive now, especially when I think of how I treated my four kids. But then I accepted it as the way things were, as natural. I never rebelled. Not once.

At the age of ten, Antigone Paget contracted rheumatic fever. A combination of her father's anxieties and the conservative medical opinion of her family doctor led to her spending most of a year convalescing in bed. She had no symptoms and no limitations, yet her father requested that she attend a local college, live at home, and even after graduating stay near home, owing to fear of her health and to the need for her parents to protect her.

I caved in. I couldn't tolerate the strong sense of guilt I felt. (Should I say, I was made to feel?) My father, but my mother, too, would get so upset if I didn't do what was expected of me. And what was expected of me was to stay in the family, to place the family ahead of my own person. I had this great need to break away, to go out on my own. Finally, after several years of feeling unable to make the break, that is I couldn't decide, I just did it. But that comes later.

The strong message to me from childhood was not to upset Father because he was such a worrier. I don't know if I was ever told worrying would make him sick or simply that it made his nervousness worse. But I felt that I could hurt him if I worried him too much.

Religion was important here.

We were fundamentalists—believers. I was trained to believe in the reality of sin, in the need for self-control and penitence and God's grace. I was told it was good to be submissive to God's laws. I literally believed in the devil and felt if I didn't control my feelings he could take control of me. I remember how college changed all that. Now those ideas became metaphors. But then they weren't symbols at all. They were the real thing. And they reinforced that sense of oppressive control. I kept my questions about religion secret. I kept my own needs and resistance and in fact myself secret.

I had a model for this, for keeping powerful secrets, for bottling my need to break out, to rebel within. When I was seven a neighbor began, he began, to molest me. I tried to tell my parents, but they wouldn't believe me. Finally he stopped. But all the while I learned to keep secrets. I keep a private place and have a hard time expressing my own needs, my inner anguish and hurt. I've never worked this out. There is a lot of unexpressed anger in me, I've learned. About this. About the way my parents overprotected me. I still have the feeling deep in me that if I criticized my parents something terrible would happen to them. It is as if the words themselves could magically make something awful occur.

Ultimately, Antigone Paget did break away. "I up and decided to become a fashion designer in some distant, romantic place, and live in Italy. Well, I didn't get to live in Italy, but I did get to Chicago, and I did work for an art gallery." This act was the strongest Mrs. Paget had taken to get out from under the oppressive control of her father. "It scared him terribly. And I worried about how upset he got." But she did live on her own, fulfilling at least a small portion of her dreams and fantasies for a more independent life.

"Eventually I caved in again. I left the job in Chicago, but only after I had begun training as a painter. I returned home and met my husband. I had at least begun a career of my own, though I hadn't gotten very far."

Looking back after many years of married life, Antigone Paget believes she had not individuated, had not developed a strong enough self-identity when she married. "I was old enough. But I hadn't found myself. Now the priorities were different. But they still weren't mine. Before, my father's fears came first. Now my husband's academic career took precedent." Three months after a miscarriage, Mrs. Paget became depressed, with symptoms of sadness, irritability, weakness, fatigue, insomnia, and loss of appetite. Retrospectively, these symptoms suggest that Mrs. Paget had developed a major depressive disorder. But she was not, at the time, diagnosed. After several years of inconclusive medical workup and a variety of ineffective treatments, the symptoms disappeared.

It did leave me changed, however. There was something sad and hurt that got buried deep, deep within me. An inner pain. Sometimes over the years, out of the blue I would feel it well up. A great sadness, a loneliness, a feeling of loss and hurt and desperation. Then I would let myself go and not so much cry as wail. A deep lament.

An active feeling of guilt was accentuated by this experience inasmuch as her illness led to repeated hospitalizations barely six months after she and her husband adopted their eldest son. This meant that for some months she was unable to take care of her son. When she mentioned this guilty feeling, she cried: "I wanted to be the best mother and have trouble when I think I made mistakes. I didn't know about bonding. It has had a bad effect on him. He is retiring and hesitant. I feel it is my fault."

Mrs. Paget's husband, like her father, expected his wife to defer to him, and she did. They moved frequently early in the marriage for *his* schooling, *his* first academic posts, *his* teaching appointment, *his* career development. Antigone Paget had little input into the decision making. She was expected to tolerate this pattern, and she did, keeping the anguish to herself.

The accident made me think of my own death and how I was spending my life. I never talked much with my husband about the pain. It became like so much else in my life—something horrible to keep silent about. But something had changed. The feeling of physical pain, which became so unbearable, carried another significance—of inner pain—and it made it necessary to do something, to act.

During the third year after the accident, she decided to separate from her husband. Subsequently, she has lived by herself, eking out a living from her paintings; the children, who now are grown, first stayed with her, then went to live with her husband. Currently, they either live independently or are away at school. All wish their parents to reunite. And now Antigone Paget is at the point of making the decision whether to return to her husband or divorce him. "Hard to answer what the decision will be. When I get close to going back I become very fearful that we will never really connect on a really deep level and things will return to where they were before, very quickly."

She speaks of the major concerns that led to the separation as

alienation, lack of communication, real resentment undealt with, under the surface, unhappiness and inability to resolve conflict. . . . I'm very lonely now. But before, I felt controlled by someone else and not able to have power and make decisions myself. I felt blotted out, effaced. Like my husband was my father—he made all the decisions. I allowed it to happen.

At the end of our talk about this looming decision, which she has repeatedly postponed, Antigone Paget became greatly upset. She asked: "You know, as a psychotherapist, this area. Will I ever be able to make a choice and resolve this thing?"

I was left with the definite sense that her pain, as terrible an experience as it is, saves her from making this ultimate decision about marriage, with all of its significance for her questions about independence and freedom. It is a decision literally too painful to make. Antigone Paget has failed to resolve her conflict, a failure that is undermining her self-confidence, amplifying her suffering, and alienating her from her world. She can't face the pain of her choice about family versus self; reciprocally, pain prevents her from making the terrible choice to break up her family or repress herself.

Here is Antigone Paget on the relationship of these aspects of her life to pain:

If I see myself completely pain free, it's someone functioning at a much higher energy level. I see myself going out into more involvements, into new areas. As for my creative work: something has happened to me in my studio since the accident. I have not enjoyed my own work as I did before. There is a definite connection between the studio and pain. Just like having to make a decision in my life, so working in the studio brings in pain.

I see pain interfering with opening my life, freeing up what is silent and hidden inside, opening myself to others. When I think of making a definite decision to end marriage, I think of new relationships. I have had ambivalent feelings about new relations with others that could control me, and I get to feel guilty again, not allowed to have these feelings. Pain controls them. All I can think of is how much it hurts.

I'm not sure I can make a go of it on my own. The loneliness is not so bad. But the pain is worse when I'm alone, overpowering. I can survive financially, though just barely. In the studio, the loneliness, the real pain, the pain of my choice, the lack of structure, all the desires I feel that threaten me, they interfere with self-discipline and getting work done.

The pain, I mean the problem in my marriage is I can't go back to having my husband dominate me. With the pain I became increasingly unhappy and needed to do something for myself. I had lost control of my marriage just like I had lost control of my body. I was powerless. I think whatever sense of self I had I eventually lost. I modeled my grandmother who always deferred to my grandfather. With the separation, power began to come back to me.

The last time I heard from Antigone Paget, her pain had worsened substantially. The verdict about moving back with her husband for a trial period had been postponed. She was unable to work in the studio. Her future looked just as uncertain as it had at the start of our interviews.

Interpretation

Each patient brings to the practitioner a story. That story enmeshes the disease in a web of meanings that make sense only in the context of a particular life. But to understand that life and the illness experience it creates, we must relate life and illness to cultural context. Practitioners are attracted to and repelled by both these narratives and the opportunity to interpret them in light of the patient's life world. They are attracted by the potential to understand how a person and the person's world affect and are affected by a disorder. Many practitioners recognize that this is the surest way to provide humane and effective care to the chronically ill. They are repelled by the fear that the story will entangle them in confusion, which may cover over the traces of disease (thus making diagnosis more difficult) or interfere with the working out of a disease-specific treatment plan.

Antigone Paget's narrative should help us see more clearly why the patient's story is central to the work of doctoring. My own role in this case was limited to that of a researcher recording that story. But as a healer, I feel certain that effective clinical work with Mrs. Paget must deal with both the pain as a bodily experience and the pain as a personal crisis. (The latter must be seen to be constrained as much by central cultural tensions as by the patient's personality.) Attention to either bodily or personal pain alone distorts the psychosomatic integrity of the problem. In my clinical experience, I have seen such a split in the purposes of care contribute time and time again to exacerbation of the problem rather than to its solution. That solution in Antigone Paget's case needs to take into account the reciprocal influence of chronic pain and the struggle for freedom—the unifying theme of her illness. Medical care for this patient should include psychotherapy (and perhaps family therapy as well) focused on this theme and its relation to her illness experience. That psychotherapy must, moreover, be an integral part of the medical treatment, not a separate activity divorced from her medical care. In chapter 15, I outline a system of medical psychotherapy organized with Antigone Paget and others of the patients described here in mind. That system places particular emphasis on the task of remoralization through the authentic witnessing of the patient's experience of illness and the interpretation of its key meanings. For Mrs. Paget, psychotherapy should entail the work of grieving for perceived losses and counseling toward the practical resolution of her paralyzing marital choice. Although Antigone Paget has received psychotherapy in the past, it did not center on these questions in the exigent context of her illness experience, and therefore it is not surprising that it did not succeed.

Antigone Paget's struggle for freedom represents the dynamics of her personal life story and her role as a representative of a class of patients. American women of the middle class who articulate somatic idioms of distress communicate their distinctive biological and psychological problems together with the shared cultural tension of an unresolved conflict between the traditional expectation of family life and the desire, intensified by contemporary social pressures, to experience personal freedom. The cultural location and social dynamics of Antigone Paget's ambivalent quest for a life of her own require more elaboration than I can do justice to in these few sentences.* Suffice it to say that a large number of women in

*See Showalter (1985) for an extended discussion of the cultural predicament of women in England over the past 150 years and its relationship to mental and psychosomatic disorders. The causes and effects are similar to those I describe for women in contemporary North America, suggesting a much longer and deeper Western cultural dilemma.

contemporary middle-class American society are under particular strain. On the one side, there is the cultural expectation that they fulfill their potential as individuals. At the surface level, this often means that they find a career, or at the least employment, outside the home. At a more deeply personal level, this injunction prescribes a quest for authenticity in self-identity and its expression (so-called self-actualization) that has been intensified in recent decades as the core moral requirement of the individual in American culture (Bellah et al. 1984). This expectation is the basis of the current commercial ideology of a consumer society, but one is mistaken to see it as a myth of television advertising. This is the cultural message most powerfully transmitted to children—it orients them to their inner development and to their changing world. For adults, it guides their assessment of their status and that of others: "Be all that you can be." It is a message that each of us internalizes, then unconsciously projects onto the experiences that surround us, so that at last we discover it as a "natural" part of the "real" world.

For women, most particularly, this cultural ideal conflicts with the equally powerful expectation of nurturance: building and investing in and anchoring the family. For professional women, this opposing moral message has in recent times become ambivalent if not pejorative. Career versus marriage, work in the labor force versus homemaking, self-expression versus love and support of others—these clichés articulate the same core cultural conflict, a double bind due to opposing values of how one should behave. Antigone Paget is stuck right here: between the horns of a dilemma that has become the crisis of her age cohort; her problem is intensified by the peculiarities of her life history and life world. What turns dilemma into tragedy is both the peculiar personal dynamics that intensify a person's need and the relative deprivation in regard to the resources necessary to make both goals achievable. The strain is expressed variously—from silent despair to explosive rage—but bodily idioms of distress are common enough to make this a subject physicians in North American society should master.

Antigone Paget's decision is to divorce or not, whether to bear the anguish of breaking up her family on behalf of her spirit or to suppress herself on behalf of the family. It is not that this lonely choice has made her vulnerable, but that she was this way before there was a choice. Her pain expresses and authorizes her indecision. A judgment, she realizes, will be fateful for her husband, children, and parents, but it may not resolve a personal problem whose roots go back to her early life, to her ancestors, and to the structure of Western society. Obligation, a word she rarely speaks, is on her mind as much as rights, loyalty as much as rebellion. Hers is a lifelong and historical conflict over autonomy and social order. As she recognizes, pain takes its meaning from these sources. There is a unity to the meaning of her illness, a coherence that in my experience is unusual. The illness, like her life, takes order from the same powerful impulse that recreates the core conflict again and again. That impulse is not neurotic repetition, whatever psychoanalysts may make of this case, but the dialectic between social world and personal experience, which persists in appropriating each new aspect of her experience into the service of this conflict. To understand the meaning of her chronic illness is to understand this psychocultural dynamic. That is to say, the unique details of her life together with the shared cultural aspects constrain her illness experience. Pain symbolizes both. Treatment requires the exploration of both.

6

Neurasthenia: Weakness and Exhaustion in the United States and China

Within the flowing garment of symptoms called neurasthenia there resided an anxious and depressed human being. But cultural pressures and family expectations surrounding this human being only deepened and prolonged the symptoms.

—G. F. DRINKA
(1984, 235–36)

Neurasthenia has two sources: the constitutional [biological] basis of the patient's personality and social forces.

—A Chinese psychiatrist
(personal communication, October 1986)

We now turn to a type of illness behavior out of vogue in today's North America, though it is common. In 1900 it was, by contrast, the medical cynosure of the age.* By *neurasthenia* was understood both weakness of the nerves and nervous exhaustion. A portmanteau term, *neurasthenia* packed together in the same category a syndrome of chronic fatigue, weakness, and a myriad of associated bodily and emotional complaints with a presumed neurological cause; as was stated then and now, it is a "real physical disease." The term was coined by the New York neurologist George Beard shortly after the Civil War, but the phenomenon had been noted in the West for a very long time under other rubrics. Fifty years after Beard gave it a new name, neurasthenia was a most fashionable

*The historical discussion of neurasthenia is adapted from Kleinman 1986, 14–35.

diagnosis throughout the Western world. Beard originally called it "the American disease"; he avowed that it was greatly increased in prevalence owing to the "pressures" of modern civilization, especially in late nineteenth-century America. Drinka captures Beard's description of the paradigmatic neurasthenic male of the Victorian age by drawing on evolutionary (social Darwinist) and electrical metaphors, which were leading cultural symbols that shaped the period's medical models of illness:

A person with a nervous tendency is driven to think, to work, to strive for success. He presses himself and his life force to the limit, straining his circuits. Like an overloaded battery, or like Prometheus exhausted from reaching too high for the fire of the gods, the sufferer's electrical system crashes down, spewing sparks and symptoms and giving rise to neurasthenia. (1984, 191)

Weir Mitchell was the most successful physician of elite women during this period of North America's immense transformation by the forces of industrial modernization. He emphasized, with characteristic paternalism, Victorian women's cultural plight, which led them into neurasthenic careers: unhappy love affairs, loss of social position and wealth, "the daily fret and worrisomeness of lives which, passing out of maidenhood, lack those distinct purposes and aims which, in the lives of men, are like the steadying influences of a flying wheel in the machine" (quoted in Drinka 1984, 201).

Sicherman, a historian of late nineteenth-century America, notes that neurasthenia came to express dominant tensions of this period: "the overloaded electric circuit and the overdrawn bank account." There was believed to be only a limited supply of nervous energy, and like money and commodities in the capitalist marketplace, social pressures were placing "inordinate demands on that supply" (1977, 34, 35). Among the many patients given the diagnosis neurasthenia were William James, Henry James, Sigmund Freud, and Charles Darwin; no doubt Beard himself would have received the diagnosis had it been around and fashionable when he was an adolescent.

Howard Feinstein, in his biography of William James, summarizes the cultural antecedants and social importance of neurasthenia:

In mid-nineteenth-century New England it [neurasthenic invalidism] coalesced from a romantic and puritanical matrix into a durable social role. Salvation through work, condemnation of illness, suspicion of pleasure, and a belief that suffering leads to grace flowed from the puritan source. Insistence on self-expression, a high valuation of leisure, and the admiration of delicacy and acute sensibility issued from the romantic. In such vigorous crosscurrents, illness had considerable utility. It provided social definition, sanctioned pleasure, prescribed leisure for health, protected from premature responsibility, forced others to care, and expressed inadmissible feelings while protecting vital personal ties. (1984, 213)

In this age of very rapid development of society, neurasthenia and other medical labels began to replace religious categories for what today would be both popularly and professionally called "stress." Society was becoming more secular; the helping professions were gaining ascendancy in defining personal problems (Lasch 1979). Rieff (1966) called this development the "triumph of the therapeutic." More psychological complaints and interpretations of distress would begin later on, to replace the bodily complaints of neurasthenia in American and European society.

Drinka (1984, 230) notes that neurasthenic patients were the problem patients of their epoch: their symptoms were persistent; they were difficult to cure; they and their physicians tacitly recognized that the illness had cultural cachet, as well as a social utility in authorizing withdrawal from or negotiations in difficult relationships. As examples of social sources of personal and group distress among the middle and upper classes in the Gilded Age, Drinka names the strict double standard of "respectable" manhood and womanhood, the high value placed on choosing a safe career and managing wisely, and the responsibility to preserve the family fortune and good name.

Neurasthenia is no longer a fashionable diagnosis. Indeed, the one-time "American disease" is officially now not a disease in North America, inasmuch as the American Psychiatric Association's *Diagnostic and Statistical Manual,* third edition (DSM-III), the official diagnostic system of American psychiatry, has banished it from the orthodox nosology to be replaced by depressive and anxiety disorders, the contemporary terminology for hysteria (somatization disorder), and various psychophysiological and psychosomatic designations. The term *neurasthenia,* though still to be found in the World Health Organization's *International Classification of Disease,* ninth revision (ICD-9), is also out of popularity in Western Europe. The persistence of culturally salient complaints such as "fatigué" in

France and "nerves" and "exhaustion due to stress" in Britain and North America, however, indicates that the phenomenon itself has not disappeared and may rather have acquired new names.

In certain areas of the world—for example, in Eastern Europe, Japan, India, and China—neurasthenia has continued to be used in its original sense as an important diagnostic label. The situation in China, where I have conducted field research, is particularly noteworthy. For there, neurasthenia, introduced from the West early in this century as a medical diagnosis, is the most common of all psychiatric diagnoses and one of the ten most frequent diagnoses in general medical clinics. On the other hand, depression and anxiety disorders are not extensively diagnosed there. In 1980 and 1983, my wife, who is a China scholar, and I conducted research at the Hunan Medical College—the old Yale-in-China Medical School and one of China's leading centers of psychiatry—to determine the relationship between neurasthenia and depression. We discovered that Chinese neurasthenic patients complain of many of the classical problems that Beard and Mitchell associated with neurasthenia: lack of energy, fatigue, weakness, dizziness, headaches, anxiety, and a wide assortment of other recurring but vague physical complaints. We also learned that most of these patients could be rediagnosed, using the American DSM-III criteria, as cases of depression or anxiety disorders. Yet their chronic neurasthenic complaints persisted even when they received effective doses of antidepressant and anti-anxiety medications. Only those patients improved who resolved a major family or work problem. Political, economic, work, family, and personal problems also played a role in illness onset and exacerbation. Our finding was that neurasthenia as a chronic illness is extremely sensitive to influences from the local life world of the patient and from the wider social system. This appears to have been the case in nineteenth-century North America as well.

Although neurasthenia is rarely diagnosed today in North American primary care or psychiatric practice, the syndrome of complaints is still to be found, and would seem to be common in the guise of "stress syndromes." The diagnostic labels are different, and so are the ways patients with these complaints are treated. I will describe two cases of neurasthenia, one from Changsha (a provincial capital in south-central China), the other from New York City. Again my focus is the meaning of symptoms and behavior to patient, family, and practitioners. Each case also brings a mirror to the culture and local social systems of its distinctive society. My interpretations of the cases will seek to understand two very different social worlds and their influence on the onset, course, and outcome of neurasthenia, and recursively the influence of neurasthenia on those life settings. Whether or not the official medical lexicon in a society treats neurasthenia as an authentic *disease,* the syndrome of chronic exhaustion is a ubiquitous *illness* behavior that can be described and interpreted for particular individuals engaged in particular situations and relationships within particular cultural contexts. Indeed, long before *neurasthenia (shenjing shuairuo),* the medical term, was introduced into the Chinese language, neurasthenia as a chronic behavioral problem was depicted in traditional Chinese medical texts. And long after it lost official status in North America, it is treated by clinicians.

First I will briefly narrate a case of neurasthenia from our research project in the department of psychiatry, Hunan Medical College, then I will expand the case description to interpret an important aspect of current Chinese society; finally, I will do the same with a North American case. A comparison of the two will offer additional insight into the meanings of illness.

A Chinese Case of Neurasthenia

Yen Guangzhen is a forty-year-old teacher in a rural Hunan town. She is intelligent, articulate, and deeply depressed. She sits immobile on the wooden stool opposite us, looking fixedly at the floor. Her black hair, tied tightly back in a bun, is streaked with white; her handsome, high-cheeked face has deep creases radiating outward from each eye. She slowly recounts for us the story of her chronic neurasthenia. Headaches and exhaustion are her chief complaints.* Sitting before us, Comrade Yen radiates weariness and

*This case is a modified and updated version of a case history published in Kleinman 1986, 134–37. When I originally wrote up this case, I emphasized the complaint of headache and deemphasized the other complaints in order to stress the chronic pain syndrome. The current description is fuller and brought up to date.

fatigue. She looks much older than she is, and at times it seems as if she has difficulty supporting her body. Her voice is weak.

There are several sources. Before the Cultural Revolution I was outgoing, active, had high self-regard. As a teenager I had been secretary of the local Communist Youth League. I dreamed of a career with the party and advanced education. My family and friends all expected great achievements. I had ambition and high goals. Then during the Cultural Revolution I was severely criticized. I had to leave my position in the Youth League. I went to the distant countryside to a very poor place.* I couldn't adjust to the conditions. The work was too hard; too little to eat. Bad smells were everywhere, and nothing was clean. Terrible living conditions!

All of this was made worse by the realization that her career aspirations were no longer tenable, that even return to an urban environment was unlikely. The daughter of intellectuals, with several generations of professionals in the family, Yen Guangzhen felt deeply the lost opportunity for a university education and career in the Communist party, sources of social mobility in China. Cut off from family and friends, books and newspapers, and initially not well accepted by the peasants, she grew aloof and solitary. As the Cultural Revolution accelerated, she occasionally bore the brunt of self-criticism sessions. On one occasion she was denied an injection by a nurse at a rural hospital who accused her of being a "stinking intellectual." She began to experience a change in personality. Comrade Yen felt constantly demoralized, and in place of her former optimism she felt hopelessness generalized to all aspects of her life. She expected only the worst to happen. She became introverted, sensitive to what she perceived as the criticizing and rejecting eyes of peasants and cadres. She began first to deprecate her goals, then herself. Hesitant where she once had been assertive, lacking confidence where she once had radiated it, Comrade Yen regarded herself

*During the Cultural Revolution millions of Chinese adolescents left their urban middle schools and were rusticated in rural communes, often remote and poor ones, where they were expected to engage in agricultural labor and learn from the peasants. Adjustment to conditions in the countryside was difficult for urban adolescents who lacked experience of the drudgingly difficult routine of rural life. Alternatively, adjustment of rural peasants to urban students was also difficult, especially when these students were seen as a drain on the limited and already oversubscribed resources of the commune. The stage was set for a culturewide crisis that has captured the imagination of creative writers in China (cf. Chen 1978; Link 1983; Barme and Lee 1979) and occupied center stage in the biographies of Chinese expatriates (Frolic 1981; Liang and Shapiro 1983). An excellent account of the lives of victims of the Cultural Revolution is to be found in Thurston (1987).

as inadequate and coped by limiting her life even more. She stayed to herself. Eventually she obtained a post as a primary school teacher in a rural town. When her native abilities became apparent to her fellow teachers, they wanted to elect her principal. But Comrade Yen declined because she feared the responsibility. She did not want to expose herself again in a situation where she might well fail and suffer further losses.

She married a native of the region who is now a peasant but was previously a cadre in a mine. They live apart, and it is clear that she prefers it this way: he resides in a distant village and she lives in the small market town. They have three children, two adolescent sons who live with their father and one daughter who lives with her mother. Comrade Yen is angry that her husband has not been rehabilitated and given back his post as a cadre; her husband has given up, declaring that he will never regain his former status. This is a chronic source of frustration, another difficulty about which she feels nothing can be done.

Her third source of anger is her daughter.

I really did not want to have her. I wanted to be alone. We already had enough children. When I was very pregnant I hit myself several times quite hard against the wall, hoping I might abort. But my husband wanted a child and I could not decide on an abortion at the hospital. Thus I blamed myself when I gave birth to a baby girl with a withered arm. I felt I caused it.*

The daughter grew up to be beautiful and very bright, an outstanding student. But her mother grieved for her because of her deformity. "In China normal people don't marry cripples. Even though she could do everything—cook, clean, play sports—I knew she would have trouble marrying." At this point in our interview, the patient silently cried, her gaze fixed on the cement floor beneath the table separating us.

Her husband, who had accompanied her, looked much older than Comrade Yen and was wide-eyed in a provincial capital he had visited only a few times before. His weather-roughened features

*From a biomedical perspective, it is hardly likely that the congenital abnormality resulted from Comrade Yen's actions during the pregnancy. But her guilt over her desire to terminate the pregnancy is fed as well by traditional Chinese ethnomedical beliefs that the thoughts, moods, and behaviors of the mother during pregnancy can symbolically impress themselves on the growing fetus.

contrasted with his wife's more refined ones. He joined her in weeping openly when she continued on about their daughter:

There is no hope for her. Even though she is one of the best students in the senior middle school, she cannot take the examination to go to the university. Her school principal and the secretary of the local branch of the party decided that only completely healthy, normal children can take the examination. We appealed to the county authorities, but they upheld the decision. There is nothing that can be done. Our daughter will live at home and do what work she can.*

There followed several minutes when the patient could not go on, as she sobbed and wept. Finally, she told us how she and her husband had arranged for their daughter to meet another "cripple" in a nearby town. But her daughter decided that she would not marry someone else who was deformed; rather, she would remain single.

Comrade Yen shared her full hopelessness with us. Often she thinks it would be preferable to be dead. Her headaches and chronic fatigue keep her to herself. She cannot face any more "stress"; it is too upsetting. "My health is too uncertain. I cannot do too much. I think only of my headaches, not of the future or the past." Comrade Yen severely restricts her world. She withdraws from all but essential responsibilities. She cannot plan any outing "because of bad influences on my health—the weather, the noise, the crowds." She feels exhausted after even limited effort. She describes this state as a general sense of lack of energy, weakness, dizziness, and apathy.

Because of her pessimistic feelings of failure and hopelessness, she circumscribes her life to school and dormitory room. Only on occasional weekends does she visit her husband. Her daughter stays with her. They appear to be like two recluses, grieving their different losses. Yen Guangzhen's world is now that of pain and exhaustion: experiencing her hurt, waiting for it, fearing it, talking about it, blaming her problems on it, feeling exhausted by it, and obtaining relief through sleep and rest. It is the pain and related weariness and other complaints that legitimize her withdrawal at work and in family life. These same complaints sanction her isolation and demoralization. Her chronic pain and exhaustion are unavailing ex-

*In the last several years the policy of discrimination against handicapped students has been changed. Now it is in principle acceptable for those with a handicap to go on to the university. But the association of stigma with disability is still widespread.

pressions of depression owing to her multiple losses. Before we departed she sent us a letter:

I feel always sad about being ill for such a long time. I feel headaches, dizziness, don't like to talk, take no pleasure in things. My head and eyes feel swollen. My hair is falling out. My thinking has slowed down. Symptoms are worse when I am with others, better when I am alone. Whenever I do anything I have no confidence. I think because of the disease I have lost my youth and much time and everything. I grieve for my lost health. I must work a lot every day just like the others, but I have no hope in what lies ahead. I think there is nothing you can do.

Three years later I received another letter from Yen Guangzhen, in reply to a request to return to the clinic for a follow-up interview. She declined with great politeness to return and mentioned that her symptoms were unchanged. She simply did not have the energy to travel, and her headaches were made so much worse by the long bus ride and the questioning that she could not undergo another interview. She had had to take a year's leave from teaching and was requesting a disability status that would reduce her teaching or give her early retirement. She had received permission to return to the city where she was raised, but her parents were aged and infirm and she did not have the strength to look after them. Even writing the letter tired her and caused her head to throb. She was being treated by a doctor of traditional Chinese medicine for an inadequacy of *qi* (vital energy).

Neurasthenia in Chinese Culture

Neurasthenia plays a role in contemporary Chinese society akin to its role in turn-of-the-century North America. It provides the legitimation of a putative physical disease for bodily expressions of personal and social distress that would otherwise go unauthorized, or worse, be labeled emotional problems and mental illness. Mental illness in Chinese culture carries strong stigma, which, unlike the stigma of mental illness in the West, affects not only the person who is ill but the entire family. The family with a mentally ill member

is regarded as carrying a hereditary taint of moral failure and constitutional vulnerability. It becomes difficult to marry off children and
to maintain the family's status in the community. Hence individuals
and families in China use euphemisms or disguising metaphors to
describe distress of a psychosocial kind so that they can avoid
carrying labels of mental illness or emotional problems. Whereas
the language of stress has displaced the idiom of neurasthenia to
serve this purpose in contemporary North American society, in
China neurasthenia has found a new and welcoming home.*

Another reason for the popularity of neurasthenia in China is that
it avoids the use of terms such as *depression,* which convey a sense
of alienation of a sociopolitical as well as psychological kind. For
instance, during the chaos of the Cultural Revolution, Mao Zedong
said that such mental illnesses were not so much diseases as they
were wrong political thinking. The label *depression,* then, until very
recently was a tricky one in China, since it indirectly conveys the
idea of political dissatisfaction, a feeling unacceptable to many in
China's morally fervent political context, where each individual is
expected to participate energetically in mass political campaigns and
local political groups (see Kleinman 1986).

Finally, neurasthenia as a concept has been fairly easy to assimilate to traditional Chinese medicine, which has since ancient times
had an interest in problems such as weakness and fatigue. These
have been attributed to problems in the flow or constitution of *qi*
(vital energy), or in the balance of *yin* and *yang* elements in the body.
After almost a century of assimilating neurasthenia to this conceptual system, traditional Chinese practitioners use it as if it were not
a foreign import but a native product of the Chinese medical system.

Yen Guangzhen's experience illumines the contribution of potent
social forces (political labels, mass campaigns, uprooting and migration, poverty, and so forth) and psychological factors (depression,
anxiety, personality problems) to the cause and exacerbation of
neurasthenia. That not all Chinese under the same pressure have
developed neurasthenia indicates that genetic predisposition, family situation, and personal development place certain individuals at
greater risk. The local social environment influences the impact of

*"Stress" is just beginning to gain popularity in China, primarily among professionals.

social forces on vulnerable persons. Some environments can shield, deflect, or otherwise minimize the effects of political oppression and economic deprivation. Others amplify these effects on particular individuals or categories of individuals (for example, the politically disfavored).

Neurasthenia has cachet in modern China. It is a diagnosis that can authorize the sick person to obtain disability benefits; it can justify early retirement; it can enable a person to change work or to move from the country to the city—in a totalitarian system where it is not easy to make such changes. Now that neurasthenia no longer has such cachet in North America, official diagnoses of chronic pain, depressive disorder, post-traumatic stress syndrome, or particular medical diseases must be used to obtain these social ends. The individual must call on illnesses that have official status as listings in the disability, medical, legal, and other institutional bureaucracies in North America.

For Comrade Yen's doctors, much of what we have reviewed is understood implicitly, though it usually is not directly discussed. These clinicians prescribe particular therapeutic regimens for treating neurasthenia symptomatically, just as they have their indigenous criteria for making the diagnosis. Intriguingly, neurasthenia patients in China occupy the same position as chronic pain patients in America: they are held to be problem patients who don't get well and who frustrate their care givers. Neither acupuncture and traditional herbs nor modern biomedical drugs are found very effective against neurasthenia. Perhaps we are viewing a dimension of chronic illness generally to which all medical systems respond with difficulty. Research with an epidemiological colleague of mine in Taiwan disclosed that even folk healers—who in non-Western societies have been reported to be effective sources of care for illness behavior problems—have their hands full with neurasthenia patients (Kleinman and Gale 1982). The problem may be that healers of all stripes run into difficulties in the long-term care of patients with illnesses that can't be cured and that exhibit powerful social uses and cultural significance.

Let us turn now to a North American patient with weakness, exhaustion, and psychobiological distress so that we may consider the question, Whither neurasthenia in the United States?

Neurasthenia in Midtown Manhattan, 1986

Eliza Choate Hartman is a slender, pale, large-eyed, sleepy-looking, long-haired twenty-six-year-old. She works as a temporary secretary in New York City for her livelihood during the day, and at night and on weekends she pursues her métier as an oboist and clarinetist. Hers is an engaging, sensitive personality with old-world charm and a whimsical comic sense, but neither vigorous nor assertive. There is something languid in the style of her movements that reminded me of "leisure" in its nineteenth-century European sense. There is also something vulnerable in her personality that periodically leaves her hesitant, a bit flustered, even at times guilty-looking. The first thing she confided to me was her feeling of embarrassment that her complaints of fatigue and exhaustion were considered a chronic illness, with all that the term conveys of disability, seriousness, and even a threat to life. Yet she quickly assured me that her symptoms are slowly "killing" her. The words she used to describe her condition were spoken one by one, with a pause between each as if to give her time to savor choices from a rather lengthier mental list: "tired," "weak," "constant, nagging dry throat," "getting out of breath," "always feeling on the verge of getting a flu or grippe," "never feeling good," "exhausted." The last was pronounced with an exaggeration of the middle syllable and a sigh of languor accompanied by a mime of dropping eyelids, lips, and head. Eliza traces the onset of her condition to a bout of mononucleosis two and a half years ago.

I wore myself right out and got mono. I was working full time as a waitress at a Manhattan restaurant. I walked about forty-five minutes to get there and forty-five minutes back. But first, before I went home, I went to practice the oboe and clarinet by myself and with a small ensemble in a loft about half an hour from my flat. I, we worked very hard. We were to appear that summer at a small music festival in upstate New York. Sometimes we played until midnight. After that my boyfriend and I walked back to the tiny flat we rented. That was even more exhausting. We were in the process of breaking up, and each night we fought for as long as we stayed awake. I never got enough sleep. Sometimes I slept in the loft. Walking back and forth, I got chilled and was exposed to rain and wind. I think that also had something to do with getting sick.

The mono really scared me. I didn't know what was wrong. Each day I felt sicker. I was so weak I couldn't walk more than a few blocks without feeling exhausted.

My body ached. And I got this very dry sore throat. I felt a heaviness in my body, and the feeling I have now, that it is harder to move, to make an effort than before. But in spite of this I had iron willpower and determination. I tried to keep going. My mind would get there first and dragged me behind. But for a month I was out of it, totally out of commission, unable to work or be with my friends or make music. Since I'm a single woman on my own that was scary for me.

The trouble is, you see, I never fully recuperated. I didn't have the time. I had to get back to work or I would have lost the only job I could find. I had this image of negative energy building up in my body, and not being able to get rid of it. I went back to the same exhausting routine and I've been sick ever since. I really need time, lots of time off, to recuperate fully, to get back my strength and my health. If I keep up the present schedule, I don't know—it's real scary; I can't seem to get over it. If I were to win the lottery, now, then I'd be able to rest and get better. Keep my schedule from not overdoing things. Work on what's important: my music. That's all. What worries me is that I feel like I could come down with mono again, get really sick. I can't go through that again—it was terrible, isolating, difficult to start over. I couldn't keep up.

Eliza feels like she is "decaying," "eroded," "not having strength, being drained." Her throat gives her a constant sense of being "red and raw." These symptoms affect her almost every day, with a respite two or, at most, three days per month. The mornings are usually good, but "by 3 P.M. I feel dragged out and my throat hurts." If she doesn't sleep for at least eight hours at night, then the mornings are bad, too. "If I don't talk. If I rest. If I sleep well and spend hours by myself. If I don't overdo the practicing, it will get better." But Eliza does not feel able to gain such control over her life. As a result, she believes that her resistance is always low, leading to frequent "colds," which further weaken her.

Eliza strongly dislikes her work as a temporary secretary. She finds the work "dull, mechanical, draining. . . . But I can't afford to stop working. It's my only source of income." Because of her debilitated condition and her need to work full time, she has had to sacrifice her music. She has dropped out of the ensemble, with a great sense of loss, and has even reduced her practice time to a bare minimum. Even with these severe adjustments, she feels she cannot find enough time in her daily schedule to obtain the rest she requires to gain back her strength.

In her quest for her lost health, Eliza has consulted a range of physicians, most notably those who practice holistic health—in which she is a firm believer—as well as health food advisers; secular counselors of various persuasions; experts in massage, meditation, and yoga; a chiropractor-dietician; a self-help group for patients suffering chronic illness; and most recently, in rapid succession, a reflexologist, a voice therapist, and a Chinese herbalist. Eliza has followed various diets, usually vegetarian, raw, and free of sugar. She has taken various antibiotics, and her medicine cabinet is full of a large array of vitamins, tonics, healing herbs, and several exotics such as tiger balm from Hong Kong and ginseng from North Korea. In light of her yearly income of $17,500, Eliza's considerable expenditures on health represent her chief expense apart from rent and food.

I spoke on the telephone with the primary care physician who had provided her biomedical care for almost two years. He listed Eliza's problems as "malaise, fatigue, and recurrent pharyngitis." When asked on a mailed questionnaire to circle the part of a figure of the human body that was affected by her illness, he put a circle around all of it. He listed her symptoms as "very severe," but her physical disability as "mild," and he thought that psychological problems and emotional distress combined in a psychosomatic disorder. This midcareer clinician felt confident in Eliza's medical management but reported at the same time his disquiet that treating her was "extremely difficult." He told me, "In the old days I think Eliza would have been diagnosed either as a neurasthenic or some kind of post-infection debility syndrome."

Eliza's major source of help (and difficulty) is herself.

I think before I was constantly looking for help or reassurance from people and it wasn't always helpful. I've been fighting my symptoms for two years—worrying constantly, trying mightily to be healthy again. My overachiever pattern that got me sick was still in gear. I felt ashamed of being sick, of falling behind, and needed to push myself. I need to let myself be sick, not push myself to be healthy, which isn't helping. You can't simply see how feelings affect your health and then jump to control their effect on you. You need to express those feelings physically, you need to create space and time to cry, rage, laugh, really get it out. Change then becomes much less of a struggle.

When I get into something like a performance, I get all wound up over things to do the next day. I really have trouble sleeping. I feel exhausted in my bones, and my throat gets sorer. Most of the time I'm worried. I can't rest or relax or get enough sleep. Will I be able to do what it takes to make me better?

My physician and his specialist colleagues don't take my past mono, lack of recovery, and fatigue seriously enough. I recently went to an infectious disease expert and felt better. Maybe they will find a virus, like EB [Epstein-Barr] virus. If this workup is negative at the hospital, well, I will have more trust in my doctor. He didn't refer me; I went on my own.

Eliza describes her symptoms as "whole-body tiredness." She regards herself as vulnerable to fatigue, lassitude, and extreme weakness if she overextends herself or fails to get adequate rest. This sense of vulnerability is constant and strongly influences her daily decisions and life style. When she begins to practice the oboe or clarinet, she often feels a wave of fatigue pass over her body. If the fatigue persists, she feels the need to put down her instrument and sleep. Sometimes, however, it is the parched throat that interferes with her playing. Deep sleep relieves the throat (as it does the fatigue), and so does warmth, resting in a warm place ("like a long leisurely warm bath"), and "staying under covers." Not enough sleep and rest, being cold, eating sugar or wheat, and playing her wind instruments for too long make her symptoms worse.

I was not able to stop and rest and get over it when I was sick. I took care of my boyfriend, not myself. I worked and worked, hadn't learned how to take care of myself. I have a lot of regret about my illness: it was totally beyond me. I feel ashamed that I could be sick that long. My real fear is that I will get really sick again. Have to start from scratch again and then will interrupt, inhibit the progress I have made that has gone so slowly and taken so long. Maybe it will be another five years before I regain my health.

Her history as elicited in psychiatric examination is consistent with a diagnosis of dysthymic disorder—chronic low-grade depression and demoralization related to her disease. The condition has become so much a part of her illness and of her life generally that it seems part of her very personality. She feels lonely, sad, angry, and desperate about her ill health and about her unsatisfactory work, abandoned music, and lack of a boyfriend. Sometimes she feels guilty and blames herself for her situation; at other times she blames her problems for causing her feelings of isolation, joylessness, and occasionally hopelessness.

Eliza's usual work as a temporary secretary is low-level typing. She calls the work "repetitive, dull, unrewarding." It is a constant source of frustration to her that there is so little time for her "true work," her music, while her job takes up so many of her hours. Her work is not up to her occupational standards, nor does it pay well; but it is all she has been able to find to enable her to maintain her independence. Nevertheless, she feels dehumanized and alienated at work. She feels that her lack of energy prevents her from finding a better job, but her fear that she could lose what she has has caused her to hesitate even to negotiate with the secretarial agency for higher pay or to work fewer hours; yet an improved work situation would be better for the life style she wishes to create. She attributes her unacceptable position to a lack of self-efficacy, a failure to be tough enough to succeed in a world that demands aggressiveness.

Eliza Hartman's narrative swings back and forth between two opposing plot lines about how her family life and childhood development contribute to her present troubles. In one version, her parents are accused of overprotecting her so that she was not prepared (and still is not) to meet the practical difficulties of "real life." In the other version, her parents (and others) are accused of not having done enough to give her the time, money, or practical help to recuperate fully. Her narrative is not so much a description of her experiences as a justification for what she perceives as a series of failures that have knocked her out of her expected life course, derailed her aspirations, and "left me in limbo."

The only child of a second marriage, between a German Catholic émigré engineer and a Quaker housewife, Eliza sums up her early experience in the Hartman family: "I was spoiled badly. The neighboring kids resented this and they treated me very harshly. My first experience of contradictions between what my parents told me about life and how it really is."

She spent most of her time with her parents,

in a world of my own: not many friends, alone. I was a good student but terrified I wouldn't do well.

I got the message from my parents: you always will be taken care of. I was raised in a middle-class life style. Had everything I wanted, but was made to feel that's how it always would be. No one ever told me living—working would be so bloody hard; that you would have to develop your toughness and strength to deal with problems. That one day you would be on your own, alone, with no one but yourself to rely on. When things really got bad I didn't get taken care of, anyway. I blame my folks for this feeling. My mother has never had to deal with what I do as a single woman and musician. She didn't prepare me for life. She never had to deal with a career, making money. She came from a privileged upper middle class background. And my father merely continued more of the same. My father should have known better. I feel resentment about the difficulty I had breaking away, becoming independent.

Growing up, I didn't have a life of my own. I did what others wanted me to do. I was wrapped in a cocoon and only now am coming out. I followed what others did. No one ever taught me to care for my body properly, to discipline myself. I was fat and sloppy.

Like a revisionist historian, Eliza reinterprets her biography almost wholly through the lenses of her current problems and her perception of the failures of her parents to prepare her to handle sickness, the daily drudgery of uninspiring work, and being alone. She feels her parents have never accepted her illness and her role as chronically ill. She believes they want her to participate with them in a collusion of silence over her exhaustion and especially her psychological state. During most of her childhood and adolescence, Eliza had frequent low-grade sicknesses and missed a great deal of school. Now she recognizes that whenever she felt seriously stressed she would amplify complaints, particularly fatigue and gastrointestinal symptoms. Her parents, she avers, never accepted her image of herself as vulnerable and weak, but they did let her stay out of school.

I was raised by my father's mother, who did everything for me. I never had a sense of self-efficacy, even in music I always had my doubts. There's an underlying stress in my life that I don't like to admit—but I'm only comfortable when other people are taking care of things. It feels right, like when my friends are working on my apartment. I have this nice sense of things being accomplished and all's right with the world. But when they leave some project for me, I have this overwhelming dread that it's going to be hard, if not impossible. I'll probably never finish it and it might kill me—this makes it a little tough to get up and go to work every day. I just don't really believe I'll survive it.

Eliza often excuses such feelings of dependency and inefficacy in handling the real-world problems she faces because they are due to or intensified by her illness. Her illness has given her a sense of falling behind, missing out on the normal development of career and relationships; and it has supplied an explanation to justify her situation. "I feel there is no time for my métier. I am pissing away time each day, just recuperating: just to physically live."

Eliza Hartman is also quite capable of standing aside and looking ironically at her failures and losses.

Sometimes I think that society is so organized so that each of us must spend all our hours surviving, we are not supposed to have time to break our concentration on the rat race and see the world as it is. What we do is fill our vision and thoughts with all the concrete details, all the things to do. That's me, all right. The illness, my work, financial problems, practicing my music. There goes my day. No time to look around, see the carrot and the stick, analyze things. Each of us needs an anthropologist.

Beneath her many theories and her persistent complaints, Eliza Hartman holds firmly to the idea that she has a basic deficit in energy, a weakness at the core—a problem in her vitality, and exhaustion of resources, a general decline in functioning. I will return to this conviction, and to her lack of insight into the strategic uses and the powerful nonverbal communication of her symptoms, when I compare the Chinese and American cases of neurasthenia.

Interpretation

We have much more information about Eliza Hartman than we do about Comrade Yen. Yet we recognize both important similarities and equally important differences. There are similarities in their bodily symptoms of distress—the weakness-exhaustion-demoralization constellation—that fit the classical pattern of neurasthenic complaints described by George Beard in Manhattan one hundred years before Eliza Hartman (living in the same borough) and Comrade Yen (residing in a radically different society ten thousand miles away) developed their disorders. The similarities are not surprising, since the biology of stress and demoralization (including changes in the brain's limbic system, the neuroendocrine system, the autonomic nervous system, and cardiovascular and gastrointestinal physiology) underlie this syndrome. Comrade Yen's condition takes on meaning within a shared popular and professional conception of neurasthenia in Chinese culture, but the picture in North American society is more complex. Eliza Hartman probably has little idea what *neurasthenia* means, and her explanation of her illness draws on a bewildering variety of biomedical, alternative medical, and popular sources. For example, her views on lack of vitality fit in well at the holistic medical center she attended, where a program of "revitalization" was emphasized. The views of that program reciprocally intensified Eliza's interest in this aspect of her illness. But in addition she made use of concepts from the stress model of illness, the hot/cold folk theory of illness, psychoanalytic psychotherapy, and much else besides. Eliza Hartman had even been treated by a traditional Chinese physician now practicing in Manhattan's Chinatown. Such is the exchange of knowledge and commodities between societies in our era!

There is also an important structural similarity in the causal nexus of both cases. Eliza and Comrade Yen have both become involved in vicious social cycles creating and intensifying demoralization and its bodily forms. In each of their lives, work, family, and personal problems are instrumental antecedents and consequents. We have here evidence of a lasting element in the human condition that is similar in Hunan and New York. The uses to which both illness careers get put are also aspects of a shared humanity.

Another important similarity is that both patients regard their illness as caused by physical factors. For Eliza Hartman, new biomedical interest in chronic viral disease offers her an up-to-date medical explanation of her chronic fatigue syndrome that removes feelings of personal accountability while encouraging the hope that biomedical research will discover a technical intervention that will cure her. There is a controversy in American medical circles as to whether chronic viral disorders actually cause chronic fatigue and depression, or whether the weakness and the rest of the neurasthenia-like syndrome arise from the patient's psychological reaction to life's problems and the search for a more socially acceptable medical excuse. This controversy is not unlike the one that swirled around neurasthenia in North America earlier in this century; consider also the current debates over whether hypoglycemia and food allergies cause fatigue or whether muscular trigger points give rise to pain. In contemporary Chinese society neurasthenia is a medical legitimation for problems that otherwise would raise serious moral questions of personal responsibility; thus disease labels play the same role for Comrade Yen and Eliza Hartman.

But there are also great differences between the two cases, differences in the particular sociopolitical, economic, and cultural systems that make of China and the United States such radically different societies. There are also striking differences in these two patients' local environments, personalities, outlooks on the world, responses to illness, and outcomes. Comrade Yen is stoic and has a no-nonsense practicality; she lives under a moralistic peasant ethos with unrefined language, harsh conditions, and an expectation that most personal problems must be endured. Her situation contrasts markedly with Eliza Hartman's: Eliza is very expressive and has a psychological orientation; she perceives a lack of practical experience and discusses life's problems archly, through the lens of her overly sophisticated, urban, upper middle class rhetoric; she expects that most personal problems can be changed. Thus the case analyses are led in different directions: Comrade Yen's more toward her social situation, Eliza Hartman's more toward her inner self. And the same differences have led Comrade Yen's doctors to focus on neurasthenia as physical disability and most of Eliza's doctors to emphasize psychological factors.

Neither person has insight into the way her chronic illness expresses and helps resolve tensions in her life. And this may be a salient similarity worldwide. The chronically ill are caught up with the sheer exigency of their problems; what insight they possess into its structural sources and consequences they are not expected to voice. This is a social fiction of the illness role. The patient, in order to legitimately occupy that role, is not expected to be consciously aware of what she desires from it, what practical uses it has.

For the treatment of "neurasthenia" in North America, psychotherapy is an appropriate intervention; in China there is hardly anything that we in the West would call psychotherapy. Social interventions would be helpful in both cases. But neither under capitalism nor under communism does appropriate social change to reduce specific social problems seem feasible. Indeed, massive social transformations have contributed to Comrade Yen's problems. Nonetheless, some of these problems may respond to change of work or highly focused interventions in workplace and family. Both cases require such interventions along with more standard psychological and medical treatments. Yet the structure of biomedical care in both cultures tends to preclude the necessary social interventions.

Comrade Yen and Eliza Hartman, like the other chronic patients whose stories I have recounted, are problem patients for their respective medical systems. There are several reasons for this cross-cultural similarity in the care of the chronically ill. Surely, frustration for patients, for families, and for practitioners can result from the sheer chronicity, poor outcome, complications, high costs, and the many other difficulties that beset effective care for this group of patients. Yet there is one source of problems in care that is close to the central theme of this book. Care of the chronically ill brings out the inherent potential for the patient's principal concern with the illness to clash with the practitioner's chief interest in the disease. And clash they often do. In the chapter that follows we will examine such conflict by observing the interaction between lay and professional explanatory models in the process of care.

7

Conflicting Explanatory Models in the Care of the Chronically Ill

We . . . are in part living in a world the constituents of which we
can discover, classify and act upon by rational, scientific, deliber-
ately planned methods; but in part . . . we are . . . submerged in
a medium that, precisely to the degree to which we inevitably
take it for granted as part of ourselves, we do not and cannot
observe as if from the outside; cannot identify, measure, and seek
to manipulate; cannot even be wholly aware of, inasmuch as it
enters too intimately into all our experience, is itself too closely
interwoven with all that we are and do to be lifted out of the flow
(it *is* the flow) and observed with scientific detachment, as an
object.

—Isaiah Berlin
(1978, 71)

Explanatory models are the notions that patients, families, and practitioners have about a specific illness episode. These informal descriptions of what an illness is about have enormous clinical significance: to ignore them may be fatal. They respond to such questions
as: What is the nature of this problem? Why has it affected me? Why
now? What course will it follow? How does it affect my body? What
treatment do I desire? What do I most fear about this illness and its
treatment? Explanatory models are responses to urgent life circumstances. Thus, they are justifications for practical action more than
statements of a theoretical and rigorous nature. Indeed, they are most

often tacit, or at least partially so. Not infrequently, they contain contradictions and shift in content. They are our representations of the cultural flow of life experience; consequently, as the epigraph to this chapter suggests, they congeal and unravel as that flow and our understanding of it firms up in one situation only to dissolve in another. Furthermore, these models—which can be thought of as cognitive maps—are anchored in strong emotions, feelings that are difficult to express openly and that strongly color one person's reaction to another's explanatory models.

The elicitation of patient and family explanatory models helps practitioners to take the patient's perspective seriously in organizing strategies for clinical care. Practitioners' effective communication of their models in turn assists patients and families to make more useful judgments of when to enter into treatment, with which practitioners, for what treatments, and at what ratio of cost and benefit. Negotiation among patients and practitioners over salient conflicts in models can remove an important barrier to effective care and almost always contributes to more empathic and ethical treatment. Practitioners' inattention to the explanatory models of patients and their families, conversely, may signal disrespect for clients, hubris in the face of alternative viewpoints, and failure to regard psychosocial dimensions of care as relevant. Such blatant disregard impedes the therapeutic relationship and undermines the communicative foundations of care. The following vignette illustrates the great clinical significance of explanatory models. This case narrative also discloses the central contribution patients and families make to the therapeutic process.

The Case of William Steele

William Steele is a forty-two-year-old white American attorney with a two-year history of asthma. His asthma has steadily worsened since its onset, and Mr. Steele is now following an extensive medication regimen that includes 20 milligrams of prednisone taken daily. He sleeps near a cool-mist vaporizer, uses various bronchodilator inhalers during the day, and drinks lots of fluids to keep his bronchial secretions moist. He has undergone allergy testing and desensitization for pollen and dust allergies, without effect. Mr. Steele has no family history of asthma, and he did not have asthma as a child, though he did experience frequent upper respiratory infections.

His doctor, James Blanchard, is an internist who serves as his primary care physician. Dr. Blanchard has explained to Mr. Steele that asthma is a disorder involving bronchial constriction that makes it difficult for patients to breathe; its ultimate cause is unknown, but allergies, stress, and sometimes—in Mr. Steele's case, regrettably—exercise contribute to flareups. He has made it clear to Mr. Steele that asthma is a chronic disorder without a cure, but one whose physiological effects can be well controlled with the proper medical regimen. Over the course of the two years, Dr. Blanchard has demonstrated to Mr. Steele that pipe smoking and drinking red wine lead to expectable exacerbations. Mr. Steele has discontinued both. Dr. Blanchard has responded to Mr. and Mrs. Steele's request for advice about acupuncture, self-hypnosis, and macrobiotic diet with the information that there is no scientific evidence that these folk treatments do any good. He has referred Mr. Steele to two specialists: a chest disease expert who concurred with Dr. Blanchard's assessment and treatment and suggested a battery of pulmonary function tests with which to follow this patient's course, and a psychiatrist who diagnosed a secondary depression owing to the asthma and the prednisone and who recommended an antidepressant medication and psychotherapy. Dr. Blanchard was reluctant to endorse the psychotherapy because, as he put it, "The patient is a Pandora's Box; who knows what will happen once the lid is removed?" He did accept the recommendation to begin low doses of an antidepressant (Tofranil), but discontinued the drug when the patient complained of side effects of dry mouth, dizziness, and constipation.

From Dr. Blanchard's perspective, Mr. Steele's progressively worsening course and the acute onset of the asthma in midlife without earlier symptoms were perplexing. He felt that there was probably an allergic cause, and he was considering further allergy testing and desensitization. Some months later, at the insistence of

Mrs. Steele, who was deeply distressed by her husband's condition, Dr. Blanchard finally referred the patient to a second psychiatrist for treatment. This psychiatrist elicited the following story.

From Mr. Steele's perspective, both the onset and the poor course of his problem could be explained. His asthma began with an attack of wheezing the morning after his fortieth birthday. On his birthday he had appeared in court to argue a difficult case, and he had been criticized by the judge several times for not providing sufficient information. As a result, he and his client had had an argument; when the argument got out of hand, the client precipitously fired him. That night William Steele, his wife, and his three children (aged ten through fourteen) celebrated his birthday. He remembers feeling greatly ambivalent about reaching "middle age"; he was under substantial stress in his legal practice (which was less successful than he had thought it would be by this time) and in his home life (his relationships with his wife, eldest son, and in-laws were increasingly tense).

I felt like everything was going the wrong way for me. My career was going poorly. My wife and I had a worsening relationship, and I couldn't stand her parents, who had objected to our marriage in the first place and constantly told my wife I wouldn't succeed. My son—oh, God! I had some kind of learning problem myself as a kid. It depressed me that he had an even more severe one and would have lots of trouble in high school. It seemed like even with the kids, things were going badly.

Well, that night, after the party, I just couldn't sleep. I tossed and turned and wondered to myself what would happen to me, to all of us. Suppose I didn't make it. Would my wife leave me? Would the kids despise me? What if I died? I had had such dreams of being a success in my life. You know, I wanted to be a great lawyer. But I feared my talent wasn't in the courtroom. The day of my birthday confirmed my fear. I'd have to give up the dream I had held since college and worked so hard at. What would I do? I felt lost and finally fell asleep.

Well, during the night I had this terrible dream, like a nightmare. There was the courtroom, with me, my client, and the judge, and also my wife, my in-laws, and my son. I got up to speak. The judge told me that I had made a big mistake. My client chipped in and yelled at me for the same mistake. Then my wife, my in-laws, my son, they all joined in, shouting: "Mistake! Mistake! Failure! Failure!" Then a huge fire broke out in the courtroom and consumed us all. I woke up coughing, choking, and there was my asthma. You can't tell me they're unrelated. I think that's the cause.

Since then it's been one damned thing after another; I feel like it's all over for me. I can't control my asthma and I can't control my life. I've missed so much work, my partners in the law firm are up in arms. I'm sucking on the inhaler, coughing,

and waving away their cigarette smoke. I can barely attend to my work. At home
I just want to be alone in my room without stress. I get into arguments with my
wife and kids daily. I just can't take it. Either the asthma will kill me, or I'll kill
myself.

Mr. Steele's wife also had a perspective on his illness. She had
taken him to a natural food store and encouraged him to try a
macrobiotic diet. Recently she had introduced him to an herbalist-
acupuncturist. She believed that the asthma had frightened him and
depressed him, that it had changed his personality.

It's been disastrous for our marriage. We don't go out. All we talk about is his
illness and medicines. He is afraid even to have sex with me because of how it may
further hurt his health. And as for the kids, he can't tolerate their normal behavior.
They fight and he starts wheezing. Our son's school problem is bad; he's dyslexic,
and Bill can't figure out how to respond. All he does is hide. He's not like he was
before. He's become frightened and completely absorbed with his symptoms. If
this goes on, I don't know what we will do.

William Steele describes his asthma as follows:

You know, it's terrible to have an attack. It's, it's like you are drowning, smother-
ing. You can't breathe. I spend a lot of time worrying about it. I do all I can to avoid
it. At the first sign of a wheeze, I increase my medications. I don't do anything for
fear exercise will bring it on, as it has in the past. What do I do? I feel hopeless.
Maybe they should just take me outside and shoot me.

Mr. Steele mentioned that as soon as he developed wheezing,
even if it was very mild, he would get a panicky feeling and fear
that he would die. As a result, he would take more of his asthma
medication than prescribed and then would often develop signs of
toxicity. He had insight into this vicious cycle but was unable to
break out of it owing to his overwhelming fear that he might die
because he was unable to breathe.

Mr. Steele had on several occasions changed his treatment regimen, without the knowledge of his physician. Once he stopped
taking a drug altogether because he felt it made him extremely
anxious, at the same time doubling the dosage of another medication, which produced a toxic reaction. On another occasion he followed the advice of his herbalist-acupuncturist and stopped his oral
bronchodilator; he precipitated an asthma attack that landed him in
the emergency room.

Both Mr. and Mrs. Steele believed that personal, work, and family problems worsened his illness. But when they raised this issue with Dr. Blanchard, they felt that he discounted its significance; he did not encourage them to seek counseling. As their marriage and family problems worsened, Mrs. Steele insisted that Dr. Blanchard refer them for psychiatric evaluation. When Dr. Blanchard delayed in the referral for psychotherapy and resisted trying a second anti-depressant (as previously mentioned, side effects had led to the discontinuation of the first), it was only at Mrs. Steele's insistence that he finally referred her husband to the second psychiatrist for treatment.

Mr. Steele's children had their own views of his illness. The oldest son feared that his poor school performance and the diagnosis of his learning disability had worsened his father's illness. The younger children thought that their frequent quarrels with each other con-tributed to their father's increased difficulty in breathing.

Mr. Steele's in-laws thought that there was a strong voluntaristic component to his asthma. They said he used the symptoms to gain sympathy from and to control his wife and children. His in-laws came from a midwestern populist background and belonged to a charismatic Catholic sect; they were outspokenly antiprofessional. They recommended natural diet, homeopathic cures, and religious healing. They remarked: "God is punishing him for something. Medical care can't work while there is some serious religious prob-lem. We had a feeling from the start he was that kind of person."

After six months of psychotherapy, marital counseling, and a course of antidepressants, Mr. Steele experienced a significant change in his asthma symptoms and psychological state. His medi-cations were significantly reduced and he was off steroids entirely. Over the next few years his marital relationship improved and he made a major career change. He gave up his legal practice and joined his father and brother in the wholesale fish business. Four years after this story began, Mr. Steele was off all asthma medication and symptom-free.

You know, I think I was right. It wasn't allergies; it was my life. I was under such stress, it makes me feel terrible to think of it. I know I was going nowhere in the law. I had to give up my dream. But I couldn't let go. I worked harder, and things went from bad to worse. I think my body was telling me that I had to make some big changes. The psychotherapy helped a lot. But it was the life change that was crucial. Now I'm in a family business, feel good about it, and don't feel the pressure to be somebody I couldn't be and do something I couldn't do. I feel in better control.

By this time Mrs. Steele shared her husband's views, but Dr. Blanchard did not. He noted that it was extremely unusual for asthma to disappear solely for psychosocial reasons. He also pointed out that onset of asthma at age forty was very uncommon. Perhaps, he argued, there was a transient allergen (a pet or a new pollen or environmental contaminant) that had been responsible for the asthma and now was gone. The psychiatrist who initially evaluated Mr. Steele also did not fully accept the Steeles' rationale for the successful outcome. While he believed that stress reduction, improved social support, and treatment of the underlying depression had contributed to the outcome, he also assumed that some other physiological change had occurred as well. The second psychiatrist, who actually treated Mr. Steele, was more inclined to accept a psychosomatic explanation; but in his view, the depression was the main reason for the symptoms and its treatment the chief source of recovery. Mr. Steele's in-laws were convinced the outcome was an act of God. In this case, family and patient explanatory models are not the same, and, indeed, the clashes among these models also contribute to the Steels' problems. But it is of special significance that, in spite of the dramatic cure, the practitioners' models refuse to accept either the patient's contribution to the outcome or the powerful effects of the psychosocial intervention.

Dr. Blanchard also does not share the Steeles' belief in the usefulness of alternative therapies or self-care. He seems at best ambivalent and at worst frankly hostile to the place of psychosocial treatment in chronic medical disease. A senior, well-respected clinician, he paid little attention either to the biography of the patient or to the patient and family perspectives, which were elicited for the first time by the consulting psychiatrist. For Dr. Blanchard, medical treatment is the prescription of medications. This is not the viewpoint of Mrs. Steele or her husband. Unaware of his patients' concerns, Dr. Blanchard inadvertently colluded in the vicious cycle of noncompliance and psychosocial distress that intensified the asthma and made the medical treatment part of the problem rather than the solution. Here we see exposed the profession of medicine's mischievous mind-body dichotomy, which assumes that only biological aspects of illness are "real" and only biological treatments are "hard" enough to produce biological change. While the remarkable outcome of William Steele's case is unusual, the contribution of professional orthodoxy to inadvertently heighten the passivity and demoralization of patients and their families is all too common in the treatment of the chronically ill.

Professional Explanatory Models and the Construction of Chronic Illness as Disease

The following interchange was tape recorded by a research assistant as she followed a patient with psoriasis, Mrs. Jill Lawler, into the office of a leading dermatologist. Mrs. Lawler is a thirty-five-year-old woman who has had psoriasis for fifteen years. She is extremely knowledgeable about this disorder, having read medical texts and even the latest research reports. She also holds a psychosomatic view of the relationship of life stress to illness, a view shared by most behavioral and social scientists and increasingly by many physicians. Because she has recently moved to a new city, she is making her first visit to this dermatologist, who is an expert in a new technological intervention to treat psoriasis.

MRS. LAWLER: I have an appointment with Dr. Jones.
RECEPTIONIST: Have a seat and fill out this form regarding your insurance and current health problems.
MRS. LAWLER (*after entering the doctor's office*): Dr. Jones, I am here to see you because of my psoriasis. I understand you are an expert in the use of a new treatment.
DR. JONES: How long have you had psoriasis?
MRS. LAWLER: Oh, about fifteen years.
DR. JONES: Where did it begin?
MRS. LAWLER: I was in college, under lots of pressure from exams, and there is a family history of skin problems. It was winter and I was wearing heavy woolen sweaters that seemed to bother my skin. My diet was—
DR. JONES: No, No! I meant where on your skin did you first notice plaques?
MRS. LAWLER: My shoulders and knees. But I had a problem for some time with my scalp that I never—
DR. JONES: How has it progressed the past few years?

MRS. LAWLER: These have been difficult years. I mean I have been under great stress at work and in my personal life. I—

DR. JONES: I meant, how has your skin problem progressed?

The reader has probably had a sufficient glimpse at this interview to be able to share the patient's frustration at getting her story across. The expert in psoriasis is interested in the illness only to the extent that it provides clues to what is happening to the disease. His style is authoritarian and interrogative. He does not acknowledge that the patient's experience with a chronic disorder makes her an expert of sorts whose insight may be useful. Indeed, by this stage of the interview, Dr. Jones was well on the way to infuriating his patient, who, not surprisingly, decided not to return. Dr. Charles Jones, whom I know slightly, does not strike me as being as insensitive as this brief transcript makes him out to be. But he is an extremely busy clinician, and this was his first meeting with a new patient whose disease problem he wished to define as expeditiously as possible so that he could determine whether his new therapy was appropriate for her case. I believe I would not be exaggerating to say that in Dr. Jones's professional view (and in that of many medical specialists) there is no notion that the patient can make a contribution to clinical judgment about the disease and its treatment. In the care of an acute problem, an interrogative style may be necessary to help the practitioner diagnose a potentially treatable disease and commence effective technical interaction as quickly as possible, especially for life-threatening health problems. But it cannot be emphasized enough that this is an inappropriate clinical method to use with the chronically ill.

Elliot Mishler (1985), a Harvard behavioral scientist with long experience in the sociolinguistic study of doctor–patient communication, refers to that interaction as the setting for a dialogue between the voice of medicine and the voice of the life world. His research and his review of the studies of many other students of clinical communication show that all too frequently the voice of medicine drowns out the voice of the life world, often in ways that seem disrespectful, even intolerant, of the patient's perspective. Since the diagnosis of disease is based on the history of illness and is a semiotic act transforming lay speech into professional categories, careful attention to the illness account is essential, even when the story is viewed in terms of narrow professional objectives (Hampton et al. 1975). When the empowerment of patients and their families becomes an objective of care, the empathic auditing of their stories of the illness must be one of the clinician's chief therapeutic tasks.

The message the practitioner indirectly transmits to patients and their families is this: your view doesn't really matter much; I am the one who will make the treatment decisions; you do not need to be privy to the influences and judgments that inform those decisions. This is a medicocentric view increasingly at odds with the kind of care patients and families want and today *expect* for chronic illness. Remember that the patient's and family's discourse is the original and most fundamental account of illness. It comprises the text that the practitioner interprets. I say to physicians, return to that original discourse! We live in a time of great concern for the practitioner's response to the patient's request. But the primary ground of care is not that response; it is rather the patient's discourse on illness. Physicians say that they listen to that discourse to diagnosis disease ("listen to the patient, he is telling you the diagnosis" is a famous clinical maxim taught to medical students). Yet practitioners must go beyond this concern, important as it is, and return to the time when as beginning medical students, with a foot in both lay and professional worlds, they audited the speech of their first patients with great intensity, with something approaching awe in respect for hearing the patient's story in his or her own words and with deep sympathy for the human condition of suffering. That, it seems to me, is the best way to come to understand the illness experience and take it into account in practice.

Professional Influences on the Recording of Disease

The recording of a case in the medical record, a seemingly innocuous means of description, is in fact a profound, ritual act of transformation through which illness is made over into disease, person becomes patient, and professional values are transferred from the practitioner to the "case." Through this act of writing up a patient account, the practitioner turns the sick person as *subject* into an *object* first of professional inquiry and eventually of manipulation. The patient's record is an official account, in the language of biomedicine, that has legal and bureaucratic significance. Medical students are trained in how to construct a case report. They are taught how to record symptoms and medical history and how to reinterpret them as an official diagnostic entity in the authoritative medical taxonomy. Each student learns to reproduce an account that meets strict criteria and has a standard format. The evaluation of student performance is based in part on readings of these reports. Over a clinical career, physicians learn to write in the record with an eye to professional standards as well as to possible legal and bureaucratic appraisal; for the record is read by other doctors and also by nurses, peer review committees, medical ethics committees, clinical pathology review groups, and—if there is a court case—by lawyers, judges, and juries.

From an anthropological point of view, recording the case is an example of a secular ritual: it formally replicates a social reality in which core values are reasserted and then applied in a reiterated, standardized format to a central problem in the human condition. Like religious rituals, secular rituals express and manipulate key symbols that connect a shared set of values and beliefs to practical action. By observing in this light the writing of a case into the medical record, we should be able to see more clearly the influence of professional values (and the professional's personal preferences) in the care of the chronically ill. To accomplish this end, I will first provide a transcript of a doctor–patient interview and then describe the wording of the physician's formal write-up in the patient's record. I don't contend that the following example is representative; indeed I believe that the degree of professional insensitivity it depicts is unusual. But I do think that the physician's overriding interest in disease and disregard of illness is, regrettably, commonplace. (Note that I observed only one transaction in a long series of transactions, the totality of which might have given a rather different impression.)

The two protagonists in the transcript are Mrs. Melissa Flowers and Dr. Staunton Richards. Mrs. Flowers is a thirty-nine-year-old black mother of five children who has hypertension. She lives with four of her children, her mother, and two grandchildren in an inner-city ghetto. She works at present as a waitress in a restaurant, but periodically she has been unemployed and on welfare. She has been married twice, but both of her husbands have deserted her. As a result, she is a single head of a household. Mrs. Flowers is an active member of the local Baptist church, which has been an important source of support to her and her family for many years. She is also a member of a community action group. In the household of eight she is the only wage earner. Her mother, Mildred, is fifty-nine and partially paralyzed owing to a stroke that was the result of long-standing and poorly controlled hypertension. Her oldest daughter, Matty, the unmarried nineteen-year-old mother of two small children, is at present unemployed and pregnant; in the past, she has had a drug problem. Mrs. Flowers's fifteen-year-old daughter, Marcia, is also pregnant. Their eighteen-year-old brother, J.D., is in prison. Teddy, a twelve-year-old, has had problems with truancy and minor delinquency. Amelia, eleven, the baby of the family, is said by her mother to be an angel. A year ago, Mrs. Flowers's long-time male companion, Eddie Johnson, was killed in a barroom brawl. Recently, Mrs. Flowers has been increasingly upset by memories of Eddie Johnson, by concern for how prison will affect J.D., and by fears that Teddy will get involved with drugs like his older brother and sister before him. She is also concerned about her mother's worsening disability, which includes what she fears may be early signs of dementia.

DR. RICHARDS: Hello, Mrs. Flowers.

MRS. FLOWERS: I ain't feelin' too well today, Doc Richards.

DR. RICHARDS: What seems to be wrong?

MRS. FLOWERS: Um, I don't know. Maybe it's that pressure of mine. I been gettin' headaches and havin' trouble sleeping.

DR. RICHARDS: Your hypertension is a bit worse, but not all that bad, considering what it's been in the past. You been taking your medicines as you ought to?

MRS. FLOWERS: Sometimes I do. But sometimes when I don't have no pressure I don't take it.

DR. RICHARDS: Gee whiz, Mrs. Flowers, I told you if you don't take it regularly you could get real sick like your Mom. You got to take the pills every day. And what about salt? You been eating salt again?

MRS. FLOWERS: It's hard to cook for the family without salt. I don't have time to cook just for me. At lunch, I'm in the restaurant and Charlie, he's the chef, he puts lotsa salt in everythin'.

DR. RICHARDS: Well, now, this is a real problem. Salt restriction, I mean a low-salt diet, is essential for your problem.

MRS. FLOWERS: I know, I know. I mean to do all these things, but I just plain forget sometimes. I got so much else goin' on and it all seems to affect the pressure. I got two pregnant daughters at home and my mother is doin' much worse. I think she may be senile. And then I worries about J.D., and here comes Teddy with the same problems startin' up. I—

DR. RICHARDS: Have you any shortness of breath?

MRS. FLOWERS: No.

DR. RICHARDS: Any chest pain?

MRS. FLOWERS: No.

DR. RICHARDS: Swelling in your feet?

MRS. FLOWERS: The feet do get a little swollen, but then I'm on them all day long at the restaurant—

DR. RICHARDS: You said you had headaches?

MRS. FLOWERS: Sometimes I think my life is one big headache. These here ain't too bad. I've had 'em for a long time, years. But in recent weeks they been badder than before. You see, a year ago last Sunday, Eddie Johnson, my friend, you know. Uh huh, well, he died. And—

DR. RICHARDS: Are the headaches in the same place as before?

MRS. FLOWERS: Yeah, same place, same feelin, on'y more often. But, you see, Eddie Johnson had always told me not to bother about—

DR. RICHARDS: Have you had any difficulty with your vision?

MRS. FLOWERS: No.

DR. RICHARDS: Any nausea?

MRS. FLOWERS: No. Well when I drank the pickle juice there was some.

DR. RICHARDS: Pickle juice? You've been drinking pickle juice? That's got a great deal of salt. It's a real danger for you, for your hypertension.

MRS. FLOWERS: But I have felt pressure this week and my mother told me maybe I need it because I got high blood and—

DR. RICHARDS: Oh, no. Not pickle juice. Mrs. Flowers, you can't drink that for any reason. It just isn't good. Don't you understand? Its got lots of salt, and salt is bad for your hypertension.

MRS. FLOWERS: Uh huh. OK.

DR. RICHARDS: Any other problems?

MRS. FLOWERS: My sleep ain't been too good, doc. I think it's because—

DR. RICHARDS: Is it trouble getting to sleep?

MRS. FLOWERS: Yeah, and gettin' up real early in the mornin'. I been dreamin' about Eddie Johnson. Doin' a lot of rememberin' and cryin'. I been feelin' real lonely. I don't know—

DR. RICHARDS: Any other problems? I mean bodily problems?

MRS. FLOWERS: No, 'cept for tired feelin', but that's been there for years. Dr. Richards, you think worryin' and missin' somebody can give you headaches?

DR. RICHARDS: I don't know. If they are tension headaches, it might. But you haven't had other problems like dizziness, weakness, fatigue?

MRS. FLOWERS: That's what I'm sayin'! The tired feelin', it's been there some time. And the pressure makes it worse. But I wanted to ask you about worries. I got me a mess o' worries. And I been feelin' all down, as if I just couldn't handle it anymore. The money is a real problem now.

DR. RICHARDS: Well, I will have to ask Mrs. Ma, the social worker, to talk to you about the financial aspect. She might be able to help. Right now why don't we do a physical exam and see how your doing?

MRS. FLOWERS: I ain't doin' well. Even I can tell you that. There's too much pressure and its makin' *my pressure* bad. And I been feelin real sad for myself.

DR. RICHARDS: Well, we'll soon see how things are going.

After completing the physical examination, Dr. Richards wrote the following note in the medical record.

April 14, 1980

39 year old Black female with hypertension on hydrochlorothiaziade 100 mgs. daily and aldomet 2 grams daily. Blood pressure now 160/105, has been 170–80/110–120 for several months, alternating with 150/95 when taking meds regularly. Has evidence of mild congestive heart failure. No other problems.

Impression: (1) Hypertension, poorly controlled
(2) Noncompliance contributing to (1)
(3) Congestive heart failure—mild

Plan: (1) Change aldomet to apresoline.
(2) Send to dietician to enforce low salt diet.
(3) Social work consult because of financial questions.
(4) See in 3 days, regularly until blood pressure has come down and stabilized.

Signed: Dr. Staunton Richards

Dr. Richards also sent a terse note for a consultation to the dietician, which read: "39 year old Black woman with poorly controlled hypertension who does not comply with low salt diet. Please help plan 2 gram sodium diet, and explain to her again relationship of salt intake to her disease and that she must stop eating high salt foods and cooking with salt."

Interpretation

The case that materializes in the written record seems quite different from the sick woman who speaks in the transcript. Melissa Flowers is reduced to her hypertension, her noncompliance with the medical regimen, her early signs of heart failure, and her medications. Gone from the record is Melissa Flowers as a sick person under great social pressure, worried and demoralized by difficult family problems (see Dressler 1985). Those problems are a reflection of the social breakdown, violence, and inadequate resources and limited life chances of the United States's black underclass. But while we might not expect Dr. Richards to include those social sources of Mrs. Flowers's multiple misfortunes in the medical record, it is deplorable that he fails to include her life problems, including the multiple family difficulties, the prolonged grief reaction, and the psychological effects of her troubled social environment. (Indeed, I believe a case can be made for describing social sources of illness in order to specify the social changes needed to prevent and treat such life distress.) But then again these are concerns that Dr. Richards either failed to follow up on with specific questions or actually stopped Mrs. Flowers from elaborating. That is to say, Dr. Richards permits Mrs. Flowers to speak about her disease but not about her illness. Physical complaints are authorized, but psychological or social ones are not. The diagnosis is, in fact, a systematic distortion of the interview: only facts that relate to the disease and its treatment are sought, allowed to emerge, and heard. The human suffering that is so much a part of this chronic illness is met with silence and seemingly denied.

Cultural issues are allowed to slip by, one after another, in a way that would be regarded as sheer clinical incompetence if the issues were biological. Mrs. Flowers uses the terms "pressure" and "high blood," which refer to folk illnesses in lower-class black American society (see Nations et al. 1985). These concepts help explain what Dr. Richards labels noncompliance; for example, high blood, a folk condition believed to result from blood rising into the head, is thought to cause headaches and is treated ("lowered," "thinned," "cut") with pickle juice. If Dr. Richards were to attend to this alternative belief system, he would have a more accurate understanding of Mrs. Flowers's behavior and would also have an opportunity to explain the biomedical view and negotiate with Mrs. Flowers to change potentially dangerous behavior. When Mrs. Flowers uses the word *pressure* she is drawing on holistic concepts that relate social and psychological pressures to blood pressure. Biomedical theory acknowledges a role of stress in hypertension grudgingly and only as a chronic long-term stressor, not as an important source of short-term fluctuations (see Blumhagen 1980).

Finally, noncompliance for Dr. Richards is a moral term indicating patient failure to *follow* the doctor's instructions. This view is predicated on a professional view of the doctor–patient relationship that is paternalistic and one-sided, a view that is increasingly rejected by popular demands for a more egalitarian relationship in which the patient is seen as a partner in decision making.

The difference between transcript and record, interview and written medical notation, is the difference between illness as the patient's problem and disease as the physician's problem. The core value structure of traditional biomedicine can be seen in this transformation of a sick person into a case. A rigidly biomedical approach to acute diseases, for which magic bullets can provide cures and getting the specific disease sorted out is essential to using the right magic bullet, is often appropriate and effective. Even for acute exacerbations of chronic disorders, where a life-threatening biological problem must be controlled, it has its place. But it is inappropriate in the long-term care of chronic illness, for all the reasons illustrated in this volume. Fortunately, a narrow professional approach, so commonplace in the past, is becoming less acceptable even in the medical profession. But it is still all too common, especially in situations where upper middle class doctors treat lower-class patients. In that context, general class relations in society are replicated in the actual medical encounter, and the political economy responsible for them enters into the clinic like the protagonists' shadows. It is doubtful that Dr. Richards would have been as insensitive if Mrs. Flowers were white and a member of his own social class.

It is important for the reader to recognize that the structure of the interview and of the clinical write-up is not idiosyncratic to Dr. Richards but is the result of his training into a professional culture; it reproduces a version of interviewing that he has learned and that I and many other practitioners also learned. That professional model, I have tried to show, is a reflection of a particular set of values about the nature of disorder, the work of medicine, and the nature of human beings that is frankly destructive in the care of the chronically ill. But putting questions of care to the side, simply as human beings we should be critical of a therapeutic method that dehumanizes the doctor along with the patient.

8

Aspiration and Victory: Coping with Chronic Illness

Woe to the man whose heart has not learned while young to hope, to love—and to put its trust in life!
—JOSEPH CONRAD
([1915] 1957, 338–39)

The patients' stories I have retold in the preceding chapters may seem to the reader excessively morbid and gloomy. There are many persons with chronic disorders and even severe disabilities who live lives of exemplary courage and often of remarkable stability and success. Such patients are not referred for psychiatric evaluation. Even anthropological studies of unselected patients may be biased by their focus on the patients whose life problems are the most formidable and whose therapeutic experiences are the most recalcitrant. It is important to balance the record with the description of a patient whose adaptation to illness is an undoubted success, whose illness problems are effectively dealt with in personal and medical settings, whose life is a model of mastery and grace under fire. To maintain one's aspirations in the face of grave adversity, to work hard to contend successfully with the daily assault of an impaired body on a robust spirit, to be victorious over the long course of losses and threats that constitute disability—these are lessons for us all, examples of what is best in our shared humanity.

Each of us, even the most advantaged, has need of all the good examples we can find. Perhaps at no time is this more true than when we must confront suffering, as only those who experience long-term, daily suffering can attest.

I have had the excellent fortune of getting to know a few individuals whose aspirations were not undermined but heightened by chronic illness and whose lives with illness can be said, without romanticizing and thereby distorting their daily struggle, to be victories. Paddy Esposito is the person whose luminous life comes first to mind.

To provide this account with the moral force it holds for me, I must set the stage as it was just before I met Paddy Esposito. The year was 1973. I was in my residency in a large university teaching hospital in New England. It was early winter; days were gray, cold, and short. The enthusiasm of fall (and of the heady initial period of professional training) had given way to a somber recognition that winter (and the rest of training) were going to occupy a very long, trying time. A survivalist mentality had set in. Interns and residents are grim survivors: pragmatic skeptics poised precariously somewhere between the disdained "soft" enthusiasms of medical students and the longed-for "hard" wisdom of seasoned clinicians. Their energies and patience are under such regular assault that they are not the exemplars of compassion most patients hope to encounter in the hospital. In fact, too little sleep for too long, combined with the tensions of being in an extended adolescence—betwixt and between in professional career and personal life—make for irascible dispositions and small visions. That's where I was then.

I had become the liaison to an inpatient rehabilitation unit that at the time specialized in the care of quadriplegic and paraplegic adolescents. One of my responsibilities was to organize and run a small weekly group therapy session at which six to eight paralyzed adolescent patients, some in wheelchairs, others in hospital beds, were placed in a wide arc around me, inside a large physical therapy room. The purpose of the sessions, at least in principle, was to assist these severely injured young men and women to adapt to their very extensive functional impairments—in some cases, loss of movement in both legs; in others, loss of all sensation and movement (including control of bowel and bladder) below the neck; in still others, inability even to breathe on their own. In fact, the meetings were sustained expressions of collective grief over such very serious losses and rage at the frustration of rehabilitation. Advice seemed to trivialize the desperate existential reality; rather than offer mutual support, the members of the group were more likely to encourage each other in unappeasably cursing their fate, their care givers, and me. I was applauded by the staff for being able to organize this outpouring of resentment in a single meeting of an hour or an hour and a half, which I was told might contain the resentment or redirect it in a more positive direction. But I had serious misgivings about what was being accomplished, and I was uncertain of how the group ought to function.

At one of the most distressing meetings, the group's members decided to talk about suicide as a legitimate potential way out of what for almost all were unacceptable present constraints and bleak prospects. After listening for ten or fifteen minutes to utter gloom— which left me feeling that the group experience would end up doing more damage than good and would demoralize everyone—I responded to my own anxiety and hopelessness by reviewing the standard case for why suicide was an unhelpful, even cowardly, and, in the rehabilitation setting they were in, impossible option. I waxed eloquent about courage and hope, and I think I even said, much as I blush to think of it now, that with the passage of time they could come to accept their condition as something they would be able to live with.

The hour was late and I was very tired. I wanted to end the meeting on a positive note; it was five o'clock on Friday and I had the weekend off, after having been up the entire night before in the emergency room. I was looking forward to taking my wife and children up into the snow country. All of a sudden, one of the youngest patients, a sixteen-year-old who had fractured his lower spine in a diving accident and who had managed to alienate virtually all of the staff owing to his unremitting hostility, shouted at me: "Fuck you, Dr. Kleinman! Fuck you! You don't have to live this way the rest of your life. What do you know about what it's like to be in our condition? How dare you tell us what to do. If you were like us, you'd want to die, to take your life, too." That outburst brought on an avalanche of anger and sadness directed at me.

I returned home after the meeting more or less in a state of shock, certain that the young man was right and I was wrong. I relived the session vividly over the weeks and months to come. I had been inauthentic. I had had no answer. I simply could not imagine what I would feel if I were at that tragic impasse. How is crippling disability made meaningful? The question reverberated in my experience, threatening what sense of meaning I had worked out to engage the chronically ill.

Patrick ("Paddy") Esposito helped me out of the therapeutic nihilism into which I had retreated. How can I best describe Paddy? He was thirty years of age, tall, extremely thin, dressed almost always in a dark blue corduroy suit with a small red flower in the buttonhole (he said that was to celebrate, because "every day is a good day"), bearded and fierce-looking, but with an infectious smile ready in an instant to breakout upon his large, expressive lips and in his soft brown eyes. You wouldn't call him handsome, but he had a presence that drew nearly everyone's eyes toward him as soon as he entered a room. And you felt good to be in his presence. There was a warmth and openness and finished courtesy to his character, and also a deep sense of calm. The ancient Chinese would say he had a plenitude of *qi* (vital energy), had found his road (the *dao*) in life, and had cultivated human-heartedness (*ren*).

Paddy was a bereavement counselor in a small suburban hospital. He spent his days counseling dying patients and their families. He had, as he was wont to say, "a way with words," which he attributed with characteristically self-mocking humor to his Italian-Irish heritage. He was single, but he had a large circle of friends. Paddy suffered from a mysterious progressive inflammatory disease (myocarditis) that attacked the smooth muscle of his heart. He was almost always short of breath. But many people commented that this was one of the least remarkable things about him. Although he had a serious incapacity—it restricted his activities, and caused severe symptoms, and eventually led to his death in 1976—he made remarkably little of it. Often in speaking with him for a few minutes, even when he was a patient in the hospital, you forgot all about his problem while you felt his wonderful openness to your own difficulties. This trait led even people who didn't know him well to tell him about their personal troubles. He seemed to be a kind of natural therapist.

He was also a man of great inner peace and, to my mind, real wisdom. Paddy had dropped out of law school after his second year, soon after the diagnosis of myocarditis was made. He had always wanted to travel around the world and especially to visit India, Nepal, and Southeast Asia, since he had a strong interest in Buddhism. He spent three years in Asia, most of the time living in ashrams and Buddhist temples. The experience had a great effect on him. Before his illness he had been, by his own admission, restless, immensely ambitious, egotistical. After he returned to the United States, his health was much worse, but in his felicitous words, "I was so much better."

He decided that his role in life was to serve others, to bring them the peace and wisdom he had found. That is why he became a bereavement counselor. It wasn't easy. The hospice movement had not taken off yet in North America. The larger hospital programs didn't want him, since he was seriously ill himself. But he persisted, and in a sense he developed his own program. He was an excellent counselor, but because he was self-effacing and quiet, he kept his successes to himself. He never developed a reputation beyond his circle of friends, and he made it clear that recognition didn't matter to him. He wasn't so much against the ego-aggrandizing, inhumane self-images of our age as he was entirely indifferent to them. He neither watched television nor read the newspapers. When asked about this, he jokingly referred his interlocutors to King Lear's words to Cordelia on the irrelevance of political ambition and social status to love and happiness.*

*I think Paddy had in mind Lear's transforming happiness at reunion, even as a prisoner, with Cordelia:

> No, no, no, no! Come, let's away to prison.
> We two alone will sing like birds i' the cage.
> When thou dost ask me blessing, I'll kneel down
> And ask of thee forgiveness. So we'll live,
> And pray, and sing, and tell old tales, and laugh
> At gilded butterflies, and hear poor rogues
> Talk of Court news. And we'll talk with them too,
> Who loses and who wins, who's in, who's out,
> And take upon's the mystery of things
> As if we were God's spies. And we'll wear out,
> In a walled prison, packs and sects of great ones
> That ebb and flow by the moon (V.iii.8–16)

Perhaps Paddy meant that his life-threatening disease was like Lear and Cordelia's prison. One could be vitally alive and happy in spite of morbidity. Indeed, perhaps he meant more than this: the disease itself could even be part of that vitality and happiness; it could be the source, not just the occasion, for wisdom. Intriguingly, another chronic pain patient, a profes-

Paddy usually followed the reference with a statement about desire being the source of unhappiness and loss the basis for transcendence. Aspiration, he said, should burn in one only for small, human blessings: friendship, inner peace, the joy of helping others, courage, the search for meanings one could live by. But Paddy wore his Buddhism lightly, and I never heard that he pressed his views on others. In fact, he seemed suspicious of easy truths and formulaic answers. Living out one's "way" was what mattered. His character was playful, not solemn; he was serious of purpose, but his style was warm. He laughed easily and heartily; he told me once that it was incredibly humorous to contemplate the heavy solemnity that the leaders of our society brought to the defense of acquisitiveness and the conspicuous consumption of frivolous goods, mere things. "And," he added, "I am regarded as impractical. Why [I can hear him laugh irreverently] is it sober and prudent to worship things?"

Paddy was not financially secure, and after he died a collection had to be raised to pay for his burial. It turned out that he donated a significant portion of his limited income to charities. He modeled his life on the Buddha; when he was in financial straits, he remarked that he had come into the world with nothing on his back and would leave that way. People, not commodities, were his life.

I never got to know him well. Indeed, much of what I know about him I learned from others. But once, when he was just entering the terminal phase of his illness, we had a long talk in the hospital. At that time, I told him the story of the adolescent cord injury group and my inability to understand how to respond to the question of bafflement and meaning in the face of so devastating a life situation. I remember, sick as he was, he laughed and told me that it was precisely situations of utter despair and terminality that were essential to create authentic meanings. He said something like this:

If you were in his shoes, you would have had no difficulty responding to him. Those kids were too young and too spoiled. They hadn't come to understand things. Perhaps it's our culture. You should know that better than me. We refuse to face the reality of suffering and death. We have powerful techniques but no wisdom. When the techniques fail, we are left shipwrecked. It's too bad I can't have

---

sor of English literature, worked through his own suffering in light of Lear's tragedy and claims thereby to have lessened his own discomfort.

a shot at those kids. I have something I would like to teach them. Something I was taught about human nature generally and myself in particular.

Then Paddy told me about his own life. He was raised in a working-class family in Southern California, the younger of two children. His older sister developed epilepsy in her teens, following a bout of meningitis. Paddy was embarrassed by his sister's fits. He tried to avoid her. Once she had a convulsion near their school. He remembers seeing her fall to the ground with her eyes rolled upward and her arms and legs jerking. People gathered around her but didn't know what to do. Paddy felt deeply ashamed and threatened. He made believe he hadn't seen what happened and walked away. He hadn't wanted to attract attention to himself. He also felt paralyzed and helpless. He didn't know what to do.

"Have you ever read Joseph Conrad's books?" Paddy asked me, after telling this story (I will paraphrase his words since I didn't tape them):

You know, Conrad wrote *Lord Jim* and *Victory* about ordinary individuals who were placed in situations where they were exposed to tests of personal courage. Both failed initially, like me. They failed because of an inability to see through the superficial fears of competence and questions of self-identity that beset all adolescents and young adults. They were too absorbed with themselves and their own reaction to things. They failed the great test, and afterwards were so deeply ashamed of their cowardice that they ran away. They ran away to avoid the responsibilities that bound them to others. But they were unable to hide, even in the South Seas. In each of their lives the test was repeated, at a time when they had unavoidably built new ties to others. Those ties, those new relationships, were threatened. And they rose to the challenge. That's the great test for each of us: to serve others and through that to better ourselves. That's me, too. I failed miserably, shamefully, because of my egotism. But I have gotten a second chance too, a chance to turn my life into a kind of victory. Maybe not the great American dream of success. Let's call it a small success. Well, believe it or not, it's this darn illness that has given me that second chance.

As I said, I didn't know Paddy as well as I would have liked. One person who did know him fairly well told me that he regarded Paddy's final years as a luminous example of the moral life. I don't know what label to give to it. But I'm convinced that Paddy Esposito's response to his illness represents the best that is in us. As W. Jackson Bate concluded of the life of Samuel Johnson: "He had given them the most precious of all the gifts one can give another, and that is hope. With all the odds against him, he had proved that it was possible to get through this strange adventure of life, and to do it in a way that is a tribute to human nature" (1975, 600).

I'm not even sure Paddy's coping (what a trivializing word) provides a useful example for others, since so few of us are likely to have the qualities and discipline to carry it out. I think that his life, though, is an answer of sorts to the deeply troubling question put to me by my paralyzed adolescent patient. Meaning is created in the context of serious illness out of the very stuff that makes up our personal and cultural dilemmas. Shocked out of ordinary reality by handicaps or the threat of death, we turn to those sources of meanings that inform our life world. Meaning is inescapable: that is to say, illness always has meaning. The experience when ill need not be self-defeating; it can be—even if it often isn't—an occasion for growth, a point of departure for something deeper and finer, a model of and for what is good.

I have rarely used Paddy Esposito's story in my clinical work or teaching. Perhaps it is so exceptional that most patients cannot relate to it. In that sense, it might even burden them with an ideal that few of us can emulate. Yet while I have met only one Paddy Esposito, I feel that there are other ways in which sick persons can (and frequently do) successfully cope with chronic disorder. These ways are more modest and highly particular. Successful coping, furthermore, is not something that can be achieved outright, once and for all. Patients and families, and, what is more, practitioners, too, struggle to cope on a daily basis. We cope well on Tuesday, badly on Wednesday morning, better Wednesday afternoon, better still on Thursday, worse again Friday morning, and so on. (See Gordon Stuart's story in chapter 9.) It is even uncertain what successful coping means in any generic sense apart from an individual's particular experience in a particular local context. What is clear is that chronic illness is an ongoing process in which personal problems constantly emerge to challenge technical control, social order, and individual mastery. Like the rest of life, though greatly concentrated and intensified, it must be taken in total without valuing one part and rejecting others: we are both courageous and weak. Few of us are heroes in the grand sense; but in a small, quiet way and in a moral rather than a military sense, there are real heroes among the chronically ill. For most of us, just dealing with the day-to-day challenges of chronic illness might be a more valid, humanly proportioned example (and test) of what Alfred North Whitehead called "direct perception of concrete achievement 'in its actuality . . . with a high light thrown on what is relevant to its preciousness' " (quoted in Bate 1975, xix). To meet one day with defeat, the next with hope, the great adversity of chronic illness with its many losses and threats surely is a moral lesson that can keep even the most indocile of us from despair.

9

Illness unto Death

O Lord, grant each his own, his death indeed,
the dying which out of that same life evolves in
which he once had meaning, love, and need.
—Rainer Maria Rilke
(from Enright 1983, 46)

They [a small elite of behavioral scientists] propose to reconcile
death with happiness. Death must simply become the discreet but
dignified exit of a peaceful person from a helpful society that is
not torn, not even overly upset by the idea of a biological transition without significance, without pain or suffering, and ultimately without fear.
—Philippe Aries
(1981, 614)

The Good Death

The patient, Gordon Stuart, is a thirty-three-year-old writer dying
of cancer. The doctor, Hadley Eliot, is a family practitioner in his
fifties who works with the local hospice. Dr. Eliot has been visiting
Mr. Stuart for six months, providing him with palliation for his pain
and other symptoms. Now Gordon Stuart has entered the final days
of his illness, cancer of the rectum with metastases throughout his
body. I listened to a tape recording of this visit. Mr. Stuart is dying
at home, in accordance with his strong wish. Dr. Eliot's care has
been crucial in making it feasible for Mr. Stuart to remain at home
in these final hours. I never met Gordon Stuart. But I feel I know
him through this taped interview. I have enormous respect for him,
as does his physician. He has given something of great value. I also

admire Hadley Eliot, who offers a kind of care for the final hours that I know I would wish to receive, but that is, in my experience, rare.

Throughout the interview, Mr. Stuart is wracked by bouts of coughing. There is a rattling sound in his chest, and he wheezes. His voice is faint but clear. He breaks off, then begins anew. I've made no attempt to enter these resonant physical emblems of death in this selection from the transcript.

GORDON: I am dying now, aren't I?

HADLEY: Yes, you are.

GORDON: I can look into my garden and see sunshine. I know that next week, maybe tomorrow, it will be shining just as brightly, just as beautifully, but I won't be part of it. I will no longer be here. Do you know, can you imagine what it—it feels like to make that statement and know that it is true for you, that you are dying?

HADLEY: I think I can, but I'm not sure.

GORDON: All that nonsense that's written about stages of dying, as if there were complete transitions—rooms that you enter, walk through, then leave behind for good. What rot. The anger, the shock, the unbelievableness, the grief—they are part of each day. And in no particular order, either. Who says you work your way eventually to acceptance—I don't accept it! Today I can't accept it. Yesterday I did partly. Saturday, I was there: kind of in a trance, waiting, ready to die. But not now. Today it's the fear all over again. I don't want to die. I'm only thirty-three; I've got my whole life to live. I can't be cut off now. It isn't just. Why me? Why now? You don't have to answer. I'm just in a lousy mood right now. You get maudlin and morally weak waiting for the end. I'm usually pretty good, aren't I? Only sometimes something young and scared breaks out. Otherwise I've become like an old man, preparing myself—but over weeks, not years.

. . .

At least this is the way I want to go: at home, surrounded by my family, my books and music nearby. The garden—ever till now I thought of a garden as something you look out into in order to escape the solipsism of your self. Things moved and you saw them. That reflects my trade. Writing is experiencing of fantasies, working out visions, struggling for the right word or phrase. But now I think of my garden as a setting into which you project your feelings in order to organize them. You order what is inside by looking into an outer, ordered space. Make sense? Or am I speaking gibberish?

HADLEY: It makes sense, a lot of sense.

GORDON: I told you earlier, you remember, I couldn't take it if it affected my mind. Thank God, it hasn't. At least so far.

(There ensues a very long silence.)

It occurs to me that I've always handled big problems in my life by first running away—then, after the energy was dissipated, thinking about them. Now there's no running away. I can't escape this. I can't get away from the feeling that I am dying. There is a feeling to it, you know. A definite inner sense of things running down, getting weaker, losing something vital. I'm not sure that does justice to it, but it's there.

When they first told me about the cancer, I went out and got drunk. I couldn't assimilate it. I felt reasonably good. The only sign was the blood in the stool. I thought this was an immense discrepancy—between the word *cancer*, a kind of death sentence, and how I felt at the time. Well, eighteen months later, I guess the person meets the diagnosis. I look horrible, and feel that way, too. . . .

I've been trying to write down my feelings. But I simply don't have the energy or the concentration. I forget what I've gone through. All the hours in clinics and waiting rooms, the hospitalizations, one test result more depressing than the next. The inexorable course of things. The feeling there is something not me in me, an "it," eating its way through the body. I am the creator of my own destruction. These cancer cells are me and yet not me. I am invaded by a killer. I am become death. I really don't want to die. I know I must. I will. I am. But I don't want to.

(There is another long silence.)

HADLEY: Do you want me to turn this tape recorder off?

GORDON: No, don't. This helps me feel I will leave something behind. Not quite up to the vaulting ambition I've had, but something nonetheless. . . .

I want to thank you, Hadley, for the time you have spent, the things you have done. I know I couldn't be here without you. I couldn't take dying in a hospital. It goes against the grain of everything I value: nature, home, life, that which is human and tender. Thank you, Hadley.

HADLEY: It's you who is doing it, Gordon.

GORDON: I know that. No one can die for me. . . . When I heard the word *cancer*, I knew it was a death sentence. But there are ways of dying and ways of dying. I suspect if we had a choice we would all go quickly. Cancer makes us think of a lingering torture, a being eaten away from inside. And that is what it's been like for me.

(At this point, Gordon Stuart and Hadley Eliot talked about practical matters: drug dosages, Gordon's living will, plans for the funeral, a paper Gordon had written that he wanted Hadley to send out to friends and staff in the hospice.)

GORDON: I want to talk about something else, Hadley.

HADLEY: Go ahead, Gordon. I've got time. I'd like to hear.

GORDON: I think too much can be made of death. Take my parents. I hardly see them. They can't take it. After I go, it will be very hard on them. But some moments like this, I feel ready to make an end, a final stop. We come into life, we spend an awful long time growing up, and then we go. The cycle goes on. New faces to replace the old. It can almost make you believe in the migration of souls. Even an atheist like me has to make some sense of it. Could it be that we are solving some still unknown evolutionary conundrum? All our flailing and worrying must be for some purpose. What purpose was my life, my illness, my death? I'm still working that one out. It certainly can't be—grace under fire or coming to some big understanding. It must be something more intimate. Death perhaps is the meaning of life. Only when we think of it in the real terms of our death do we realize this is the ultimate relevance. You see, Hadley, death is making me into a philosopher. Maybe it's because you are such a good listener and I get such a good feeling after talking to you. I think I'm ready, Hadley. If I could will it, I would die now—in midsentence, ironically, with the best part left unsaid. You can go now, Hadley. You done good today.

Gordon Stuart died ten days after this interview, at home, with Hadley Eliot in attendance. Hadley Eliot told me:

Gordon died a good death. He was clear right up to the end. He had fortitude and character and died as he lived, very much his own person. He was no less angry, not accepting at the end, but he kept his sense of irony, his way with words. He seemed to grow into whom he wanted to be. His death confirmed his life. If you weren't there, you would say the death of a thirty-three-year-old man just beginning his career was a tragedy. But for those of us privileged to be there, tragedy is the wrong word. Anyhow, it's a word Gordon hated, thought it maudlin; and at the death, he so ordered things that it is not a word that came to mind. He was a model for me. I would wish to do the same for my own death.

The Killing Fear of Death

Julian Davies is a sixty-three-year-old architect who has suffered his second heart attack. He was well until shortly after his fifty-ninth birthday, when he began to experience anginal pains. A month later he suffered a heart attack. His recovery was uneventful, and within two months he returned to work. Until his second heart attack, four years later, his life was "back on track." I was asked to see Julian Davies by his cardiologist, Samuel Medwar, because Dr. Medwar felt his patient had given up and was not participating in the program of rehabilitation, in spite of being in a stable physiological condition without serious aftereffects. I saw Mr. Davies three weeks after his heart attack.

A short, obese, bald man, reclining in his pajamas and silk bathrobe in a huge leather chair in his suburban home, Mr. Davies greeted me with a nod of the head and downcast gaze. His wife hovered around him, straightening the blanket on his lap, refilling his water glass, offering him advice not to overexert himself, and regarding me with obvious suspicion.

I first asked Mr. Davies about his physical condition, and he assured me that he felt no pain or other serious symptoms. I then told him that he seemed to me somewhat depressed. He shrugged. I asked if he felt hopeless. He nodded. I asked if he had given up. He said, "Maybe." I asked why. Mr. Davies looked directly at me for the first time since I had entered the room. He told me that he knew he would die from his heart condition, and therefore he believed there was no good reason to follow the rehabilitation program. Mr. Davies reached out and grabbed my arm. His eyes were dilated, and his face was covered with perspiration. He seemed terrified.

He was. In a whisper, Julian Davies told me that he was terrified of dying. He cried. He held his head in his hands. He grieved openly for his anticipated death. His wife intervened, admonishing her husband for getting upset and me for upsetting him. Mr. Davies waved her away. He and I talked for another twenty minutes. During that time, he reiterated both his pessimism that he would not get better and his terrible fear of death. I asked him why his reaction to his second heart attack was so different than that to his first. He answered that his first was so mild he never believed his cardiologist's warning that it was a "real attack." In fact, after returning to work he decided not to comply with the rehabilitation plan because he could not believe there was anything seriously wrong with his heart. The second heart attack changed all of that. The pain was severe, and for the first several days in the hospital he felt so extremely weak he became convinced that life-threatening damage to his heart had occurred and that he could not survive. The realization made him panic. He was shocked that death could occur at the slightest strain or overactivity. He feared undertaking the rehabilitation activities, even taking responsibility for his own care.

Mr. Davies's mother had died in childbirth when he was eleven. He recalled his mother's death as a horrendous blow to the family, a crushing loss that had left him deeply wounded. His father had died a lingering death after a heart attack twenty years ago, weakening over the course of months, developing arrhythmia followed by heart failure, and finally dying from a pulmonary embolus. Mr. Davies confided to me that he felt helpless to prevent his condition from following the downhill course his father had taken. At night he awoke in terror that he would stop breathing or die in his sleep. He was obsessed with the fear.

Mr. Davies could not talk to his wife about his alarming thoughts. He accepted her deep concern and mothering as an additional sign that his condition was critical, or as he told me, "terminal." He could not accept the reassurance of his cardiologist, which he interpreted as professional dissembling. Before I left Mr. Davies, I asked him specifically if he were convinced he would die. He told me, again with horror in his gaze, that he was convinced. I tried to talk Mr. Davies out of this conviction, but quickly saw that I was getting nowhere.

After returning to my office, I called Dr. Medwar to express my concern that Mr. Davies had in fact given up and had a delusional conviction that he would die. I was aware of George Engel's (1968; 1971) writings on this problem, and had consulted on two patients who had died unexplained deaths associated with the conviction that they would die. My experiences had left an indelible impression and I knew that this was an emergency. I recommended a brief psychiatric hospitalization, which I argued should be arranged as soon as possible. Dr. Medwar visited Mr. Davies but was unable to convince him either to enter a psychiatric hospital or to see me again. I called his home, but his wife refused to let me speak to him.

Two weeks later, Dr. Medwar called to tell me Mr. Davies had died: suddenly, without a clear-cut cause, a day after he had examined him and found his condition unchanged. At that examination Mr. Davies had amazed Dr. Medwar by getting on his knees, in a state of great agitation, and begging the doctor to take his life with a drug overdose so that he would not have to die so agonizingly slowly. That same day Dr. Medwar had tried to talk Mrs. Davies into letting me or another psychiatrist visit the house to determine whether Mr. Davies was psychotic and would require involuntary hospitalization. Mrs. Davies had refused the request. She told Dr. Medwar that she knew her husband was dying, that it was so fearful a topic they couldn't talk about it, and that she wanted him to spend his last few days in peace at home. Dr. Medwar was unable to change Mrs. Davies's mind, even though he reviewed the medical evidence with her and concluded that Mr. Davies was not in life-threatening danger but rather had developed an obsession. Dr.

Medwar, deeply affected by his patient's death, asked me if this was
a case of "psychological death." We will return to the question at
the end of this chapter.

Death in Another Country

The year was 1977. The place, Taipei, Taiwan. I was conducting
field research, when I learned that a senior physician of my acquaintance, Dr. Song Mingyuan, one of Taiwan's most progressive
medical educators, had several months before been diagnosed with
metastastic carcinoma of the head of the pancreas, and was nearing
the terminal phase of his illness. On a Saturday afternoon, I pur-
chased a small gift box of mountain tea and carried it, together with
a copy of an academic journal I had recently begun editing, to his
home. His adult children, grandchildren, and brothers were present.
My Chinese colleague received me with great politeness and asked
me why I chose to honor him with this unexpected visit. I began to
tell him of how I heard about his illness when I was abruptly cut
off by his brothers; they told me that Dr. Song was all right, that
there was nothing for me to be concerned about. For the next hour
we talked of many things, but never about the cancer, or the treatment, or the fact, visible for all to see, that Dr. Song was severely
cachectic and deathly ill. Before I left I managed to ask Dr. Song
about his treatment. He seemed embarrassed by my question. I
repeated it in English, believing that he failed to comprehend my
Chinese. "Don't ask me about such things. I don't know anything
about it. My family is in charge of this thing." As I departed, I asked
his brothers, who were in an adjoining room, about his condition.
We whispered back and forth. They told me that all treatments,
including traditional Chinese as well as Western medicines, had
failed. Their brother, they knew, was dying, and they were beginning to make plans for the funeral and the family's future welfare.
I asked whether Dr. Song knew. Perhaps, they said, but this matter
was now out of his hands. It was the family's responsibility. One
must not speak about such things in front of him, they reminded

me, treating me as if I were an insensitive adolescent, unaware of ritual and custom.

I did not see Dr. Song again before he died several months later, but two colleagues who did—both old friends of his—had similar experiences. Family members, none of whom were in the health field, made all the key decisions. Dr. Song acted as if he were unaware of what was going on, though clearly he realized that he was dying.

Interpretation

We have here three instances of death in the course of chronic illness. In the first example, Gordon Stuart invites us to be a witness to his last days. His medical treatment has failed to stop the progressive development of his cancer; but his relationship with his doctor continues until the moment he dies. Dr. Eliot has switched objectives from curing his patient's disease to managing the chronic course of suffering. In the end, the doctor's work is to assist his patient to die a good death. This is a traditional task of medicine in the West, although it has been usurped by medical technology's mandate to keep the patient alive at any cost. Gordon Stuart and Hadley Eliot have agreed not to allow Gordon's terminal period to become technologized. Gordon Stuart is assisted to die with dignity in the intimacy of his home. The care of the dying makes the personality of the practitioner and the quality of the patient–doctor relationship the major modes of therapy.

Nonetheless, no concern with therapeutic technique can prepare patient or family or practitioner for the final hours. The remarkable quality of the taped interview between Gordon Stuart and Hadley Eliot is the participants' struggle to maintain authenticity, to avoid sentimentalizing or in other ways rendering inauthentic a relationship centered on the most existential of problems. Hadley Eliot has no answers to Gordon Stuart's questions. Nor does Gordon expect, or even want, Hadley to try to answer. What this marvelously humane physician provides for his remarkable patient is intense listening. Empathic witnessing is a moral act, not a technical procedure. Dr. Eliot's skill lies in his ability to hear Gordon's story, to reflect the power of the questions, to allow his patient to maintain irony and a critical analytic sense, and to build tentative understandings out of the crafting of words in the face of a final assault on the integrity of his body-self.

That approach to dying makes a great deal of sense in the context of Gordon Stuart's life; it might not be appropriate for others of us for whom a more specifically religious or less intensely self-aware approach would be more suitable. Taking into account their own sensibilities, the practitioner, family, and dying person must work out an appropriate and desired way toward death. The practitioner must not press the patient toward some model of dying that is undesired and invalid in the patient's life. I fear that this happens routinely, and I applaud Gordon Stuart's negative assessment of mechanical models of the stages of dying. There is no single, timeless pathway toward death that is most serviceable for the dying person. An individual's course of death, like that of life, may take dozens of different turns, circle back to the start, or enter a state previously unknown. The practitioner cannot know in advance where the patient is headed or what is best. The pathway and course of action should emerge from the doctor–patient relationship or should be something determined by the dying person and the family. The practitioner does not (cannot) bring a teleology (a doctrine of final causes and ultimate meaning) from medicine. If such a teleology comes from the physician, it is from a religious or cultural background, not medicine.*

Not everyone would want to undertake Gordon Stuart's course. Some people would be frightened or otherwise repelled by his self-imposed demand that he be fully conscious of his end; that his death be as uniquely individual as his life; and that the final discourse be his own. The work of culture is powerful here. Contrast Gordon Stuart's terminal trajectory with that of Dr. Song Mingyuan. In Chinese culture, among tradition-oriented families like Dr. Song's, the family is the locus of responsibility, and that locus extends to include aspects of the person that in the West are regarded as

---

*Ezekiel Emanuel helped clarify for me the role of teleology in care. Much the same point is made by MacIntyre (1981), Rieff (1966), and Lasch (1977).

sacrosanct to the individual. Dr. Song turns over to his family all the decisions in the course of his cancer, in spite of the fact that he alone is medically qualified and even an expert on chronic illness. Even the way I have put it is ethnocentric: Dr. Song does not "turn over" responsibility; it belongs to them, not him. In the end, Dr. Song is part of an immortal vehicle—the Chinese sensibility about the family—which existed before he arrived on the scene, in which he occupies a temporary place, and which after he departs continues on with his descendants and ancestors. The discourse and consciousness of death in that culturally organized family context are radically different from Gordon Stuart's experience. (Although Gordon dies at home with his parents and friends around him, they play a much less pervasive part in his experience, which is ultimately the death of a lone individual. Chinese often find this aspect of American life strange and repugnant.) It can be held against this conclusion that I neither knew Gordon Stuart nor had access to Dr. Song's intimate experience. I concur. But other experiences and my reading of the literature convince me that we are viewing a major divide between North American and Chinese cultures.*

Julian Davies illustrates yet another response to death: fear and terror. The story of his parents' deaths contributes powerfully to his personal response, but there are other factors as well. Mr. Davies and his wife have developed a tacit *folie à deux* about his condition.† Perhaps because of a severe depression or other psychiatric problems, Julian Davies has become convinced that he will die; he has given up; he is in a state of malignant panic. There is a great deal of controversy over the pathological mechanisms that underwrite psychogenic death.‡ Obviously, in a patient with a serious heart disorder, a deadly episode of arrhythmia, pulmonary embolism, acute heart failure, or other process resulting directly from the dis-

---

*The evidence comes from the work of psychologists (Bond 1986), psychiatrists (Tseng and Hsu 1969; Lin and Eisenberg 1985; Kleinman and Lin 1982; Tseng and Wu 1985), social scientists (Hsu 1971; Li and Yang 1974; Parish and Whyte 1978; Potter 1970; Wolf 1972), and historians (Metzger 1982). The traditional conceptions and responses to death in Chinese culture insofar as they are interpersonal have been well studied and are effectively reviewed by Watson (in press a; in press b) But dying and grieving as personal experience among Chinese have, to the best of my knowledge, not been studied.

†*Folie à deux* is a shared delusional system, even a shared psychosis, between two or more individuals.

‡The controversy extends to the question of whether psychogenic death (self-willed and voodoo versions especially) actually occurs (Lewis 1977; Reid and Williams 1985).

ease itself can occur. Although these factors may occur independently to cause sudden cardiac death, Lown and his colleagues (1980) have evidence that psychophysiological factors are frequently responsible. Inasmuch as there was no autopsy, we do not know what actually happened in Mr. Davies's case. But there is a controversial body of medical and anthropological literature on psychogenic, self-willed, and voodoo or magical deaths, which suggests that individuals can come to believe they are socially dead—a belief shared by their social circle—and can die in a psychophysiological reaction. Engel (1968; 1971), conducting research at the University of Rochester, has identified in patients with serious chronic illness a complex of "giving-up, given-up" that correlates with unexplained sudden deaths. Hackett and Weisman (1960; Weisman and Hackett 1961), working at Massachusetts General Hospital, found that surgical patients who strongly believed they would die in fact died much more frequently than other surgical patients. Mr. Davies seems to combine several of these syndromes: he is convinced he will die, he gives up, and he suffers morbid anxiety about death.

I describe these cases as examples of one particularly important aspect of the meaning of chronic illness. Illness can mean the threat of death or the experience of dying. In my experience, fear of dying—though not at Mr. Davies's level of morbid preoccupation—is common among the chronically ill and their families. For many patients with chronic illness the fear comes as vague, amorphic ruminations that are crystallized when patients enter a terminal stage of their disorder or when there is a severe exacerbation of symptoms. It is important to remember that most patients with chronic illness do not have an acutely life-threatening problem and that many, perhaps most, will not die of their chronic illness. Indeed, there is an old saying among clinicians to the effect that nothing is as effective at teaching a person how to live a long life as the experience of chronic illness. For some patients, convictions of dying or giving up are not delusional perceptions of their current situation, but rather perhaps early premonitions and remarkably sensitive recognitions of mortal, though subliminal, bodily changes. In the gray zone of serious but not life-threatening chronic illness, such perceptions may be accurate reflections of extraordinary psychophysiological sensibility. For most, however, such a sixth sense responds to emotional reactions, personality type, life situation, and even cultural background (for example, Jews have been shown to be more fearful of symptoms and the threat of death than Old Yankees) (Zborowski 1969; Zola 1966).

If there is a single dimension of illness that can teach us something valuable for our own lives, then it must be how to confront and respond to the fact that we will all die, each of us; this was Paddy Esposito's lesson (chapter 8). I have referred several times to chronic illness as a moral lesson, an obdurately edifying grain in the human condition across cultures.* There is no better example of what I mean than the sick person's coming to terms with death. As the experience of Gordon Stuart teaches, this is a complex reality, one that cannot (and must not) be reduced to a simple answer. If we learn anything as auditors of Gordon Stuart's final words, it is that death is an awesome process of making and remaking meaning through which we come to constitute and express what is most uniquely human and our own.†

---

*Although in chapter 8 and this chapter I explicitly describe cases of dying patients, death is an issue in the lives of most of the patients who appear in this book. The subject of death and dying historically and across cultures is dealt with in a number of fine volumes and articles (see Aries 1981; Schieffelin 1976; Bloch and Parry 1982; Levy 1973; Keyes 1985; Obeyesekere 1985, Madan 1987). These anthropological and historical accounts disclose a great diversity in the ways death is conceived of and responded to; but they also disclose similar problems of bafflement, suffering, and social order that must represent the constraint on cultural particularization of universal psychobiological processes in experience and the core requirements of social life (see Kleinman and Good 1985).

†Consider another example, Noll as quoted in Stjernsward et al.: "I knew I had cancer. They advised an operation and I declined, not because of heroism but because it did not agree with my view on life and death. I had no alternative. They should have taken out my bladder, irradiated me, and the whole incident would give me a 35% chance of survival, mutilated and for a limited time. We are all going to die. Some of us very soon, others much later. My experience is: we live a better life if we have it as it is, namely, for a limited time. Then it hardly matters how long the life prolongation lasts, when all is lost in eternity" (1986, 1).

10

The Stigma and Shame
of Illness

The normal and the stigmatized are not persons but rather perspectives.

—Erving Goffman
(1963, 138)

My starting point is always a feeling of partisanship, a sense of
injustice.

—George Orwell
(cited in Crick 1980, 406)

The Nature of Stigma

Few etymologies usefully decode the significance of contemporary
terms; not so for *stigma.* From the Greek, "to mark or brand," *stigma*
referred to marks that publicly disgraced the person. Goffman,
whose book on stigma is very pertinent to chronic illness, claims,
"The signs were cut or burnt into the body and advertised that the
bearer was a slave, a criminal, or a traitor—a blemished person,
ritually polluted, to be avoided, especially in public places" (1963,
1). Among the later meanings are religious notions of stigma as the
bodily marks of God's grace and the medical definition, that signs
of disease are visible stigmata of the pathology (for example, a
particular type of skin rash signifies smallpox). Eventually, *stigma*
shifted meaning to refer to a person marked by a deformity, blemish, or ugliness. Goffman (1963, 2) notes that in more recent times,

stigma has come to refer more to the disgrace than to the actual bodily mark. The change in meaning is an instance of a more general process of psychologization of experience in the West, through which metaphors of distress and other human problems that were once bodily have become mental.

If the source of stigma is publicly visible, stigma is "deeply discrediting"; if concealed from others, the stigma renders the affected person "discreditable." In either case, it is internalized as a "spoiled identity," a feeling of being inferior, degraded, deviant, and shamefully different (Goffman 1963, 3). Goffman also points out that "persons who have a particular stigma tend to have similar learning experiences regarding their plight, and similar changes in conception of self—a similar 'moral career' " (1963, 32). He is referring to problems, such as colostomy, cerebral palsy, epilepsy, mental retardation, and disfiguring and crippling afflictions, that create problems in the presentation of self and a conflict between candor and seemliness.

Diseases that stamp powerfully disconfirming cultural meanings onto the sick person stigmatize in the same way as Hester Prynne's scarlet letter, the yellow Star of David sewn to the sleeve of a Nazi concentration camp victim, or the dunce cap forced on the heads of intellectuals during public ceremonies of degradation in China's Cultural Revolution. Stigma may be literally inscribed into the skin in the classical Greek sense of the term, as in the instance of the leper's collapsed bridge of the nose and amputated extremities, which are a living icon of a deeply discrediting disease. A disfiguring deformity and the bizarre actions of florid mental illness stigmatize because they break cultural conventions about what is acceptable appearance and behavior, while invoking other cultural categories— of what is ugly, feared, alien, or inhuman.

Stigma often carries a religious significance—the afflicted person is viewed as sinful or evil—or a moral connotation of weakness and dishonor. Thus, the stigmatized person is defined as an alien other, upon whose persona are projected the attributes the group regards as opposite to the ones it values. In this sense, stigma helps to define the social identity of the group. In certain societies, so powerful is the stigma brought to the patient by the culturally marked illness label that it affects all his relationships and may lead to ostracism: leprosy, even more than untouchable caste status in rural India, is like this; so is AIDS in present-day North America. In China, the stigma of mental illness is so powerful that it attaches not only to the seriously mentally ill but also to their families. In principle, traditional Chinese held, if a person is mentally ill, his ancestors doubtless were affected, his siblings share in the family moral taint, and his descendants are at risk. Hence, marriage go-betweens were supposed to rule out of the pool of eligible bachelors and maidens the siblings and offspring of psychotic patients. In nineteenth- and early twentieth century Europe, mental retardation, epilepsy, and mental illness were thought of as a degenerative trait passed down through the generations in families of "low evolutionary level," and the "science" of eugenics aimed to prevent their propagation.

In stigmatized disorders, the stigma can begin with the societal reaction to the condition: that is to say, a person so labeled is shunned, derided, disconfirmed, and degraded by those around him, though usually not by the immediate family. Eventually, the stigmatized person comes to expect such reactions, to anticipate them before they occur or even when they don't occur. By that stage, he has thoroughly internalized the stigma in a deep sense of shame and a spoiled identity. His behavior, then, becomes shaped by his negative self-perception. Nancy Waxler (1981) has shown how Sri Lankan patients infected by the leprosy bacillus learn to feel and behave like lepers. The patient may resist the stigmatizing identity, or he may accept it; either way, his world has been radically altered.

Rudolph Kristiva's case in chapter 4 illustrates another process of stigmatization. The stigma begins not with the societal reaction to him, but rather with his own acceptance of a stigmatized identity. In that situation, stigma is not brought to the person through the cultural significance of the illness label; instead, Rudolph Kristiva's homosexuality, ethnicity, and personality disorder, as it were, lend the stigma to the illness behavior and mark him as different, defective, and ultimately discreditable. In the very brief descriptions that follow, I sketch the effect of stigmatized illness or other conditions (visible and concealed) on the individual. Then I turn to a related situation: instances in which patients feel shame, not because of the cultural meaning of illness, but rather in response to the reactions of family and especially health professionals. Patients may feel shame in any illness for which they interact with care givers (see

Lazare 1987). For the families of the chronically ill (and the disfigured and disabled) and for the health professionals who treat them, an acute sensibility to stigma and shame is a necessity. That sensibility is a commitment to what is at stake in the care of the chronically ill: namely, a willingness to help bear the burden of the lived experience of suffering.

Six Who Bear the Shame of Illness

HAROLD DOWD

Harold Dowd is a twenty-eight-year-old New England baker. He was born with a large, disfiguring reddish mole—a so-called port wine stain—that covers almost the entire left side of his face. Harold Dowd has an anatomical abnormality, but he does not have an active disease process. The mole holds no health significance, nor is it hereditary. Furthermore, Harold neither refers to the mole as a disease nor regards it as such. Yet he has developed a set of illness behaviors to cope with this huge skin blemish. The facial disfigurement has become a lifelong "burden" and to Harold's mind a "handicap."

He told me that his earliest memories are of family members staring at or touching his mole. He recalls his mother's visible embarrassment when his older brother and sister called attention to it. He remembers overhearing his parents discuss how he would be received by students and teachers at school: they were afraid that he would be made to feel different and would have difficulty making friends. Their fears were confirmed. Harold feels, in retrospect, that his diffidence and difficulty in interpersonal relations stem from that time. His first day in school was, he says, "disastrous." The other children surrounded him, making fun of his blemish. The teacher had to intervene frequently the first week to help Harold participate in activities: "No one wanted me." After that, things improved, but Harold was well on his way to what he calls his "minute-to-minute consciousness of being different—shocking people who have not seen me before." He knows that response will follow any encounter. He waits for it, anticipates it, and feels shame when it occurs, just as he felt it that first day of school, twenty-three years ago.

Harold has met others with similar facial disfigurements who seem to have adjusted much more successfully to their deformity. Still, he believes that his own life has been "spoiled" by it. He has internalized a sense of being "ugly," "marked," "strange," "not normal," "not one of us." This has intensified his sensitivity to rejection. Though he has a few good friends from high school, he feels that their acceptance, like his family's is exceptional. It is not close relationships that bother Harold, but rather his entry into any new social group, his interaction with a new bank teller, a new waitress, a new postman. They all stare at him, and the old feeling of shame returns. Harold told me that if a blemish can be hidden by clothing then its effects can be limited, but when a blemish is as visibly disfiguring as his there is nothing that can be done.

Harold holds his mole responsible for what he takes to be great constraints on his life: he could not work in a setting where there were new faces to confront; he has never been able to develop a close relationship with the few women he has admired; and he generally avoids activities that put him in situations where others may stare at him. He has undergone behavioral therapy with a psychologist to reduce his sensitivity to the blemish, but without success. Harold recognizes that his is a problem that can be mastered by a more confident, less morbidly sensitive approach to others; yet he has never been able to act that way. Rather, each new situation makes him feel discreditable, calling into question a fragile self-identity. "I am marked for life. I look in the mirror and I feel ashamed. I stare at myself, too, like everyone else. It has ruined my life."

HORACIO GRIPPA

Horacio Grippa is a thirty-two-year-old homosexual teacher with AIDS. When I interviewed him, in early 1985, he was about to leave the hospital, his disease in partial remission but his life in disarray. When it became known that he was suffering from AIDS, he was dismissed from his job. Later his landlady ordered him to vacate his apartment. Finally, his parents told him that he could not come home. He was in a lawsuit with his private medical insurance company, and he was not sure that the company would pay his hospital bill. Deeply depressed, he had been referred for psychiatric help. Mr. Grippa was angry about the way he was being treated.

The nurses are scared of me; the doctors wear masks and sometimes gloves. Even the priest doesn't seem too anxious to shake my hand. What the hell is this? I'm not a leper. Do they want to lock me up and shoot me? I've got no family, no friends. Where do I go? What do I do? God, this is horrible! Is He punishing me? The only thing I got going for me is that I'm not dying—at least, not yet."

SUSAN MILO

Susan Milo is an attractive, tall, unmarried twenty-five-year-old white secretary with ulcerative colitis who has recently had a large part of her colon surgically removed. She is being instructed in cleaning and caring for her colostomy. She has become depressed at the prospects for her future life. She told me:

I feel so embarrassed by this—this thing. It seems so unnatural, so dirty. I can't get used to the smell to it. I'm scared of soiling myself. Then I'd be so ashamed I couldn't look at anyone else. I've met four or five colostomy patients. They seem to be doing so well. But none was my age and unmarried. Who would want a wife like this? How can I go out and not feel unable to look people in the eyes and tell them the truth? Once I do, who would want to develop a friendship, I mean a close one? How can I even consider showing my body to someone else, having sex? Now they tell me the colitis is gone, together with my bowel; but what is this I'm left with? It's a disaster for me. I feel terrible, like a monster. I see my folks. They cry; they feel so bad for me. They can't talk about the future. What future?

DANNY BROWN

Danny Brown, a freshman in college, tells me how easily patients can be made to feel shame in the clinic. How, without thinking, health professionals contribute to the dynamics of shame. Danny has severe eczema on large parts of his body.

When you take off your clothes, and, and, and are stripped to your nakedness, you first feel shame. Shame at how you look. At exposing what is such a private part of you. Shame at how the nurse and doctor look at you. Shame because you are not normal, not like others; and, well, because, because where else do you expose yourself to others' eyes? But the clinic nurses and doctors seem so insensitive to how you feel. Sometimes they keep talking while I'm standing naked in front of them. I don't feel comfortable with a woman looking at my skin. Once they even called in a group of medical students. That was the worst! I felt like a curiosity, you know, a—something like the Elephant Man. I wanted to hide my face. There were two or three young women, just a few years older than me, in that group. Oh, it was terrible. Most of the time I avoid taking a shower in the dorm when others are around. I don't want anyone to see how bad my skin is. How different I am, how ugly. I had to stand before those medical students like, like a thing to gawk at. Damn that doctor for putting me through that. He never considered how I might feel. All I am is "an interesting case."

THE ELDERLY LEPER

I remember the first time I visited a leprosarium. It was a large one, in a rundown condition, most symbolically sited on Taiwan. It was separated from the road by a large hill: cut off, hidden, isolated. I went to one of the clinics, and even with my medical training I felt threatened by what I saw: such severe wounds and disfiguring mutilations. I wanted to visit patients in their small shacks. I remember how an elderly woman with a severely deformed face and no fingers turned away from me. I thought she was angry at my intrusion. It was not anger but shame. She didn't want an "honored foreign guest" to see such horrible deformity. Her family had rejected her, even though she was no longer infectious and, in principle, was free to return home. She had resisted discharge, because she had no place to go. She was unacceptable to the outside world, she told me. Her family did not want others to know about her and "laugh at them." She had learned to make a life for herself in the hospital. The other patients looked as deformed as she did. She, like them, was a leper. This is where she belonged.

It was impossible, the hospital director told me, for such patients to reenter society. The fear of leprosy was too great; the family would suffer. Patients knew this. So they gave up thinking about leaving. They wished to avoid the heckling of children, the humiliating stares, the curses, and the fear. As Chinese, they were extraordinarily sensitive to shame. And now, he told me, they had what they considered the most shameful of disorders.

PAUL SENSABAUGH

He was tall and very thin, and he always dressed in the same black suit, red tie, and porkpie hat. His grin was a seemingly constant part of his expression. But it set him off as different, too. He always looked down or away, never directly at you—like a kid who is too embarrassed to look you directly in the eye. He had two reasons for his unusual behavior. First, he didn't like others to see the scars from his brain surgery. Second, he had trouble answering questions and was embarrassed by his slowness in speaking and comprehending. Paul Sensabaugh had been a typical young husband and father when he had the terrible accident that rendered him brain-injured. He had been married for five years, had two young children, and held a clerical job in an insurance company. A truck hit his car and smashed it into an iron guardrail. Doctors said he was incredibly lucky to be alive. He was in a coma for weeks. There was at least one episode of profound physiological shock, and it was thought that this, as much as the injury to his frontal and temporal lobes, had caused the personality change and mental deterioration. He had become childishly impulsive and silly. He had difficulty getting his thoughts out. He seemed to have become, his wife said, "simple-minded."

Paul Sensabaugh was too disabled to work; his wife said, "It was like having a third child in the family." Mrs. Sensabaugh felt bad, but she divorced him anyway. She had her own and her children's lives to look out for. She and the children were so ashamed of Paul that they went to court and were able to take away his visitation rights. He never sees them now.

He lived alone, in a single room in one of those predatory hotels that spring up like weeds near large hospitals to take in the mentally ill and mentally retarded and alcoholics who have no other place. His welfare check went directly to the hotel's manager, who also acted as a legal guardian. He gave Paul an allowance, and also made sure he got enough to eat and that his room was clean.

For a period of months I saw Paul once a week. At first, flipping through the lengthy medical record, I wasn't sure what the reason was for his regular visits. Later I learned that the hospital was part of his world, the clinic visit his major activity of the week.

His day was so simple you really couldn't believe it when he described it to you. But there it was: get up, shower, dress, walk out of his room, say good morning to the manager behind the hotel desk, and walk across the street to buy the daily newspaper. Buying the paper was, he told me, his major fun of the day. There was warmth and sensitivity in Louie, the old black man who ran the newspaper kiosk and sold him his daily paper: he called Paul "handsome" and asked him why he was all dressed up and where he was going. This had gone on for years. Paul felt comfortable enough to raise his head a bit and give a short answer. In fact, Paul could not read much of the newspaper because of problems in his visual field. He bought it, I believe, because of the importance of a stable daily ritual and, quite simply, because for six days of the week this two- or three-minute interaction was his chief human contact. Then he went to have breakfast at the hospital cafeteria, a cavernous, impersonal, unattractive dining hall, where everyone recognized him but no one spoke to him. He sat way off to the side of the huge, poorly lit hall, by himself. He took a long time over breakfast. After he finished, he took his "walk": a long perambulation of his part of the city. He arrived back in his room in time to wash up before lunch. Then he returned to the anonymity of the hospital cafeteria. After that it was time for his nap, followed by a much shorter walk around the block, and then television watching in his room. Dinner took him back into the hospital. After eating, sometimes he would sit in the lobby of the hospital watching and listening to others, but always indirectly, his face behind a magazine or newspaper. After he walked home to his hotel, he generally stayed inside. He used to like taking an evening walk, but a few months before I met him he had been robbed by a gang of adolescents who kept calling him names like "queer," "nuts," and, worse, "half-wit." So he stayed in and watched television. Once each week, the hotel manager checked his room, gave him his allowance, and explained to him how much money he had in his account. That took about fifteen minutes, Paul estimated.

His big event of the week, the thing he waited for, was visiting the clinic. He dressed for the event by putting on a black vest or a gray sweater under his black suit jacket; sometimes he bought a carnation in the hospital's gift shop and had the volunteer on duty pin it to his lapel. I had inherited Paul from the clinical fellow whom I had replaced, and I passed him on to the fellow who followed me, doubtless as had been done several times over the years. Paul didn't have much to say, but he liked the repetition each week of the same

questions and had become good at answering them, as long as they
were asked slowly and in the same order. He was thrown off balance
by novelty of any kind. Simply rearranging the sequence of the
questions overtaxed his concentration and recall. He told me that
actually he just liked to sit and hear the doctor talk. Over time, by
reading his enormous record and by slipping in a new question here
or there and giving him a long time to think it over, I was able to
learn a lot about Paul.

Possibly the most important information was that he so easily felt
embarrassed. He knew that he "wasn't right in the brain," and he
tried hard to cover over his impairment, because, as he told me at
least once each week, he "didn't want people to laugh." Paul pre-
tended that his was a normal life and that he was "independent"
and "on my own." He wanted desperately to pass as normal, like
any of the other people who ate in the cafeteria, or visited the
hospital, or bought a paper from Louie. But his incapacity was so
visible that even he had to admit that he wasn't normal. "But not
that different, either," he would add.

I felt a great sadness each time I saw Paul: a sense of a life so
utterly alone, so devoid of human contacts. But I don't think Paul
saw it that way. For him it was a struggle to do all the things he had
to. His feeling was not one of sadness but shame, because he knew
that he was different and that everyone saw him this way, and he
wanted to pass as competent in spite of knowing that he was inadequate. His day was a good one if he could get through it believing
that no one had stared or laughed at him or treated him "like a
child."

I came to realize just how often he was shamed: by children in
the hospital who gawked at him and mimicked his behavior; by
patients or families who avoided sitting near him; by the hospital
security personnel, who had a habit of making faces when he
walked by; by the woman at the cash register who would say,
"Come on, get goin', we can't wait all day while you count your
change"; and worst of all, by the janitorial staff who called him
"dummy." I found myself contributing to this pattern, inadvertently. I had so many patients to see; there was so little to talk about
with Paul that was medically relevant; I would cut the interview off
halfway through. Then I would see such a look of humiliation on

Paul's face, as if to say: "I did badly, didn't I, doc? I don't even know how to be competent at being a brain-injured patient, do I?" Paul Sensabaugh's personality had become immature and his cognitions seriously limited, but his sensitivity to others' reactions was intact. His constant effort was to show others and himself that he was no less human than they. I often wondered: a hospital is organized to protect physically those patients who are in wheelchairs, or who are blind, or who need oxygen or special diets or assistance in caring for themselves; but is there anything in a hospital, to say nothing of the world outside, that protects a patient's sense of shame?

Disability, as Zola (1982) among others has shown, places the disabled person in a difficult situation. His world is no longer the same. Others react to him with great ambivalence, ranging from gross inattention to embarrassing overconcern. Few lay persons, family members, or health professionals are able to accept the disabled person on his own grounds. They expect him to try to "cover," "pass," or normalize his status. Paul Sensabaugh's brain injury left him incompetent in a number of the routine skills of life. But he had fashioned a world for himself. As he used to tell me: "I'm an adult. I'm the same as the others. I can look after myself." Most central to his view of that world was his need to "be like the others," not to be seen as different, not to be ridiculed, rejected, or made to feel inhuman. The work of the doctor in this situation should be to try to understand the boundaries as well as the possibilities of that world, to respond to the disabled person's needs and potential on his own terms, and to do what he can to avoid making the person feel like a freak or not fully human.

I saw Paul Sensabaugh weekly for forty-five minutes for over a year. I can remember only one conversation that went much beyond the regular round of questions, the answers to which he had long before committed to what memory remained and which he would savor as he repeated them, as if they were his gift to me. One cold January day, there was a heavy snow and my train was delayed. Paul waited for several hours, until finally I arrived to find a waiting room full of patients. I excused myself as best I could, then took Paul into my office. I apologized to him and explained that because so little time was available and so many patients were waiting, I could only speak to him for a few minutes. He didn't appear to understand. What hurt him was my brusque manner and the short-ening of his allotted time. This session, he tried to explain to me, was the most important event of his week, something he waited for with great pleasure and organized his week around. And he had something extraordinary to tell me: he had been robbed again. He was so proud to tell it to me that at first I couldn't get the sense that this event had actually happened to him. I thought it might have been something he had seen on the television, dreamed, or even hallucinated. When I finally understood, I told him it would have to wait for the following week. There was no time now.

He looked so terribly hurt, like a disappointed child. I didn't know what to do. The nurse kept buzzing me that there were patients who needed to see me immediately. Yet I felt I couldn't let Paul leave so wounded. I explained to him my dilemma, to which he said something like this:

That's OK, Dr. Kleinman. I'm accustomed to it. I'm just a small person. I'm hardly a grownup anymore. I know the truth. [Now the sheepish grin had left his face and he was crying.] I'm not all together, up here. I'm a half-wit like they said, aren't I? The world is too fast for me, isn't it? The people are too big. And when they get angry they can hurt you, can't they? It really is too dangerous a place for me. Maybe I should live in a home, you know what I mean, a home for people like me.

I felt a deep sadness break like a wave. I think my eyes teared; I may well have cried with him. Then I felt anger—not at Paul, fortunately, but at the injustice experienced by the weak, the timid, the vulnerable in a world of maneaters. I soon consoled myself with the thought that that wasn't the whole story. Paul himself had been the beneficiary of compassionate care. But I couldn't help feeling that it was me, not Paul Sensabaugh, who should have felt shame.

11

The Social Context
of Chronicity

The tenderness with which you have been pleased to treat me,
through my long illness, neither health nor sickness can, I hope,
make me forget; and you are not to suppose, that after we parted
you were no longer on my mind. But what can a sick man say,
but that he is sick? His thoughts are necessarily concentrated in
himself; he neither receives nor can give delight; his inquiries are
after alleviations of pain, and his efforts are to catch some mo-
mentary comfort. Though I am now in the neighborhood of the
Peak, you must expect no account of its wonders, of its hills, the
waters, its caverns, or its mines; but I will tell you, dear Sir, what
I hope you will not hear with less satisfaction, that, for about a
week past, my asthma has been less afflictive.
—Samuel Johnson
(quoted in Boswell [1799] 1965, 1347)

The Double Bind

In a series of insightful essays on her experience as an anthropologist working in a dialysis center for patients with chronic kidney
disease, Linda Alexander (1981; 1982) drew on Gregory Bateson's
idea of the double bind in social relationships to describe the conflicting demands placed on the seriously ill by their care givers: first,
be independent, not passive and dependent, and be active in your
care; *but* when you have a serious exacerbation, place yourself sub-
missively in our hands, and we will blame you for what you did or
failed to do to worsen your disorder. Alexander shows through case

descriptions how the double bind disorients patients and creates guilt feelings. Those responses interfere with effective care and over time can demoralize patients and their families, thereby contributing to chronicity. Jeffrey Longhoffer (1980) describes much the same phenomenon among patients and their families in a bone marrow transplantation unit. Perhaps the problem is a structural component of high-technology, specialized treatment settings. Patients are expected to be active collaborators in their care in the outpatient phase; but when they are in need of emergency room or inpatient therapy, they are expected to revert to passive compliance with treatment controlled entirely by physicians and nurses. These aggressive/regressive phases of patients' behavior have their analogue in the general care of the chronically ill and in the relationship of patient to family and friends.

Matthew Timmerley is a thirty-six-year-old black postman with chronic kidney disease caused by diabetes. Mr. Timmerley had this to say about his care in a dialysis unit:

> The signals are constantly switching. They tell you to run with the ball and help plan the plays, then when the situation changes they take the ball away from you and tell you to stay out of the decision making, leave it to the experts. It can be terribly frustrating. Do I leave it up to them, or do I take part? When I'm well, they're constantly pushing me to do more and be responsible for the care. When I get sick, they tell me I brought it on myself by doing too much. You can't win.

Phillip and Genia Wilson went to the genetic counseling clinic of their local teaching hospital after Genia delivered a baby with multiple birth defects who died soon after birth. Genia described their visits as follows:

> Frankly, it was very confusing and upsetting. They explain enough to you so that you are supposed to make decisions about future pregnancy. But there are so many improbables, so much based on probabilities and less than complete information, you feel very uncertain. How can we make the decisions? We're not doctors. They either baby you when they explain things, as if you knew nothing, or they throw you into the pool and expect you to swim on your own, with not enough lessons and no practice. Also they don't take into account your emotions. It was terribly upsetting giving birth to our baby with all these problems. We felt exhausted, betrayed, and grieved her death. You can't hear things in an objective way under that pressure, let alone formulate decisions. I think it's a kind of pseudomutuality. We wanted someone to act like a real doctor and help us make the decisions in the realities of our life. Not dump everything in our lap. Then

what? If things turn out badly, we did it, we're to blame, but I guess they are off the hook, legally.

Kevin O'Mannix is a fifty-two-year-old Irish-American insurance executive with chronic obstructive pulmonary disease, an outcome believed by his physicians and his family to be the result of more than thirty-five years of extremely heavy smoking. His wife, Martha, a college-educated housewife and mother of their adult children, three daughters and a son, comments on the effect of Kevin's disease on the family:

> He keeps putting us in a bind. On the one hand, he is so self-absorbed by his problems he seems remote from us and yet wants attention. On the other hand, when we ask him, no, beg him, to stop smoking, he tells us to stay out of this—it's his problem. But it's not his problem alone. It is ours, too. And if we didn't respond to him, he would accuse us of not caring about what happens to him. What to do? Do we mollycoddle him? Or are we supposed to shout and argue our point of view?

The O'Mannixes' son, George, a law student, sees the double bind placed on the family as part of the chronicity of the disorder.

> This is very much the structure of our family, anyhow. Dad is authoritarian, yet sometimes he seems to treat Mom as if she were his mother, and at that time he wants us to help out or take over. It's always been this way. The illness has just made it all that much clearer. I think it's not good. It sustains his smoking and messes up what treatment program has been prescribed. If you want to know my view, I'd have to say, this hot and cold cycle is part of the problem. I'm sure it has made him worse off. And for us, it's impossible.

[We will return to discuss family responses to chronic illness later in this chapter.]

In the Pain Center

For several years I supervised the psychiatric liaison with a major chronic pain center. In the center's inpatient unit a conference was held each week to review the status of cases. The conference was chaired by an anesthesiologist cum pain expert, and it included up to fifteen other participants from relevant fields: rehabilitation medicine, psychology, nursing, social work, physical therapy, occupational therapy, psychiatry, and other medical specialties (for example, for a particular case, orthopedics or neurosurgery). The treatment plan evolved as an attempt to combine biomedical and behavioral approaches for patients with severe pain problems who had failed to improve with conventional medical and surgical treatment. The hospitalization of many of the patients was paid for by the state workmen's compensation program or other disability programs.

The weekly meeting took place in a narrow, rectangular room with one set of windows opening onto the outside and another onto the ward itself; the room functioned as a dayroom for patients and their families. There were often not enough seats to go around for our group. What seats there were had been arranged into an elongated oval, the closest approximation to a circle possible in the crowded confines. The meeting was presided over by the anesthesiologist who headed the inpatient pain unit. He sat with his back to an outside window. To his left and right, hedging him in, as it were, sat the behavioral psychologists who did much of the unit's treatment. Then came the rehabilitation physician and other medical specialists, followed by nurses, the social worker, physical therapists, and the occupational therapist. The non-M.D. professionals tended to sit with their backs to the windows opening onto the unit. The psychiatrist often sat with the social worker and nurses, sometimes with the other medical specialists, and occasionally on a bolster or stool in the middle of the oval. As a case was discussed, the patient's chart would make its way from one professional to another as the patient was described, now from the standpoint of biomedicine, now from that of behavioral psychology, now from that of physical therapy, and so forth. Straightforward cases early in their stay on the unit were discussed in less than ten minutes. Difficult cases could take up to half an hour.

The structural arrangement is not a bad metaphor for the structural tensions in the management of pain patients. The anesthesiologist and his biomedical model were in charge. But, in fact, in most cases the behavioral assessment and treatment program were a more important aspect of the patient's care. Thus, there was a constant challenging and rechallenging of behavioral perspective by biomedical perspective and vice versa. The nurses, physical therapists, occupational therapist, and social worker often had more important information to contribute than did the medical specialists, but they clearly occupied a lower status and were overruled by the physician pain experts. Symbolically, they sat with their backs to the patients in the ward, and though in other settings they served as advocates of patient concerns, in this unit they went out of their way to identify with the points of view of the professional staff. Alliances would congeal and dissolve between the different disciplines. Psychiatry's marginal status in medicine was reflected in the seating arrangement: one week in with the medical specialists, another week off with the nonmedical professions, and occasionally alone in the middle of the group.

Although most of the patients were depressed or anxious, these psychiatric problems were minimized or reinterpreted by the pain experts as behavioral consequences of the pain and concomitants of chronicity. By the time a case discussion moved around the circle to the psychiatrist, the medical and behavioral pain experts had usurped most of the available time; with all the other disciplines trying to comment, precious little time was left. Paradoxically, then, the patient's psychiatric condition and the illness meanings and experiences were addressed, almost always grudgingly, in the last minute or two of the case discussion.

The behavioral psychologists, who often were able to help patients who had given up hope, tried to outdo the physicians in their tough talk and attempts to appear coldly scientific. They referred, for example, to the main psychological test employed by the unit as the "X-ray of the headbone," and interpreted it as if it provided a valid reading of the patients' intentions, fears, and desires— which, of course, no paper-and-pencil questionnaire can uncover. They spoke of environmental stimuli worsening or maintaining the chronic course. They called pain a behavior rather than an experience. And they viewed the patient and family as manipulating each other and the medical system. I often found their assessment crude, self-serving, and even more dehumanizing than the biomedical approach. For in the behavioral therapist's analysis, patients were often stripped of the protection of the sick role and viewed as little better than manipulators and malingerers.

Neither the physicians nor the psychologists spent much time thinking about the effect of the pain on the family or social network. When the family was discussed, it (as well as the work setting) was viewed as a hotbed of deviance. I don't want to leave the reader with the impression that the biomedical and behavioral approaches were unhelpful. As I have noted, they often benefited patients who were in terrible situations. Yet they routinely failed to examine adequately the issues described in this book. To my mind, that failing significantly limited the value of the care; it led to certain predictable abuses and contributed to a dangerous claim of near-omniscience regarding a health problem for which very little is known and success is limited at best. Even the social workers and the nurses presented a desocialized picture of the patient, leaving out most of the story of how their pain had influenced and been influenced by their life experience. In the one or two minutes left for his presentation, the psychiatrist had no chance to cover this ground adequately; when he tried to do so, the anesthesiologist and behaviorists made clear that what they really wanted from the psychiatrist was discussion of appropriate psychopharmacologic treatment.

There were ghosts present in the room. I'm sure of it. For each case discussed, the shadows of the players in family tragedies and comedies and melodramas in the workplace seemed to float in the corners of the room, unseen and unheard. Because the social world of pain was not adequately examined, there was little chance the behavioral interventions could identify some of the most central determinants of the experience of pain, problems that were likely to undermine the treatment regimen once the patient left the wholly artificial circumstances of the hospital and returned to the real world. In this sense, the way that pain is configured and treated in the biomedical *and* behavioral paradigms that now dominate pain programs contribute to the chronicity of the problem. In both visions the patient is dealt with as if he were either a billiard ball shot around a pool table by unseen forces or a sociopathic spider entrapping care givers, disability experts, and family members in a web of his own spinning, pulling threads to manipulate now one faction, now the other, sucking all of them dry.

Consider the case of one patient in the program. Helen Winthrop Bell is a twenty-nine-year-old minister's wife from a rural area in

Georgia. She has had chronic pain in her arms for six years. She has undergone eight surgical procedures, has been treated with more than two dozen medications—two of them prescribed narcotics to which she briefly became addicted—and has been in the care of four different primary care physicians. She has already "failed" two local pain clinics. Mrs. Bell is at the end of her first week in the inpatient pain unit. The discussion of her case at the pain conference lasts thirty-six minutes. First, the anesthesiology resident reviews the past medical history and the results of X-rays, nerve and muscle tests, blood studies, and various physical examinations. Then one of the behavioral psychologists reads the results of the psychological test battery: depression, anxiety, bodily preoccupation, hysterical personality traits, and very substantial anger. Everyone shakes his head knowingly, and a few jokes are told to indicate what an extremely hostile and difficult patient Mrs. Bell is. It is noted that the pain seems to be an effective way for her to get angry at her husband. The social worker reports that Mrs. Bell is extremely difficult to interview. She denies all problems, even though there are reports in the medical records that she doesn't like her life as a minister's wife and has been on the verge of considering divorce. There are also reports that the cost of pain evaluations and treatments has exhausted the family's insurance and savings, and that her relationship to her husband is cold and aloof. The senior psychologist adds that the couple's sex life reportedly has come to a halt and that the patient's pain has been observed by the ward staff to worsen at the times her husband visits. He interprets this as evidence that the patient is "using" her pain to manipulate her marital relationship. The nurses jump in at this point with further impressions of the relationship between the Bells: evidence, it turns out, that is greatly contradictory. They have been observed arguing, but also holding hands and praying together. The rehabilitation physician, in a dry and caustic voice, indicates his skepticism that the patient is trying hard at the physical therapy he regards as essential to her rehabilitation. He doubts that the level to which she raises her arms and the length of time she exercises (never more than ten minutes) represent her best efforts. He implies that she is undermining her rehabilitation and that no one is willing to "call her on it" because they fear her anger. The physical therapists corroborate his

point, though one of them has her doubts. The occupational therapist is of an entirely different point of view: she believes the patient
is overdoing it, trying too hard and thereby placing her arms under
too much strain.

An argument ensues among the fifteen professionals present,
with nine in favor of the first point of view and the remainder in
favor of the other. (Usually pain cases do not elicit such strongly
differing points of view, nor are they expressed with such vehe-
mence. When heated discussions did arise on the unit, however,
they frequently escalated, revealing the core structural tensions and
personal antagonisms, in large part because the chief of the unit was
indecisive and not well respected.) The neurosurgeon suggests that
even though Mrs. Bell has had eight surgical procedures—and these
have, if anything, made the pain worse and significantly limited her
range of motion and functioning—it might be necessary to consider
a new and admittedly experimental surgical procedure that would
"attack the source of the problem itself": namely, those areas of her
brain that are likely to be transmitting and amplifying pain signals.
One of the residents waggishly asks if that will remove her anger
center, too. The orthopedic surgeon is in strong disagreement with
his neurosurgical colleague. This woman, he concludes, has had too
much surgery already, and is suffering, in large part, from all the
damage done by the surgery. The neurosurgeon shoots back that he
only meant that the *possibility* for stereotactic brain surgery should
not be ruled out. The chief anesthesiologist admits that nothing has
seemed to work, including the nerve blocks and analgesics. The
junior behavioral psychologist points out, however, that though the
behavioral treatment program has only reduced the daily pain from
an 8 to a 6 in the patient's pain diary, it is still early in the course
of her treatment and the trend is in a positive direction. He adds that
the patient uses her anger to undermine the treatment program.
There is a dispute about this, since one of the nurses feels the patient
is "cooking the books" to make the pain seem less severe on paper,
while her "pain behavior" is very much the same as when she
arrived on the ward. Another nurse breaks in, saying: "We all know
what chronic pain patients are like: they are all angry and self-
destructive. What's so special about Mrs. Bell?" The head nurse
says she is special because she is so hostile and negative. Maybe we

should discharge her before she causes a major problem on the unit, she suggests. "Do you psychiatrists have anything you want to add?" asks the chief anesthesiologist. "We only have a few minutes, because we have three other cases to get to," he cautions.

That's where I came in when I participated in this pain conference one spring afternoon in 1979. I could have told the group that Mrs. Bell satisfied the diagnostic criteria for major depressive disorder, a treatable psychiatric disorder. But she had met these criteria for three years and had been treated on numerous occasions with appropriate doses of antidepressant medication without significant effect on her depression or pain. I could have told them that I had also interviewed her husband and had found him to be even more profoundly depressed than his wife. He had cried when he spoke of marrying a healthy, outgoing, lively woman who for most of their married life had been consumed by her illness and its treatment. He was at the end of his energy and personal and financial resources. He loved his wife but didn't know what to do. Her pain problem had affected every aspect of their lives and had deeply impaired his work as a minister. He knew it was blasphemous to state, but he felt God had let them down. He was unable to accept the chronicity of the pain, which sapped their vitality day by day, year after year. His wife had become so terribly absorbed by the pain that she was unaware of what he was going through and inattentive to their two small children. She was unable to do even the lightest housework. Each day she withdrew to her room for long periods of time, unable to tolerate any noise or the usual commotion of a young family. Mr. Bell had lost confidence in the future and in the medical system. He had also began to doubt his own future.

I could have told the group about my interview with Mrs. Bell, which was fairly typical of her interactions with the staff. Mrs. Bell did not want to speak to me. She told me she did not have a psychiatric problem nor any other problem except for her pain. She denied that psychological factors were at work deepening her pain and the disability it caused. She told me there were no problems in her marriage or in her role as a mother. She was enraged at the behavioral program, which treated her like a "convict," and at the physical therapists, who were demanding more of her body than it could tolerate. I asked her how she had learned to deal with the anger "created by the pain," the rage that was so visible to me. Mrs. Bell shouted at me to leave the room, accusing me of provoking her and yelling that she was most definitely *not* angry.

I spoke with several of her primary care physicians, each of whom told me that she had eventually left their care—after numerous failed treatments and the side effects of surgeries and drugs—with such tremendous anger that they were convinced she would try to sue them, though she hadn't. They in turn had gotten so very angry at her that they felt relieved when she left them for another doctor, because they felt that their hostility to her would impede further care. I could have reported these talks at the conference.

I could also have reported a chat I had with Helen Bell's older sister, Agatha, who told me that Helen had been angry all her life; before the pain it was her relationship with their parents and with her that elicited Helen's anger. She also told me that that anger was often expressed indirectly through chronic bodily complaints: first, headaches or backaches; later, her arm and shoulder pain. Agatha Winthrop told me that in their family no problems of a personal or family kind could be openly talked out.

I decided, given the very limited time, there was nothing further to be gained reviewing these problems. I told my colleagues, rather, that in my view we were part of the problem. I pointed out that the pain center itself had now been taken up in the angry, self-defeating relationships that characterized Mrs. Bell's life. We were now in the same situation as her many doctors, her husband, her sister, and other family members. The way to understand this very difficult case was not by acquiring more information about Mrs. Bell, though privately I felt sure a more adequate understanding of her personality would be of help, but instead by studying the pain as a language of communication in a system of social relationships. In the one or two minutes given to me, ironically, it would be possible to review this subject—so central to her illness, yet so peripheral to our discussion—because we had learned so very little about her social world, there was pathetically little to discuss. Her pain might be usefully looked upon as a metaphor, as some had suggested, but of what we had little idea. Our knowledge couldn't be completed by interviewing Mrs. Bell, though her notions, if we could get her to relax her defenses long enough to tell us, would be part of the picture. We required a mini-ethnography of her relationships with husband, children, sister, parents, and key members of her local community—a systematic description of the meanings of pain in those relationships. Such an ethnography, I quickly added, would take some days to develop, and perhaps it would be most easily worked up after she returned home. After all, home, not the artificial hospital environment, was the real setting of her pain.

I couldn't get any further. The chief anesthesiologist thanked me for my intervention, reminded me that time had run out, and asked if I didn't really want to see her receive the latest psychopharmacologic agent. He gently chided me for my utopian suggestion. Mrs. Bell was here on the ward and "something has to be done with her now."

My purpose in recounting this case is to illustrate a major limitation of the so-called integrated, multidisciplinary care of chronic pain patients, a limitation that it shares with other of the social environments of medical care for patients with chronic illness. That limitation is the result of a failure to assess adequately the actual social environment in which illness is experienced, complicated by the tendency to avoid confronting the fact that the social environment of the treatment unit is only one component of the patient's local social system. Furthermore, information gained about the patient's behavior in the clinical setting is biased.

Chronicity is not simply a direct result of pathology acting in an isolated person. It is the outcome of lives lived under constraining circumstances with particular relationships to other people. Chronicity is created in part out of negative expectations that come to be shared in face-to-face interactions—expectations that fetter our dreams and sting and choke our sense of self. Patients learn to act as chronic cases; family members and care givers learn to treat patients in keeping with this view. We collude in building walls and tearing down bridges. We place complex individuals in simple, unidimensional roles (the disabled, the life threatened) as if this were all they are and can be. We turn our backs on poisonous relationships. We become part of demoralizing situations, and add unhelpfully to feelings of threat and fear.

To understand the contribution of the social environment to

chronicity, to the swings of symptoms and disability, we must be able to see the patient suspended, as it were, in the web of relationships that constitute a life world, including relationships with the health care and disability systems that frequently impede the transition from impaired role back into normal social statuses (see Kleinman 1986; McHugh and Vallis 1986; Osterweis et al. 1987). Chronicity is viewed by several of the protagonists in this book as like being in limbo emotionally and interpersonally. What patients and families mean by this evocative, yet unappreciated, term is crucial to rehabilitation. Theirs is an intuition that illness involves rites of passage between different social worlds. Social theorists have modeled this movement as "trajectory" (Strauss et al. 1983) and as "cultural performance" (Frankenberg 1986). But I prefer patients' images of the journey through limbo.

The chronically ill often are like those trapped at a frontier, wandering confused in a poorly known border area, waiting desperately to return to their native land. Chronicity for many is the dangerous crossing of the borders, the interminable waiting to exit and reenter normal everyday life, the perpetual uncertainty of whether one can return at all. To pass through this world of limbo is to move through a "nervous" system, a realm of menacing uncertainty. For some the passage is not so difficult; for others it becomes routine like so much else in life; yet for others it involves despair at being stuck in a place one has come to hate and fear. This image should also alert us to the social nature of chronicity: the entrance and exit formalities, the visas, the different languages and etiquettes, the guards and functionaries and hucksters at the border crossing points, and especially the relatives and friends who press their faces against windows to wave a sad goodbye, who carry sometimes the heaviest baggage, who sit in the same waiting rooms, and who even travel through the same land of limbo, experiencing similar worry, hurt, uncertainty and loss. Social movement for the chronically ill is back and forth through rituals of separation, transition, and reincorporation, as exacerbation leads to remission and then circles back to worsening, and so on.

The practitioner's image of chronicity must be built up of different accounts of the illness and of the sick person, and where possible through direct observation. Not unexpectedly, the practitioner will learn that patients' and families' views of the meanings of illness are interpretations of a complex, shifting reality, different aspects of which are more influential on course and outcome at different times. Lacking such mini-ethnographies of the changing contexts of illness and care, we are in the dark about the potentially remediable social sources of distress and disease. Most health care is carried out in the dark, for precisely this reason. Not surprisingly, therefore, health professionals routinely make ineffective use of knowledge about illness that, if systematically collected and interpreted, could have a profound impact on the care of the chronically ill. In chapter 15 I will return specifically to this matter by proposing a clinical ethnographic methodology that practitioners should incorporate into their care of patients with chronic illness.

The Consequences of Illness for the Family

The protagonists in our accounts of the meaningful experience of chronic illness have been patients and their doctors. But, as a number of these stories attest, the family often is a major player in the illness drama. We may not hear of the family when we listen to the patient, because of the self-absorbing and isolating quality of the experience of chronic illness, captured in the quotation from Samuel Johnson at the head of this chapter. Yet there can be no doubt about the consequences of illness for the family, when the family members themselves are asked.

Dalton Moore is a seventy-three-year-old retired lawyer whose wife, Anna, developed Alzheimer's disease almost a decade ago. Because he is wealthy, Mr. Moore has been able to pay for live-in nurses to help care for his wife. Because he is deeply committed to caring for his wife in the family setting, Mr. Moore has refused to place her in a nursing home, an action that has frequently been recommended. His grown children report that Mr. Moore devotes most of his day to caring for Mrs. Moore, even though she is no longer able to recognize him as her husband.

I couldn't let Anna go to the nursing home. Maybe it's selfish of me. But I think this is what she would want. She told me that when this darn disease started; she said, "Dalton, please don't put me in an institution if it gets bad." I promised her I wouldn't. It has broken my heart to see her mind go. It's as if, I can barely say it, she were gone already. She can't recognize me or the children. If it weren't for the nurses, I don't know what I would do. I can't cope myself. I've learned to feed her, bathe her, even take her to the bathroom. I've given up all my interests and our friends. I think people think I'm batty for doing this. But we were so close. She and I were everything to each other. I believe strongly in the family. My parents did. My grandparents died at home. And my brothers and I took care of our parents at the end. But this is the worst. To see the mind go, so that there are no memories, it, well, sir, it is a living hell!

Our children come and they cry. And I cry. We reminisce about old times. We try to recall what Anna was like before this happened. But I can see it wears them out just being here for a day or two. They've got their own troubles. I can't ask them to help out any more than they do already. Me? It's made a different person out of me. I expect you wouldn't have recognized me if you had met me ten years ago. I feel at least ten years older than I am. I'm afraid what will happen if I go first. I haven't had a half hour free of worry and hurt for ten years. This illness didn't just destroy Anna's mind, it has killed something in me, in the family, too. If anyone asks about Alzheimer's, tell them it is a disease of the whole family.

Mavis Williams is a forty-nine-year-old architect and mother of three. She is a single head of household; eight years ago she and her husband of fifteen years divorced. Her oldest child, Andrew, age twenty-three, suffers from inherited muscular dystrophy. Now in a wheelchair, he is progressively losing control of his speech, arms, and upper body. The disorder first appeared when he was nine years old, but it seriously accelerated when he was twelve. It is incurable. His neurologist's prognosis is a slow decline of motor activity over three to five years, with subsequent mental deterioration and death.

I met Mrs. Williams not through clinical consultation but in the course of a field research project. I had administered several questionnaires to her to ascertain her reaction to her son's illness and to obtain her evaluation of its effect on their family.

Dr. Kleinman, I hope you don't mind me saying this to you, but I found the questions ridiculous. I filled in all the little boxes, but I think the questions are superficial. You really want to know what impact my son's illness has had? All right, then, you need to get at the way it has torn us apart, divided me from my husband, affected each and every one of us and our plans and dreams. When the questionnaire says, "Has the effect on your relationships with your spouse or your children been minimal, moderate, serious," or whatever it says—you know the question I mean—what does that have to do with a family turned into a cauldron? With explosions of rage, with a daily grief that sucks your eyes dry, with turning away hurt and empty? It is the totality of its effects, its all-encompassingness that you should study. And especially its deep currents of desperation and failure. There is a little voice in me which, if I knew you better, would scream at you: Doctor, it has murdered this family.

There is no stability; we can't work it through. Andrew's illness doesn't end. It tortures him; it does the same to us. John, my husband, blamed me. It seems to come from my side of the family. John collapsed, literally collapsed. He couldn't handle it or do anything for any of us, even himself. He ran away and drank. He was no help, no help at all. But I can't really blame him. Who can expect to meet a test like this? It is the daily struggle to stay on top of it. I blame me for being absolutely, totally incapable of separating any part of me from Andrew's suffering. I have no free space, no private and protected place to get away and call my own. It has taken all of me. What is a mother to do? Between this horror and working to support the family I have, I really have, no—no—time! Zero time for me.

Look at Barbara and Kim [her other children]. What have their lives been like? Guilt because they are normal. Anger, intense anger because Andrew has required so much of my time and energy. I have had, I'll admit, precious little left over for them. But they can't express any of this. How can you, when the person responsible is dying slowly, day by day, in front of your eyes? So they can't express it to him; they take it out on me! Like John does, like Andrew does, like I want to also—since there is no one else strong enough to take it.

OK, tell me. How do you convert this into a +3 or −3 answer, to a decimal? How do you compare it with other people's reactions? I insist it is illegitimate to make comparisons. We are not things. This is not an "interpersonal problem," a "family stress"—this is a calamity! I do not exaggerate. Before Andrew's disaster we were like everyone else: some days good, some bad. Then we had problems. But looking back, that was a kind of paradise I can hardly believe was real. Now we are burning up. I sometimes think we are all dying, not just Andy. Even my parents and brothers and sisters have been more than "affected," Dr. Kleinman. You look around you—you look! This, what you see, this tomb, our family's tomb.

Jenny Heyst's experience is almost the obverse of what Mavis Williams has gone through. Mrs. Heyst is a sixty-three-year-old housewife whose husband, Samuel, has suffered from chronic lymphoma—a slow-growing cancer of the lymphatic system—for twelve years. The mother of two and grandmother of four, Jenny Heyst believes that her husband's tumor, as she calls it, "saved our marriage—maybe our family."

She told me in the course of the same research project:

I know Sam and I were about to split up before he was diagnosed. We were going in separate directions. He had his interests, I had mine. Then the tumor was found. It was a shock. We were numb. We cried and cried, and we began to talk like we hadn't since the early days of our marriage. I began to see him differently. I think the same happened to him. Our eyes were half opened. He wouldn't agree with me, but sometimes I really do think God did this to bring us together. Well, if He did or didn't, we did come together. And not just Sam and me—the kids, too. They were off on their own. You know how it is when you are in your mid- and late twenties. You begin to loosen the ties. You think less and less about your origins and more and more about where you are and where you are heading. They were into new careers and starting families of their own. Well, amazingly, this thing, this tumor, had the same effect on them it had on us. They started calling up, visiting. All of a sudden they were big on family get-togethers. And attentive—my, oh yeah, they were attentive. We joke about it, Sam and I. Maybe the kids weren't prepared for a tumor, I mean a cancer that goes on for a long time. They were thinking maybe of a year or two. But here it is twelve, almost thirteen, years, and Sam is still going strong. But the best, the very best, thing is that really *we* are going strong; all of us are into this together.

Chronic illness is nothing if not various, as many-sided and differing as our lives. That is why, if we are to understand the meaning of illness, we cannot focus on the content. That is too various: it is Jenny Heyst and Mavis Williams and hundreds of thousands of others, each of whose illness story is different. Instead, we must inquire into the *structure* of illness meanings: the manner in which illness is made meaningful, the processes of creating meaning, and the social situations and psychological reactions that determine and are determined by the meanings.

The family consequences of illness have this in common: each family must make sense of their experience, come to terms with it. In so doing, all the things that distinguish a family as unique are replicated in that process of imparting meaning to experience. Cultural and ethnic differences, social class and economic constraints, and a host of other factors will manifest themselves in this work of making illness a part of a family's construction of reality. Understanding the influence of illness on the family necessitates understanding the family itself, not just the illness. When the family becomes the focus, it will be seen that illness influences relationships as profoundly as it does individuals.

In this chapter, I have looked at three kinds of social contexts within which illness is lived: treatment settings that place certain groups of the chronically ill in double binds, a multidisciplinary pain center, and families. I did this to demonstrate that illness is not simply a personal experience; it is transactional, communicative, profoundly social. The study of illness meanings is not only about one particular individual's experience; it is also very much about social networks, social situations, and different forms of social reality. Illness meanings are shared and negotiated. They are an integral dimension of lives lived together. Had we examined work settings, schools, or other of the major institutions of society, we would have arrived at the same point. Illness is deeply embedded in the social world, and consequently it is inseparable from the structures and processes that constitute that world. For the practitioner, as for the anthropologist, an inquiry into the meanings of illness is a journey into relationships.

12

The Creation of Disease: Factitious Illness

For a wounded spirit who can bear? . . . Imagine what thou canst, fear, sorrow, furies, grief, pain, terror . . . dismal, ghastly, tedious . . . it is not sufficient, it comes far short, no tongue can tell, no heart conceive it. 'Tis an Epitome of hell.

—ROBERT BURTON
The Anatomy of Melancholy, 1621

There are a small number of sick persons who suffer from severe psychiatric problems—usually hidden from all but intimates—that for various reasons lead them to induce illness in themselves. Illness-generating actions may include self-bleeding, self-injection with various bacteria, adding blood to urine or stool samples to mimic a serious disorder, heating a thermometer to fake fever, and so forth. The individual will disguise the behavior and often undergo elaborate biomedical diagnostic evaluations and treatment, at high cost to the medical system. The former label for such behavior was Munchausen's syndrome, named for Baron Munchausen (1720–97), an adventurer known for his fantastic tales of exploits; in current psychiatric parlance this problem is called factitious illness.* For many sufferers this abnormal behavior becomes chronic, a way of life. Unlike malingering, it does not yield a practical financial or other social gain. Rather it complicates an already deeply disturbed life.

Gus Echeverra has such a problem. When I first met him, he was a thirty-year-old historian who was on an inpatient medical unit for evaluation of a respiratory disorder associated with anemia. His biomedical workup had been so inconsistent and strange that only a heretofore unknown disorder of the lungs or a self-engendered illness seemed plausible to his physicians. The hospital he was in was known for its systematic and complete medical evaluations, and Gus Echeverra had had an enormous variety of tests to determine the precise nature of his disorder. Not surprisingly, several tests had resulted in serious complications: the sternal bone marrow sampling had produced a deep infection in his chest wall, and the liver biopsy, performed by an inexperienced resident, had caused internal bleeding. During the course of this lengthy and complicated hospitalization, Gus became deeply depressed and requested to talk with a psychiatrist. I happened to be the psychiatrist on call that day.

When I reached his unit, Gus requested that we find a private room where we could talk undisturbed by the busy medical team. When we got there, he pleaded with me to get him out of the medical unit as soon as possible. He blurted out his fear that in trying to find the cause of his problem the residents would inadvertently kill him. I arranged for Gus to enter the inpatient psychiatric unit after he confided in me that he had caused his own illness by a combination of self-bleeding and pouring a saline solution down his own trachea.

What follows is Gus's story as he told it to me both in the hospital and over the course of a year of psychotherapy. At the end of that time he dropped out of care, so the story he told me fifteen years ago has no ending. I retell it because Gus's tale, as strange as it is, has something to teach us about the relationship of chronic symptoms to human misery.

---

*Factitious illness can also be grouped under syndromes of deliberate self-harm, which include as well repetitive self-mutilating behaviors such as cutting and burning the skin (see Favazza 1987). These syndromes may occur in the context of serious mental disorders, like schizophrenia or borderline personality disorder, or as autonomous disorders; or they may not result from illnesses but may be culturally prescribed behavior such as ritual scarification.

Gus Echeverra was the last child born to Puerto Rican parents in Chicago, in one of America's most notorious inner-city ghettos. His mother gave birth to Gus when she was in her forties, years after delivering her next-youngest child. She referred to Gus as an undesired "spirit" baby, and she told him and others that he would therefore be different, difficult, and doomed to a bad future. I remember her telling me as much on the telephone, adding: "Spirit babies is stubborn, ornery, and evil. Look what he done to me."

An impoverished, hard-working woman with a deep paranoid streak, Mrs. Echeverra told Gus from the time he was a young child that she had had a stroke during the delivery that left her with a mild weakness of her right arm and a somewhat more serious paralysis of her right leg. As a result, she walked with a pronounced limp and was impaired in the full use of her arm. For this outcome, Mrs. Echeverra held Gus responsible. She told him repeatedly that he had caused it. She also told him that he was a mistake, her misfortune, that he had ruined her life, and that he would probably destroy his own. From the time Gus was four years old, Mrs. Echeverra left him at home while she went out to work as a housemaid. She was usually away from very early in the morning to late at night, and sometimes she was gone for days at a time. When she left, she locked Gus in the small apartment and expected him to care for himself. When she returned, she would beat him if he had dirtied himself or made a mess in the house. Sometimes his siblings were home to help him, but most often they were gone. His father, an unemployed drug addict, was rarely home, and when he was he beat Gus and his mother and took what food and money he could find. Gus was frightened of his mother, terrified of his father, and independent from an extremely early age. From the age of six he would shop for himself and even cook eggs and other simple dishes. From the age of seven he began to earn money shining shoes, running errands, and doing odd jobs.

Having been a short, obese, cautious, friendless child who had little experience playing with others, Gus believes that if he had not become self-sufficient so young he would have died from malnutrition and general neglect. He was precocious, and his teachers soon recognized his great intellectual skills. Academic achievement became the focus of his life, but he remained wary of adults and other children. His aloof behavior, intense interest in books, and friend-lessness made him an object of ridicule by his schoolmates, who derided his physical weakness and intellectual gifts. A great source of humiliation was the behavior of his father. On one occasion, his father entered the school under the influence of street drugs and began to threaten the teacher in Gus's class. His schoolmates, recognizing this notorious character, taunted Gus until he ran away, vowing that he hated his father and mother and would live by himself. Very soon this is what Gus, remarkably, accomplished: at the age of fourteen he found a room of his own and supported himself by working after school and on weekends.

Because of his obsession with the blame his mother placed on him for her disability, Gus began as a young teenager to frequent the local medical library, where he read as much as he could understand about stroke and its relationship to birthing. He had to see, as he told me, "if it were true that I was to blame for Mother's problem." Urged on by the same need, he obtained a job as a clerk in the hospital where his mother had delivered him. He worked hard to gain access to hospital charts stored in the record room. One day he located his mother's old chart, and he proceeded to find ways to read it. But again he could not be sure whether it confirmed his mother's accusation or exonerated him from the deeply wounding guilt. Gus divulged that in retrospect he could see that this feeling had poisoned his sense of self, bending his thoughts and emotions.

When Gus was about eighteen, the feelings of guilt and self-hatred became associated with bouts of panic and insomnia that were unrelieved by street drugs. Gus would stay up whole nights, studying part of the time and spending the rest brooding over his past. So intense did the feeling of anguish and self-contempt become that Gus felt an overpowering urge to hurt himself. Knocking his head against the walls of his small, barren rented room was insufficient. One day he stole several venipuncture needles from the hospital. He stood over the wash basin, put a tourniquet on his arm, jabbed his swollen veins, and let the blood pour out. Almost thirteen years later he would claim that until that day he had no idea of producing an illness in himself. He discovered, however, that puncturing his veins and watching the blood flow relieved the intensity of his feelings. Finally, after weeks of daily bleedings, he began to feel fatigued and exhausted. He went to the hospital clinic, but he did not tell his story to the physician who examined him. Rather, he claimed that he had no idea how he had become so anemic.

Gus obtained the first of what would prove to be many hospitalizations for diagnostic evaluation. He remembers enjoying watching the doctors "run around and not be able to figure out what was wrong." Gus had the feeling that he was getting back at doctors for what had happened to his mother. This sense of just revenge persisted through dozens of hospitalizations. For Gus had entered on a course of self-inflicted illnesses that matched the originality of his imagination. Gus's academic brilliance had led to a college scholarship, an outstanding undergraduate record, and graduate work in history at a prestigious southern university. Over the years Gus's factitious disorders escalated as he induced anemia and then developed the terrible ritual of pouring saline down his bronchial tubes to cause repeated pneumonias and eventually a chronic fibrosis of the lung tissue. At several of the country's leading hospitals, doctors often suspected self-inflicted illness, but Gus was never caught or directly accused. Sometimes Gus would run away from a hospital during a detailed workup. But most often he stayed for as long as it took to confound the investigation, even though the hospitalization interfered seriously with his academic, financial, and personal life.

In each instance Gus felt that he was fully in control of his disorder. He carefully controlled the substances he aspirated to produce significant but limited pathology that worried his physicians but did not seriously threaten his life. But his experience at the hospital at which we met was exceptional. There he felt he had lost control over events. He told me, "I feel they won't give up until I'm dead and they have the autopsy results."

The illnesses brought him somewhat closer to his mother. (His father had died from the complications of drug abuse.) When Gus was hospitalized, Mrs. Echeverra would turn her destructive paranoia away from her son and project it onto his doctors. She also tried to help her son recover from his illnesses, often taking him into her home and caring for him in the recovery period. Nonetheless, she kept the fixed idea that he was ultimately responsible for the awful complications of giving birth to him, and that his fate was doomed by the evil character he had acquired as her spirit baby.

Gus Echeverra had learned to live two entirely separate lives. At the university he was seen not only as an excellent scholar but also as a responsible member of the academic community; he spent hours tutoring minority students and teaching in outreach programs in a local inner-city community. At the same time, Gus's personal life became increasingly bizarre. He had many superficial friends but hardly any intimate ones, certainly none to whom he could talk about his problems. From adolescence he had kept an image of a naked Amerindian who was being tortured by a brutal Spanish master. This sadomasochistic image of the violated native had been his only childhood confidant: like him it was solitary and rejected by others. For Gus it passed from a loved object to a fetish that he took with him wherever he moved and that he learned to converse with about his inner wounds. His "friend," he confessed to me one day, observed the masochistic rites he performed to harrow his body and consoled him for the savage expiation of his guilt.

At the start of our therapy sessions Gus was psychotically depressed. He was suicidal and had active hallucinations and delusions. But this state rapidly passed with the help of antipsychotic and antidepressant drugs and the talk therapy. However, over the course of a year it became apparent that he was suffering from a severe personality disorder that was not improving. The self-inflicted illnesses stopped for the first nine months—the longest period since he was eighteen. In the psychotherapy, we worked our way through the painful details of his life story. Gus turned his powerful imagination and professional historical skills toward the prospect of interpreting the familial sources of his implacable guilt and the morbid icons of his ritual atonement. As I got to know his life, I began to see connections that rendered his self-injurious behavior interpretable, though not acceptable. I felt a desperate desire to save him—a danger sign in therapy. I could affirm his suffering but not his fierce self-punishment, which I insisted had to cease. Near the end of the year, I realized he was having difficulty telling me that he had begun again to exact his terrible revenge. When I confronted him with my suspicions, Gus became angry. He told me he would not be dependent on our relationship, but would independently decide when he would stop. After telling me this, he simply did not come again and I lost contact with him entirely.

For Gus Echeverra chronic illness had deeply idiosyncratic meaning that can be understood only in the alienating context of his extraordinary intrapsychic life. I see him at the deeply tragic end of a continuum. The personal significance of illness is always important, but often it is dominated by the kinds of social and cultural significance I have illustrated in the preceding chapters. However, in many individuals the psychological meanings are the most powerful influence on the course of the illness. Even among this group of patients, self-inflicted illness is very uncommon.

I have encountered fifty cases of factitious illness in a career devoted to chronic illness. Only a few were as strange as that of Gus Echeverra. His story may have sent chills through my body and challenged my own sense of reality, yet it taught me that compassion can overcome revulsion to bridge, however fragilely and incompletely, radically different life worlds. That is a lesson clinicians learn in one way or another, usually through the more mundane reality of caring for ordinary lives lived with illness. Factitious illness points to something darker, more driven, less appeasable, less given to reinterpretation as simply cognitive or affective reaction to illness. Each case of factitious illness discloses deep fissures in our inner world, a scarred soul who demands terrifying reenactment of the felt experience of suffering. The words *depression, anxiety, guilt,* and *anger* do not do justice to the deeply indwelling, self-defeating psychic forces that create and intensify the experience of illness. There is still something important left unsaid, an aspect of our unique character usually hidden even from us, that can make of life a living hell and of illness a life.

13

Hypochondriasis:
The Ironic Disease

It is the copying that originates.
—CLIFFORD GEERTZ
(1986, 380)

By definition, hypochondriasis is that disease in which there is no disease. In contemporary psychiatry it is classified as a chronic condition in which the patient persists in his nosophobia (fear of disease) in spite of medical evidence to the contrary: the patient fears he has a disease, but the physician finds no evidence that the patient's fears are based on the existence of a pathological process. In the dualistic terminology of biomedicine, the patient has an illness experience without the biological pathology of disease. To diagnose hypochondriasis, the practitioner must become convinced that the disease the patient fears he is suffering from is not present. For hypochondriasis to become chronic, the practitioner must also be unable to convince the patient of this fact, because if the patient comes to accept the medical evidence that he is not suffering from the disease he fears he is experiencing, then he no longer has the disease hypochondriasis. For the purposes of this volume, hypochondriasis is of interest because it illustrates the shifting relationship between the meanings and experiences of patients and those of practitioners. In hypochondriasis, there is a gap between those lay and professional meanings and experiences. That semantic and existential divide puts expectable tensions between doctors and patients under greater strain. The results are frustration and conflict, but also ironic insight.

Hypochondriasis creates a reversal of the archetypal medical relationship in which the patient complains of illness and the physician diagnoses disease. Rather, in hypochondriasis the patient complains of disease ("I fear that I have cancer of the throat"; "I'm convinced I'm dying of heart disease"; "I know, I just know I've got an autoimmune disease"), and the doctor can confirm only illness.

The patient, in the classic textbook description of hypochondriasis, is not supposed to doubt his fear of having a disease in which his doctors do not believe. But in reality, few hypochondriacal patients are psychotic in this way.* Thus, they have some degree of insight into the gap between what they believe to be wrong and what the practitioner believes is not wrong; the hypochondriac's persistent fear is based not on the certainty of a delusion but on the profound uncertainty of persistent doubt. He can't convince himself or be convinced by the physician that disease is *not* present. This is why hypochondriasis leads to so many futile tests of biological functioning: the hypochondriac knows that no test is complete or precise enough in its ability to define disease at it earliest, most minimal stage and thus to offer absolute certainty that he is free of disease. It is ironic that hypochondriacs, faced with medical disbelief, are forced to act as if they lacked irony.† The sufferer of hypochondriasis may be an extremely humorous person in his day-to-day world, but in the physician's office he is stolid, self-righteous, and unable to laugh at himself. If he acted with an ironic smile in the medical encounter, he could not portray his problem as a serious one. Rather, both he and the practitioner would dissolve in laughter over the patent absurdity of their conflict. Thus, the hypochondriac must maintain the social fiction of not doubting his own doubt, when perhaps the most disturbing part of the experience of hypochondriasis is the patient's intractable doubt that his belief is correct. Of course, there are certain patients with this condition who do seem genuinely to lack a sense of irony about their

*There is an uncommon form of hypochondriasis in which the patient lacks insight and his nosophobia has all the characteristics of a delusion (a fixed false belief that is not shared by others), namely, monosymptomatic hypochondriacal psychosis. The remarkable thing about this disorder is that the psychosis is limited to this single aspect of experience.

†"Simulated ignorance" is the original ancient Greek meaning of *irony*.

complaints—who, as it were, take the body overly seriously, humorlessly, and with dread.

The patient often claims that his illness behavior is unique, which is why he feels it fails to fit into established biomedical categories, but in fact it is all too apparent to the clinician that the hypochondriacal behavior is a remarkable copy of the language and experience of every other patient with the problem he has seen. The patient's intuition that the illness is unique and the doctor's counterintuition that the disease is a copy of textbook examples is a conflict not limited to hypochondriasis: many doctor–patient relationships in the care of the chronically ill reproduce this central tension. The contradiction creates predictable problems in communication within the therapeutic relationship. In fact, the perceptions of both patients and practitioners are correct. The conflict arises because they are talking about two distinctive modes of experiencing reality. Patients' behavior superficially replicates what they share with others who harbor the same pathology. However, patients' behavior also expresses the distinctive meanings in their lives that come to shape the experience of illness as most decidedly theirs and not someone else's. The essence of effective care for the chronically ill is reintegration of what is unique and what is a copy into holistic care.*

The treatment of hypochondriasis includes persuading patients that instead of having the disease they fear they have, they are suffering from a psychiatric disorder.† Hypochondriasis can be an edifying irony for the practitioner. He knows that it is not, as the official (DSM-III) diagnostic criteria of the American Psychiatric Association claim it to be, a disease entity. Rather, it is a symptom found in a wide assortment of psychiatric conditions, running from schizophrenia and depression to anxiety and personality disorders. The biomedical practitioner also knows that he contributes to the problem, inasmuch as he has been trained to act as if he can never

---

*Perhaps no other word in recent years has been more abused than *holistic,* which gained popularity as a gloss for psychosocially attentive as well as biomedically competent care but has been transformed tendentiously into a commercialized slogan for selling a brand name of medical care. I use *holistic* in its earlier sense.

†Patients who begin with somatic hypochondriasis are increasingly being transformed into psychological hypochondriacs. In my experience, this is a dangerous and undesirable change, because there are so few benchmarks in psychiatry, unlike the rest of medicine, to disconfirm a patient's (or a psychiatrist's) concern that a certain disease process is present.

be entirely sure there isn't a hidden biological lesion responsible for the patient's symptoms. A gnawing doubt that the ultimate test has not yet been employed is part of the physician's professional skepticism as a medical detective. Hence, the hypochondriac's doubt has an exact complement in that of the practitioner, who knows at heart that, in spite of trying to convince the hypochondriac to the contrary, he can never be completely certain himself that the patient doesn't have a disease. Clinical work is a matter of probabilities, as is biology, unlike physics (Mayr 1982). The physician is never 100 percent sure. Usually 90 or 95 percent is good enough, but there is always room for doubt. The hypochondriacal patient elicits the physician's doubt and makes him decidedly uncomfortable. Perhaps this is one of the reasons why physicians often find such patients irksome.

The following cases exemplify my points. The case descriptions include only those aspects of the four patients' lives that demonstrate what is ironic in illness meanings.

The Hidden Disorder

Arnie Springer is a thirty-eight-year-old unmarried systems analyst for a small computer company. For fourteen months Arnie has been visiting physicians because of fear that he has cancer of the bowel. During that period, he has consulted his primary care physician more than twenty times. That physician eventually referred Arnie to a gastroenterologist who performed upper and lower gastrointestinal X-ray studies, along with gastroscopy, sigmoidoscopy, and enteroscopy (that is, direct visualization with fiber-optic scopes of the entire large bowel, rectum, and stomach). On his own, Arnie Springer has visited two other gastroenterologists who have repeated these examinations and given him a CT-scan (computerized axial tomography, an even more precise type of X-ray examination) of the gastrointestinal tract. Arnie was referred to me by a surgeon whom he had consulted to discuss whether laparotomy (surgical exploration of the abdomen) might detect a cancerous growth.

Arnie Springer and his primary care physician have reached an impasse.

He is basically a nice guy, and I'm sure he is a competent doctor—at least I think he is—but he just won't believe me that I could have an intestinal cancer. There is after all a lot of the small intestine that isn't well visualized by endoscopic or X-ray techniques. How can he be sure I don't have cancer? Not when you take the different layers of the bowel into account, and if the tumor were a real small one. Well, tell me, short of taking out the entire intestine and examining it under the microscope—actually an electron microscope might be necessary if we were to discover a tumor in its earliest phase—well short of that, how can he or you or the other doctors be sure, I mean 100 percent certain, I don't have cancer?

When his physicians challenge Arnie's approach to disease and talk about probabilities, they may be on firm scientific footing, but as far as Arnie is concerned they have lost their case.

You see, supposing it is 99.9 percent sure that a certain test can disprove cancer, there would still be that tiny bit of uncertainty, wouldn't there? Just that little bit, and that would be all it would take to have the disease. And, of course, there is no test anywhere as accurate as that as far as the intestine is concerned.

Arnie is also well prepared for the other medical ploy, the one that suggests the problem is a question not of cancer but of anxiety. He made that clear to me at our first meeting.

I know you are a psychiatrist, Dr. Kleinman. But, you see, my problem is not psychiatric but medical. I have lots of gastrointestinal symptoms, and I'm worried I may have cancer, cancer of the intestine. The studies have been normal, so far that is. Anyway, my, I mean the last doctor I saw, Dr. Lewis, a surgeon, recommended I see a psychiatrist, because he—like my regular physician and the other specialists I have visited—thinks my concern is, well, unreasonable. I mean they feel I am obsessed by this fear that I may have cancer. Now that's the problem. I know I'm anxious about this, but wouldn't you be if you felt like I do that there was the possibility of a cancer—potentially treatable if caught early—but you couldn't convince your doctors?

Arnie Springer does not have a delusion about intestinal cancer.

I'm not entirely sure it's there. In fact, often I think it can't be there with all these negative tests. But then I began to get my doubts. The more you go into this thing, the more doubts you have. I'm a Ph.D. in applied physics and a systems analyst. Now when I read the medical literature on the detection of cancer, I'm appalled, I mean really appalled. There are so many possibilities for false negatives [tests that give a misleadingly normal result by failing to detect existing pathology]. The science is really not all that good. And this probability thing is, well, for a physicist, deeply problematic. I mean, in physics we work with laws. Biomedicine doesn't have any real laws. Now probability is good enough if you're estimating the frequency of a problem, its prevalence in a group, perhaps. But probability is really unacceptable, at least to me it is, when you want absolute confidence about an individual, i.e., me.

Indeed, Arnie Springer occasionally can laugh at his intense preoccupation with intestinal cancer.

It really is absurd. What the hell am I doing challenging the experts' diagnoses and worrying so much about what everyone else feels is a figment of my imagination? I mean, it's laughable, it really is. Or it would be if I weren't spending so much time and money, my own money, on this thing.

I know it's an obsession. I really do doubt my own worry. I can look on at what I'm doing and think to myself, "This guy is mad." But the symptoms are real enough, though probably nonspecific. And the worry is there; I can't get rid of it. Sometimes—I can tell you this but could never tell my doctors or they would throw me out of the office—I am amazed at how upset I get and how seriously they take my worry. Other times I feel like I have to convince them or they won't believe me. What an absurd position to be in. I doubt them when they tell me, "There is nothing to worry about, you are OK," and I doubt them when they tell me there may be something the matter and they need to do more tests. After all, the exposure to X-rays is dangerous; even the scopes can perforate your colon. After I get through convincing them to do something, then I worry that I may be creating problems by what I convince them to do. I really know there is a good reason I'm here talking to you.

Arnie Springer has been hypochondriacal for a long time. Ten years ago persistent headaches led him to believe he had a brain tumor. After three years he came to accept his physician's diagnosis of chronic tension headaches. After that, he developed a fear that he had skin cancer. Inasmuch as he has many nevae (moles), Arnie went through repeated skin biopsies to rule out melanoma—all of them were normal—and even consulted a plastic surgeon about the possibility of extensive skin grafting. He recalls being fearful even as a child that he might be suffering a "hidden disorder."

That's the thing, Dr. Kleinman, the feeling I have is that this thing is hidden and we have got to find it. It's lurking there in the dark. It's a scary feeling, kind of like when you were a kid and afraid of the dark at the top of the stairs. I'm a systems analyst, you know, and I am always trying to organize things, make them better ordered. I guess you could say I don't like disorder, not even professionally.

The metaphor of the hidden disorder is pervasive in his complaints. "I feel a vague, cramping, queasy sensation, like pressure in my small intestine, you know the part of the bowel that's hidden, can't be seen too well by the GI [gastrointestinal] specialist, that part could have a hidden growth, a cancer." And almost always it is associated with the idea of cancer as a hidden killer.

You see, if we don't find it—I mean, if it stays hidden, then grows and metastasizes—silently, you know—it could kill you, I mean me. . . . You see, Dr. Kleinman, I can't accept that in a world as scientifically sophisticated as ours we can't be sure there isn't a hidden killer. With all the technology we've got, I want to know, and I want control over this possibility.

The Utterly Serious Worrier

Wolf Segal is a forty-one-year-old unemployed businessman with a strong conviction that he has a serious heart disease. He has visited emergency rooms of local hospitals more than ten times in the past eighteen months. Each time he complains of chest pain, numbness in his hands, shortness of breath, rapid breathing, and palpitations. He feels as if he is going to die.*

"They think I'm a nut, I'm sure they do. I can sense they are laughing behind my back, but I'm utterly serious about this problem. Each time I feel like I am dying."

Wolf Segal is worried about many things. He worries about finding a job at a level suitable for his skills. He also worries about the pressure he has put on his wife, a bank officer, to support them both. He worries about his parents, who are getting old; his investments, which have not been doing well recently; and his tennis game, which has never done well. But most of all, Wolf ("Just call me Wolf; I'm actually just a sheep in wolf's clothing, but call me Wolf") worries about his body: "It's deteriorating. Age is part of it; not enough exercise. I like eating too much. Cholesterol: that's what

---

*These symptoms are all consistent with panic attacks, a form of anxiety disorder. Previously this was called hyperventilation syndrome; now panic disorder is known to be one of the causes of hyperventilation.

gave my father his heart problem, and mine is the upper limit of normal." Wolf used to worry about hyperventilation—a long-term problem—asthma (he doesn't have it, but his grandfather did and his brother does), and diabetes ("It runs on my mother's side of the family"). He even worries about anxiety: "I'm an utterly serious worrier, the original worrier. Until you see me, you don't know what worrying is about." But for eighteen months his chief worry has been his heart: "They tell me I'm normal, completely normal. What nonsense! If I were normal, would I have the chest pain, the palpitations, or the numbness in my hands? They think I'm normal. Me! I know I'm not."

Wolf has been going to the same internist for almost ten years. He is the same physician who treats Wolf's father and mother.

Now Harry, that's my doc, he has a problem with me. He says that I am too serious about this heart condition. That I should relax, not worry so much, step away from it and it would go away. "Wolfy" (he's known me a long time), he says, "don't worry about it. There's no problem with your heart. It's with your nerves. Relax. Take your wife out to dinner. Have a good time." You'd think he didn't know me. When I have a problem, I worry. This is a problem, so I'm worried. Is he tellin' me this isn't a problem?

It is an odd experience speaking to Wolf Segal. You begin to think you are about to break out in laughter. It's as if he were a caricature of a hypochondriac, an ethnic one, to boot. But you realize after a while that Wolf, at least while he is in the office, is utterly serious.* He has no sense of humor about his fear of disease. About other things Wolf has, to say the least, a mischievous twinkle in his eye. He likes repartee, and he spices his remarks with a jaundiced earthiness that is endearing. But with respect to his symptoms he is an enormous bore. He goes on and on, often repeating himself several times, totally preoccupied.

I suggested to Wolf Segal that his problem was psychophysiological, a mixture of hyperventilation and panic and their physiological concomitants, and I suggested that treatment of his anxiety disorder and the personality characteristics that contributed to it could reduce the intensity of or actually remove his hypochondriasis. He acted as if he were stunned:

*I thought Woody Allen's performance in the movie *Hannah and Her Sisters* was reminiscent of Wolf Segal, but not quite as funny.

Doc, you mean I've seen you three times and *you* think there is nothing to worry about, too? The worrying is a personality problem or an anxiety disorder? I grant you I'm a worrier, anxiety neurotic if you like, but a hypochondriac? Me? Wolf Segal, who would give his right arm to be rid of these attacks of pain? A stoic, not a hypochondriac! If it sounds to you like amplification—is that the word you used?—I can assure you that's not what it feels like. I'm worried about a real problem in my body. Psychological problems I've got no time for. I wouldn't bother to worry about them. Maybe I emphasize the symptoms here so that you will know what it is like, what I am going through—torture. That's what it feels like. Not many people could stand what I go through. The heart, it's the problem. The other worries, they are something else. Put them aside. I've come to you with the real problem, my heart disease, and you treat me like Harry does. You don't believe. That hurts. Let me tell you about the symptoms I had after lunch today—and I didn't go to the emergency room, either. . . .

The Single-minded Interpreter

Gladys "Di" Isfahandiarian is a forty-nine-year-old unmarried Armenian-American interpreter for a large international organization in Washington, D.C. She was born in the Soviet Union and is fluent in seven languages: Armenian, English, Turkish, Persian, French, Italian, and Russian. She gives a history of more than fifteen years of chest discomfort: pressure, tenderness, dull and sharp pains, but mostly a feeling of "discomfort"—a term she expresses in all seven of her languages. "The terms are more or less similar—a vague, unsettling, apprehensive feeling in my chest, around the heart, it seems." For most of the fifteen years she has experienced these symptoms, Di has visited doctors for what she fears is heart and lung disease.

Probably it is both. It runs in the Isfahandiarian family. I am also a smoker, so there it is. . . . It is astonishing, almost unbelievable, but in all those years not one of the doctors could find anything wrong. I have undergone very many tests. Sometimes one shows a small abnormality, but in the end nothing. It is a terrible experience to go through all these years of illness and be left with, what? How shall I say it? Stripped of your identity. In limbo, you might say. I am neither well nor ill. My illness has no name. Oh! I have been told it is "stress-related," "psychosomatic," "hypochondriacal"—in other words, in my imagination. That is nonsense! If it were in my mind, would I feel it in my chest? Ridiculous! So why am I visiting a psychiatrist, and not the first either? To see if "psychological factors play a role and can be treated," says Dr. Tahardi. Well, what better way can I spend my time but speaking to a psychiatrist? Excuse the irritability, but much as I am delighted to meet you, and for certain will learn from speaking to a professor, my problem is in my chest, not my mind.

Di is a charming, cosmopolitan, well-traveled professional woman. But she begins or ends each of her well-turned statements about herself with either a description of her symptoms or a review of her fears of the consequences of her condition.

Probably I will die. They will say I lived too soon for medical science to define the nature of the pathology. "Isfahandiarian disease" they will call it perhaps, inasmuch as I seem to be an original. But that is only too foolish. My family is filled with people with the same problem. And they tell me in the old country this is a common problem. If I don't die from it—and there is no evidence I am that sick—I will be incapacitated. Already it takes up so much of my time, interfering with all sorts of activities. Even my interpreting is hampered.

Don't tell me about stress, doctor. And please don't speak about depression and anxiety. These are not the problems, I can assure you. The problem is here, right here, in the center of my chest—the heart and lungs are injured. Why do you need to know about my personal history? What possible relationship could it have to heart and lung disease?

I am thinking of willing my body to science. Perhaps only then will it be determined what is wrong with the cells, the tissues. But what tragedy! For when they discover the disease, I will be dead. Too late for me.

During the course of our several meetings, I found it extremely difficult to turn the conversation toward Di's feelings or personal life. I did learn eventually that her "heart and lung disease" is worsened by her tempestuous relationship with her long-term boyfriend, Nikki Kashli, who seems always on the point of marrying her, only to break off and beg for more time to "think about it."

What could he be thinking about? For eight years? Yes, yes. Nikki could be a reason my disease is worse. You are right. Look at what he is doing to my heart, and the lungs as well. He is a scoundrel! In The Magic Mountain one of Thomas Mann's characters says that passion is disease, or something like that. But I don't believe it is the cause, only one of many reasons my disease worsens.

In the last of our three meetings, Di complimented me: "I am pleased to see that you now ask me how my disease makes me feel? So you know now that you are dealing with a person with real disease. You must write this to my doctors. You can help me convince them that I am a heart and lung patient!" In that same session, Di told me:

> You are trying to interpret my illness one way, and me another. I feel there is a problem in translation, and here I am, the expert. I am talking about physical sensations—discomfort, pressure, a vague feeling of, of discomfort—you are talking of metaphors and double entendres. This is not a semantic disease; it is a disease in my body. Can the mind be in the body? I don't believe it. But then again, passion is in the heart we say, and if passion is a physical state, perhaps it worsens the disease already there. You are making me confused. The problem is simpler than you think. It is a heart and lung disorder.

The Memorializer of Death

Phillips Bingman is a fifty-five-year-old professor of the humanities in a large West Coast university. He is a tall, extremely thin man with close-cropped gray hair, wire-rim glasses, and prominent black eyebrows; his large face is made to look even larger by the thin bowties he wears. For the six years following the death of his wife from leukemia, Professor Bingman has been, in his own words, "obsessed with the radical realization that I am dying." He believes that his disorder is

> an imbalance, a fundamental imbalance in hormonal secretions. That is the problem. I have had thyroid disease for many years. Only one of the doctors I have visited could detect it. It seems to be transient, and extremely mild. For all I know it could be just an acceleration of the aging process. But my energy is running down. I can feel the life force petering out.*

Professor Bingman is the first to add, however: "The disease is not what bothers me. We all must die. And I feel myself confronting death. I know I am moving inexorably toward the grave. Every day I think of death, and it is a terrible burden. A cold hand has hold of me and won't let go. I feel death in my skin and in my bones." Phillips Bingman does not meet the criteria for depression or any

*The likelihood is that Bingman never had thyroid disease, but he did have one or two abnormal results in the dozen or so thyroid tests he has undergone. This is consistent with the probability of random laboratory error. I do know from his current internist that there is no laboratory evidence of active thyroid disease or clinical reason to suspect its presence.

other psychiatric disorder. But somehow hypochondriasis as fear of disease does not capture his true concern, which is less about the disease he believes he has than about death.

I am a memorializer of death. Like the Chinese literati of ancient times who wrote memorials to the emperor on various problems affecting the Confucian state, I hear myself memorializing death. I see it coming in so many different ways. I feel its slow, steady movement within. I am not delusional or hallucinating. I am just extremely sensitive to a process that I'm sure affects us all. I wish to hold it in place or delay its progress. I am, I am the first to admit, frightened of dying. I saw my wife die. It shocked me. Then I began to sense it in me. When I visit doctors, what can I say? Help me, please, I am dying and I am terribly fearful of dying? Perhaps I should say I see too clearly what everyone else disguises. But in my case the disease may be aging too rapidly, death coming on prematurely.

There are so many ironies. I know the literature, the great works on death. I read and reread them: Plato, Cicero, Marcus Aurelius, the early church fathers, Shakespeare, even modern authors. What good does it do? It certainly doesn't relieve my fear; it may worsen things. I also know it is a weakness, a moral weakness, a spiritual sickness, to be obsessed with death. But I seem to have identified the physical sensations that are those internal transformations through which we come to die. *Identified* is wrong. I should say learned to perceive and am now unable to cease observing. I feel like a naturalist watching a garden enter winter. I feel Petrarch's "freeze in summer," but it isn't love or lust but death, quite simply death, that I feel. I don't know what kind of help you give for this sort of thing. Fear of the physical experience of dying—premature, precocious fear. But it has taken over. I am no longer an historian looking at death from the outside; I am the history itself of a death.

Interpretation

It is possible—and, for the physician trained to do it, very easy—to write up a patient's case history or, as in the preceding cases, to select and arrange quotations from a transcript in order to demonstrate the classical signs and symptoms of a particular disease. And I am convinced that the same filter the doctor employs to write the case account is present in his professional mode of listening and inquiring about a patient's problems. From that welter of troubles, the classic disease is fashioned like a sculpture—in this case, a reproduction. Were I to describe these cases in their rich complexity, the differences between them would become more apparent. The trick for the master clinician is first to diagnose and treat the disease, so that the patient receives appropriate biomedical treatment, but then to regard it as an artifact of his diagnostic training in the symbolic forms of biomedicine. Technological intervention may ameliorate or even cure the disease but not the illness. To treat illness, the healer must dare to meet the patient in the messy, confusing, always special context of lived experience.

Disease is a psychobiological process of copying: it duplicates signs, symptoms, and behaviors. The paradox in human disorder is that out of such universal processes comes something specific to a culture and unique to a person. Surely, Arnie Springer, Wolf Segal, Di Isfahandiarian, and Phillips Bingman share nosophobia and other attributes of hypochondriasis. Yet that very fear of disease is elaborated into the "hidden killer," "utterly serious worries," "Isfahandiarian disease," and "the history itself of a death." In much the same way, each person in the context of shared culture creates an original identity out of similar patterns of dress, etiquette, food, aesthetic preference, and (in this instance) disease. Illness meanings, I submit, illumine the manner in which the transformation of the individual out of the group, the particular out of the general, occurs. Those meanings are both created by *and* create the transforming dialectic that makes Wolf Segal who he is and Di Isfahandiarian who she is.

Arnie Springer's illness experience is redolent of the mainline American cultural themes challenged by cancer: the secular engineering view of the world, the expectation of precise control over the physical environment and the body, the unwillingness to grant that life is inherently risky, the fear of hidden killers in our cells (and in our streets). Phillips Bingman also seems to locate a fearsome Western cultural image: after muscular and lithe youth and the robustness of early middle age pass, we move down the long slope of decline at the bottom of which death awaits us. Aging has become a disease in the contemporary West; Professor Bingman's exquisite yet morbid sensibility is as much a creation of that cultural transformation of normality into abnormality as of personal processes. Wolf's and Di's expressions are more ethnic, and thereby replicate more particular, less generalizable idioms and metaphors.

Nonetheless, the process of creating originality out of copying is the same.

The physician and family care givers are situated in the gap between copy and original. There is a great danger when they recognize only the copy. Medical journals and lectures are filled with comments such as "the hypochondriacal patient is . . . ," "all nosophobic patients are . . . ," and so forth. But even with what little I have done to sketch personal detail, Arnie Springer, Wolf Segal, Gladys Isfahandiarian, and Phillips Bingman can be appreciated as an odd lot to put under a single rubric. Their irrepressible humanity continues to break through as a celebration of remarkable differences: not just in who they are but in how they live their chronic illness. No diagnostic rubric should be authorized to describe those individuals and their illness experiences one-dimensionally, in a look-alike caricature that is carried over into treating them as if they were the same. The purpose of a diagnostic system, after all, is to guide treatment of a disease through a recognition of patterns. It is not meant to be a perfect representation of types of individuals or a guide to caring for their life problems. It is also the case that the copy should not be denied, the diagnosis jettisoned, lest the disease go untreated. There are similarities in the fears of hypochondriacal patients that can be treated if the fears are properly diagnosed and if the care givers are educated in what to do. But to provide humane care, healers must not lose sight of what is unique to each patient.

The ultimate irony in hypochondriasis is that it reminds us of a tension between the nature of life problems and the professional and family systems that respond to them. Mastery of the craft of healing—whether by the doctor or by the patient's spouse—like mastery of any other craft, begins with the memorization of rules, copying copies. That is the stage of the novice. What the master practitioner (and the accomplished family member) has learned is how to improvise from those copies, how to move beyond stereotyping and caricaturing, with all the dangers implicit in such routinization, toward healing, which is a fundamentally humanizing art.

Treating hypochondriasis is notoriously difficult. It is easy to see how practitioners and family members can joke about patients in order to relieve their own sense of inadequacy and failure. Not just the patient's disease, but the practitioner's and family member's response, is a copy. That copy of the therapeutic relationship often is demeaning and rejecting. Even the best of intentions may contribute to a worsening in the patient's condition: excessive concern can encourage a trajectory of help seeking with unnecessary hospitalizations, costly tests, dangerous treatments, and frustration on all sides. What can I recommend?

I have found that maintaining one's own sense of irony is a barrier to feelings of therapeutic helplessness and rage. Working with hypochondriacal patients and their families explicitly to increase their awareness of the multiple ironies we have reviewed can be a means of reducing the more disabling consequences of this chronic condition. I urge that hypochondriasis be treated as a language of distress and that care givers be taught to work within that language to use the same metaphors patients use. An approach to the language of hypochondriasis could be a useful complement to psychotherapeutic explorations of the life tensions and intimate pressures that intensify patients' fear of disease and their doubt of their own and their doctors' judgments. The systematic exploration of the meanings of hypochondriacal illness can become the basis of a therapy that also focuses on the ironical position of the protagonists as actors and onlookers simultaneously. Such therapy is still a long and difficult and uncertain passage. Many cases just barely manage to pull through, in large part because they are periodically revivified by a sense of the ironic.

14

The Healers: Varieties of
Experience in Doctoring

To write prescriptions is easy, but to come to an understanding
with people is hard.
> —Franz Kafka
> ([1919] 1971, 223)

As a physician, I am aware of how draining and threatening
empathy for helpless, injured people can be. I know how hard it
is to hold on to compassion when all of one's invested power and
energy seems helpless against the tide of fate. . . . As a patient,
I felt more alone, more helpless, more terrified, and more enraged
than I now believe I had to be.
> —Judith Alexander Brice
> (1987, 32)

Men that look no further than outside think health an appurte-
    nance unto life and quarrel with our condition of being sick,
But I who have looked at the innermost parts of man and known
    what tender filaments that fabric hangs on oft wonder that we
    are not always so,
And considering the thousand doors that lead to death do thank
    my God that I can die but once.
> —Thomas Browne
> *Religio Medici*, 1643

Eight Medical Lives

The following brief sketches of the clinical lives of eight physicians
can hardly do justice to the manifold work of doctoring among the
chronically ill, or to the variety of practitioners routinely encountered by the chronically ill. It would take an entire book to depict

adequately the range of experiences of clinicians. Even this truncated account, however, compels the recognition that care of the
chronically ill is difficult yet specially rewarding, that who the practitioner is as a person is as essential to care as the personality of the
patient, that taking care of those with chronic suffering is far different from what is projected in our society's dominant technological
and economic images of health care.

The great majority of social science studies of doctoring examine
either the socialization of the physician in medical school and residency training or the influence of professional norms and personal
preoccupations on the patient–physician encounter (see Hahn and
Gaines 1985). They study how physicians learn to deal with uncertainty or with failure (Fox 1959; Bosk 1979). They study problems
in the application of technology or ethical dilemmas in practice
(Reiser 1978; Veatch 1977). They study the language of care
(Mishler 1985) or the transformation of formal textbook knowledge
into the rank-and-file professional's working technical knowledge
(Freidson 1986). Like the study of illness experience, studies of the
experience of doctoring are principally external accounts, more concerned with the influence of social forces (which are indeed powerful) than with the actual workings of care. Where care is the subject,
the relationship between patient and practitioner properly moves
to center stage.

Practitioners often feel that these externalist academic accounts,
for all their analytical power, leave something out that is of vital
salience for them: namely, the internal, felt experience of doctoring,
the story of what it is like to be a healer. Physicians have turned to
fiction and essay to convey this inner world of the clinician. The
ethnography of the physician's care lags far behind the phenomenological description of the experience of illness. We know more about
the patient than the healer. We do not possess an adequate scientific
language to capture the essence of the doctor's experience. What the
doctor feels is most at stake—what is most relevant to practice—
slips through our crude analytical grids.

An examination of the meanings of chronic illness would be
dangerously incomplete without the voice of the healer, the practitioner's account. In chapters 7, 9, and 11, I have briefly featured
physicians whose practice has either facilitated or impeded the care

of the chronically ill. Now I write of care from the perspective of the practitioner. Inasmuch as I share this experience, this is my perspective, too. Perhaps if we can get it right from the healer's point of view, we can achieve a higher degree of discrimination in our understanding of what makes care of the chronically ill sometimes such a heartening success and at other times such a dispiriting failure.

THE WOUNDED HEALER AND THE NEED TO BE OF USE

Paul Samuels is a fifty-two-year-old internist in a large midwestern city. He is in private practice, a member of a four-man group that shares evening, weekend, and vacation call. Each day he sees between twenty-five and thirty-five patients in his office and in the hospital. He begins work at 6:30 A.M. with hospital rounds, and ends the day in his office at 7:00 P.M. On Saturdays, he sees patients in the morning only. On Wednesday afternoons, he teaches medical students in the general medical clinic of the medical school, then works in the library, catching up with the professional literature. Every fourth night and weekend, he is on call for all the patients in the group practice.

Paul Samuels's chief interest is the care of patients with serious chronic medical disorders. Such patients constitute most of his practice. Paul attributes this interest to his having grown up with a diabetic father who died, following progressive complications of the disease, when Paul was twelve. He also believes that his own experience with asthma since the age of twelve has made him a more compassionate and effective care giver for the chronically ill.

It came on like a bolt out of the blue, while my father was dying. I've lived with it ever since. You might say it was my first clinical teacher. In fact, I think my sickness and my experience of Dad's made me a doctor. No, medical school made me a doctor. But those experiences made me a *healer*.

It took years before I learned to control my illness. Asthma made me feel different as an adolescent: hesitant and vulnerable. I couldn't come to terms with it at first. I was embarrassed to be sick. But, like Dad's death, I worked through the pain and the loss. Finally, I did it. I knew, even though it was still there, I had it licked. I think in that experience are several big lessons. First, I learned about illness as a life burden, a threat to your sense of confidence and control. Then I learned how to live with it. Get enough rest. Plan my life around it. Avoid the things that precipitated an attack. That must be what Osler had in mind when he said the chronically ill learn how to live a long life. Finally, I learned a great lesson in caring for others. To be wounded himself, the healer knows what suffering is like. There is no better training in the experience of illness. There was also something else tied to being ill and also caring for Dad. There was a need to be of help. To be of use gave me a sense of who I was. It kind of morally centered my identity. And it's been that way ever since.

Dr. Samuels's colleagues are unanimous in their praise of his commitment to and work with patients. One said:

He is your old fashioned doc, all right. His life is devoted to practice. He works hard to hone his skills. He spends more time with patients than anyone I know. He visits his patients in their homes. He stays as late as necessary to see everyone who comes for as long as he can. He seems to thrive in what makes most of us burn out. For me he is a model of what is best in medicine. But he is not infallible or someone from another planet. No, I think it's his humanness that is special. He is chronically ill himself. He knows what it's like to be there himself. You can see it in the way he prepares himself to meet the needs of his patients even if they can't express them.

Said another colleague:

If I had a serious illness, I'd want Paul to be my doctor. There is a courtesy, a quiet sensitivity, in his character. How often do you see that together with real technical competence? I think it must make patients feel that he is specially concerned about them. We all do pretty much the same thing, but he affects them more. Speak to his patients; they will tell you. What makes him so rare is the sense they have that he will do everything for them, and a little bit more.

I did speak with some of his patients, including a thirty-five-year-old contractor with diabetes.

You mean Doc Samuels? What makes him so darn good? I don't know, but they ought to patent it. He is the genuine article. He listens. Doc Samuels knows what you're going through. I don't know, it feels like—well, you know, like he's there with you, right with you while you go through a bad spell, an emergency. He wants you to get better. Sometimes I think I feel like he needs you to get better.

Said another patient, a working-class woman with cancer:

How can I explain it to ya. I don't feel it's what he do so much as what he don't do. He don't get impatient. I never seen him irritable or cold. Hell, now that I think of it, in my experience that's 90 percent of the problem with medicine. From the receptionist to the nurses and specialists, they got no time for ya. He's, why Dr. Samuels, is the opposite. I mean, he's got a hell of a lot of patients, real busy. There ain't so much time. But I guess what he do during the time he's with ya is what counts, what is most special about him. Dr. Samuels cares what is happening to ya. He remembers what ya been through. Ya feel good just bein' with him. Hell, sometimes I can feel better just talking to him on the telephone. The symptoms, the pain it gets less listenen' and tellin' him.

A tall, angular, balding man with a close-clipped salt-and-pepper beard, Paul Samuels is a family man with few interests beyond his family—his wife, four adolescent children, aging parents, and three brothers and their families—and his patients.

Medicine doesn't interest me nearly as much as people. In fact, I almost dropped out of med school because I found all the science dull and irrelevant. I wanted to take care of real people, not occupy my time with chemical equations and microscope slides. I work hard at keeping up with the latest developments. I want to be technically first rate. After all, that's what patients need. But that is only the mechanical aspect of care. I feel what really counts is the human aspect. That is both a lot tougher and a lot more rewarding. It is a great privilege being a healer. Entering patients' life worlds and listening to their pain, helping them make sense of their suffering, helping them to cope with the burden of disease—all that is what makes my work rewarding. Frankly, I can't think of not doing it. In some way, I need to be a healer, I need to be of use to others. That's my self-image. I guess you would say that is my identity. Doubtless it has something to do deep down with the guilt I felt in not being able to help Dad. Maybe it also has to do with my sense of self-worth: in adolescence I was pretty uncomfortable, uncertain rather. I felt kind of lost. I think becoming a care giver changed all that. It is what is most meaningful in my life. I don't mean to sound romantic or nostalgic, but this is not simply a job. It is a way of life, a moral discipline.

Paul Samuels's wife Rita uses different words that reveal some of the difficulties this healer's commitment creates for his family, but she also confirms her husband's self-image:

I, I mean we, the kids and I, used to get real upset with Paul, with the way he gets taken up into his patients' problems. And do some of them have problems! I mean Paul can't let go like other doctors. He worries about them. They are important to him. Maybe—or at least I used to think so—maybe too important. Sometimes I think he would be lost without his patients. Sometimes I wonder what would happen if we retire. But I don't think he could retire. He'd lose something that anchors him, just like he would if something happened to our family.

THE BURDENS OF CARE

Andrew M. Spier, a rotund, smiling figure, is a forty-six-year-old internist in a large metropolitan community hospital. He is a specialist in gastrointestinal disorders. Andy Spier started off in medical research but became a full-time practitioner six years ago, primarily for financial reasons. He still regards himself as more academically oriented than most of his peers, and in his spare time he is participating with several of his former colleagues in a clinical epidemiological project on chronic liver disorders.

What I need, to be perfectly frank, is a sabbatical from full-time clinical work. Then I could get back to my academic interests. I just don't have the time I need for them. What is more, I feel like I am burning out of clinical work. There is only so much you can tolerate—all the problems, the calls, all the patients and families. I didn't bargain for this when I went into private practice. I had no idea it would be so hard. By the end of the week I feel I can barely stand it anymore. This is definitely not what I went into medicine for. I'm more intellectually inclined. Here I'm a high-price mechanic and nurse rolled into one. If it wasn't for the money, I'd get out, go back to research in the laboratory. The more I get away from it, the more I realize I was happiest when there were no calls to family members, no listening all the time to people complain. Everyone seems to want something from me. I feel the need to protect myself, my involvement with patients. If I could only do, just do the cognitive side and leave the emotions, the family, the whole mess to someone else. I feel like patients are sucking me dry. They want so much, every one of them. If this keeps up, I'll either burn out in another year or two or become a danger to patients and myself.

NIGHT THOUGHTS OF A HEALER

Hiram Bender is a sixty-five-year-old family physician; he is a ruddy-faced, slow-moving native of the area of New England where he has practiced for almost forty years. Dr. Bender, who writes essays and short stories under a sobriquet, is an intellectual who has thought hard for many years about the moral lessons of medical practice. A noted local raconteur, Bender spent one long winter evening with me soliloquizing about the intractably human nature of illness. He talked about the menacing modern transformation of medical care. He offered dozens of luminous cameos from an immense store of professional experience in support of his contention that healing is rooted in an archaic human endeavor whose ancient lineaments—shamanism and priestly functions and poetic insights into the darker side of man's soul—are more a part of religion, philosophy, and art than of science.

Don't get me wrong. I'm not against science. Far from it. If I've learned anything these forty years, it's that we physicians need all the science we can get and master. But that is not really what the practice of medicine has been and still is about. You read William Carlos Williams—as great a practitioner in my mind as an artist. He got it right. Care involves you almost always in a tangle of relations, a web of personalities, a—as rich and pungent a stew of humankind as there is, including our own fears, aspirations, and needs as healers. This is . . . the messy world of deep emotion and human actions. Intellectuals like us are, are more comfortable talking about the model of the text as a model of human behavior, illness as theory. Well, theory is crucial to illness, all right; but illness is about pain, blood loss, skipped heartbeats, fears that can't be easily expressed, panic, downright terror. It is about action, not just thought.

A few weeks later, I had the invigorating opportunity to observe Dr. Bender in practice for a day. I asked more about his ideas of care between cases and at the end of an exhausting day. I have selected the following observations from many hours of talk.

I think for the doctor who can tolerate ambiguity and the sheer uncertainty of chronic states, there is, there is no longer the threat of failing or the threat of death; rather there is a, a basis to understand the human nature of human nature. . . . In a few clinical encounters there is the whole gamut of emotions and intruding moral dilemmas that take an entire novel to unfold. Each patient is a story. The doctor enters that story like a traveler lost in a forest, and more quickly than in the rest of life he learns to find his way. That recognition of the living structure of a life narrative is one of the greatest gifts that work as a physician can provide. You start with jaundice. You learn it is a pancreatic cancer—cancer of the head of the pancreas blocking the bile ducts—you then learn about the life struggle of a cancer patient. Then it's no longer a cancer patient, but Julia Jones, John Smith, Bill Schwartz—their families, their marriages, their work, their hopes, their terror, their world. You leave medicine behind and enter a life. . . . Medicine is concerned with the problem of keeping you alive; but serious illness asks the question for you, What is life for?

Medicine must be at heart a moral enterprise. How else would anyone be authentic in this thing for years on years? Oh, I don't mean the doctor is a moral paragon—far from it. Doctors are the same as the rest of mankind: greedy, envious, easily threatened, and dangerous when pushed too far by the sheer . . . exigency of living. But to care for humans is to be *human* and to see the limits and failures and also successes of our small humanity writ large in the struggle to help someone who hurts and fears and just plain is in need. The moral lesson is that this is what our life is about, too, what we must prepare for. I think at heart it's about the simple realities in life that all of life covers over because they are precisely that: too simple, too real.

Sometimes I hate what I do, but most of the time I accept it as a way of life that has made me, given me a special vision of our shared humanity. Not always ennobling; often downright negative. But frequently enough as inspiring in a poetical way as anything I have read or heard of. I don't know what will happen to this side of medicine as we make medical practice so highly technical and so dominated by cost accounting, bureaucratic rules, and an adversarial relationship with patients. Perhaps we are killing what is best in this ancient profession, like so much else in modern living. We replace intuition and emotion and moral passion with ever more minute rationality and turn questions about ends—the big ends: death, disability, suffering—into tinkering with technology. Leaving us where? I don't know. In my darker moments I think we are at the end of medicine as I know it and value it. But then again, you are talking to a crotchety old man at odds with the images of his age, annoyed by an itch he can't locate, a bad spot that burns like all evil but can't be pinpointed. A corrosive, corroding grain at the human core that is pushing us over the edge.

A few months later, Dr. Bender visited me and we ended our colloquy with a final interview. Just before we parted, he insisted I take down this statement as a final thought on doctoring.

Somewhere, one of the rabbis of old said that the world is good if we only don't lose our hearts to it, but bad, awfully bad when we do. Being a doctor has made that seem true to me, not only in the experience of illness but in the experience of doctoring—something we know all too darn little about. You need time away and out from both kinds of experiences. I guess technically we say you need the mask of medicine, the professional persona, to distance yourself from what otherwise can overwhelm you. When you doctor in the practical world of sickness, you can't think about these things. You've got to act. You've got to make tough choices. Say awful truths. Stand there and do things that cause as much pain as they help. Well, but later, at night, you begin to think. No persona or mask then. Then it hits you: all the complexity, the threat to your sensitivity of the realities of personal tragedy and the social consequences of your actions. After midnight, the professional protection is gone. You, you feel very alone, vulnerable. The magnitude of the moral effects of your decisions and actions become upsetting images, intruding thoughts that keep you awake or, worse still, become dreams, nightmares. That is the hour of truth for the clinician. For most of us who struggle to be authentic in our work it is bad enough. But for those who hide their humanity behind professional and institutional barriers, who can't handle the human side of sickness, it must be awful. No one prepares you for this, this assault on your sense of being—a much more troubling and difficult-to-shake feeling than the self-questioning about the limits of our professional competency.

THE REVOLUTIONIZING ENCOUNTER

Lenore Light is an intense twenty-nine-year-old internist who comes from an upper middle class black family and works in an inner-city ghetto clinic. Her clinical experience has been the first sustained contact she has had with what she calls

our black underclass: the poorest, the most miserable, the most chaotic, the oppressed and oppressive reminder of where we have all of us come from.

It has radicalized me; it is a revolutionary encounter with the social sources of mortality and morbidity and depression. The more I see, the more appalled I am at how ignorant I have been, insensitive to the social, economic, and political causes of disease. We learned about these things in the abstract in med school. Here it is a living reality, a medical hell. What we need is prevention, not the Band-Aids I spend my day putting on deep inner wounds.

Today I saw an obese hypertensive mother of six. No husband. No family support. No job. Nothing. A world of brutalizing violence and poverty and drugs and teenage pregnancies and—and just plain mind-numbing crises, one after another after another. What can I do? What good is it to recommend a low-salt diet, to admonish her about control of her pressure? She is under such real outer pressure, what does the inner pressure matter? What is killing her is her world, not her body. In fact, her body is the product of her world. She is a hugely overweight, misshapen hulk who is a survivor of circumstances and lack of resources and cruel messages to consume and get ahead impossible for her to hear and not feel rage at the limits of her world. Hey, what she needs is not medicine but a social revolution.

Come into our ER [emergency room] and see case after case after case of alcohol-related violence, drug abuse and toxicity, chronic illnesses unattended to for years, health habits of the kind, the kind that must break the body down, and fragmented, alienated lives. Come and see it. And what can you do but go home and cry and promise yourself there has got to be some way to prevent another generation from succumbing, to save the children. This experience is making me over into something, someone else. Franz Fanon must have come out of some world like this.* What can I do?

THE CYNIC

Benjamin Winterhouse IV is a pediatrician in a wealthy suburb of a large northeastern conurbation who specializes in adolescent medicine. A fourth-generation physician in an old New York family with an illustrious medical tradition, Ben is quick to describe himself as a cynic:

Yeah, I'm cynical about medicine. How can you not be? The medical-legal crisis makes all of us run scared—not just of malpractice, but failure to provide fully informed consent about medications, and even maloccurrence [lack of improvement]. What a world. Everyone expects to get better. No one is supposed to become a chronic case, an invalid, or die. Frankly, I'm tired of it all. The only thing to do in a bad time like this is keep your head down, don't make waves, and try like the dickens to not make any mistakes—and cover your ass in case you do or think you might have. You write defensive explanatory notes in the chart with one eye on peer review, the other on a potential jury trial. You try to avoid angering patients for fear they will turn on you. You go by the book. Which means you are more involved with paperwork and phone calls to drug firms, consultants, and your insurance company and lawyer than with patients.

*Franz Fanon, the author of *The Wretched of the Earth* (1968) and other revolutionary texts, was a French-trained psychiatrist in Algeria who was radicalized by his experiences during the Algerian War.

You try to size up high-risk families and refer them elsewhere. I mean high-risk in terms of quarrels and legal actions. What a way to practice medicine. It's not the way I was taught, and goes against my family tradition; but it's the only way to survive.

As for your chronic illness, everyone seems to be pushing something. Take irritable bowel syndrome in adolescents. I see lots of cases, lots. Well, one pediatrician says it's stress. Another, it's food allergy and diet generally. Another, it's family problems or school problems. The child psychiatrists say one thing; the gastroenterologists another. If you are a true-believer sort, you talk yourself into a single cure. That's how you make money, too: push a gimmick. The fact is, nobody knows the cause. The course is uncertain. The treatment is even more so. If you're honest with patients, they feel disappointed and leave your care for the latest fad. I see lots of problems like that: tension headaches, back pain, asthma, fatigue following the flu, you name it. Take eczema. I must have heard a dozen different theories from dermatologists. And the psychosomatic theories! My population is big on psychology, holistic medicine, massage, group therapy, lectures on mind-body connections, psychoneuroimmunology, acupuncture. They know all the psychoanalytic and behavioral medicine theories, including ones you never heard of. It makes me terribly skeptical and negative.

All right, I'm cynical—about a lot of things in life. I find myself doubting what patients say, especially parents of patients. Social workers are most dangerous: they think everyone is a child abuser. Drug salesmen pushing the latest pills for hyperactivity like they were selling dope. Laboratory reps trying to get you to set everyone up for screening with the latest blood tests. Even psychological tests scored by computers. You really don't know who or what to believe. I see a lot of complainers. I just don't believe what they tell me. They are too soft, too weak. They can't tolerate any level of discomfort.

You know, it has gotten so bad, I sometimes find myself daydreaming that I am no longer in practice but in some other field, not medicine. I told my kids: Don't, don't go into medicine. It has all changed. What they want is technicians or businessmen, not doctors. Let your readers hear what I have to say. Medicine is going down the tubes, along with the rest of society. I'm fed up with it.

THE COMMODITIZATION OF THE HEALER

Helen McNaughton is a thirty-nine-year-old psychiatrist in a very busy primary care unit, a freestanding component of a large West Coast health maintenance organization (HMO). A lively physician with high professional standards and smooth southern grace, Dr. McNaughton is debating leaving the HMO and opening her own office, because of her concern that the institutional structure works against "good care" for chronic patients. She spoke with a soft Mississippi accent and a slow cadence and slight stutter that I have not tried to reproduce, but which lent charm to her words and gave her images a striking effect.

Let's just consider care. Now care is supposed to be what the doctor does. But well, care has become a commodity. It is a "product" of the HMO. They measure it, cost-analyze it, and market it. It can be overused or underpriced. You, the doctor, dispense it. Y'all must not provide too much of it. Yeah, the less, in fact, the better.

If the patient gets to see you, having fought her way through an obstacle course of receptionists, nurses, social workers, psychologists, and physician assistants set up to protect you—the high-priced specialist whose care is expensive to the system—well, if the patient, after all that, if she gets to you (and really she just is not supposed to do that), why, then, the system has failed. Because we are supposed to keep patients away, not run up costs. Chronic patients are to stay out of hospitals, because it costs a lot. And when in the clinic, they are to receive care from lower paid professionals. Cost is everything. The images, the very language is financial. Well, darn it, good care is expensive. Money talk doesn't accurately describe care; it distorts it.

When I learned to become a psychiatrist, I learned to practice the best care I am capable of giving. It was a magical experience, like an artist in an atelier slowly working to perfect her work. It was—enchanting. Now it's disenchantment, like being a worker in a factory turning out a standardized assembly-line product. The HMO comes between my patient and me. It alienates us.

And if the patient doesn't get better, why then shift the blame to them. They don't want to improve badly enough. They are unmotivated. Yeah, it's their fault. Psychosomatic—has a word ever been more misused?—that's what's responsible. Anyway, it's their responsibility, not ours. I find myself spending half the time debunking these silly, misleading notions, and the other half diagnosing treatable psychiatric conditions in medical patients that are disguised by all this psycho babble nonsense, or that social workers and nurses can't diagnose.

The system calls patients clients. But the only really good one is the client who doesn't show, doesn't bother the HMO. Get rid of patients fast; that, sir, is the agenda. Frankly, I would prefer to practice where there is less, much less bureaucracy, and, yeah, more humanity. Y'all may call me a dreamer, but I know care can and should be much better than this. I don't want to talk suicidal patients into staying out of the hospital because we are already over our limit for hospitalization. I don't want to *manage clients,* I want to *care for patients.* I don't want to hide behind bureaucratic regs and physician assistants. I want to do the caring.

THE SENSITIVE NEOPHYTE

Beaseley Will is a twenty-three-year-old medical student beginning his introductory course in clinical medicine. He has just interviewed his third patient, a fifty-five-year-old laborer with cancer of the lungs.

I felt so bad for him. I mean, I just listened, and didn't know what to say. There is no question about the diagnosis. They've exhausted the treatment alternatives. This guy, this poor man, is going to die, and he knows it. The chemotherapy has just made him toxic; it hasn't touched the tumor. I listened to him and felt so bad. He started to cry. I felt like crying, too. Shouldn't show my emotions, I thought to myself. It scared me. What would I do if I had lung cancer or if my dad or mom had it? What do you say to a terminal patient? I felt so helpless, so lonely and unprepared. Am I too sensitive? Listening to him made me feel so bad. Maybe that's why doctors don't listen. How can you take it every day?

You know, I feel a kind of awe when I am with a patient. They are going through so much. And there's me just listening, trying to learn, a kind of observer but with nothing I can do. I try to compensate for the feeling of, of impotence by just listening harder, trying to show I want to understand what they are experiencing. I'm troubled burdening sick people with my needs as a clinical beginner. Someday I know I'll be able to help because of this experience. But still I want to give something back to the patients for being so helpful to me, a student.

I guess the residents think we are too innocent, too vulnerable. They tell jokes, seem hardened, inured to misery and distress. I guess I'll be like that one day, and not so far away either, from what I hear. But if so, I think I will have lost something important. Maybe because I've only been in med school for two years, I feel closer to patients. I mean I'm not that far away from being a layman. I guess you're not supposed to feel like that when you're a busy resident. It kind of frightens me. Do I want to be like them? I went into medicine to help sick people, not to put them down or avoid human issues. Yet, like in my case, those issues are so big, so threatening. What can you do about them? It must get easier than this.

A CHINESE HEALER

Gu Fangwen is a forty-nine-year-old practitioner of the ancient art and science of traditional Chinese medicine. He is bald, and has a delicate face and laughing eyes. A pale and frail physician of exquisite sensitivity, Dr. Gu runs the herbal medicine and acupuncture clinic at a large hospital in a southern Chinese city. He is an expert in the use of *qi gong* (a traditional breathing exercise) for "stress-related" problems, and he is renowned for the treatment of patients with chronic illnesses. Dr. Gu is the scion of a family that claims practitioners of Chinese medicine in each of the past seven generations. His father and grandfather were noted diagnosticians.

In the Chinese medical classics the great doctors are shown diagnosing complex cases from the pulse. They don't take a history. Rather they tell the patient and family what the complaints are from reading the pulse. I think that is nonsense! No practitioner—in Chinese or Western medicine—can help the patient unless he first understands the setting of the illness and the events that contribute to it. We must begin with the account of the patient's history. We must put ourselves in the patient's situation to understand what they feel. Now, I have been in practice for almost three decades. This is what I have learned. Chronic illness takes a long time to treat. We must proceed slowly, cautiously. The patient must be in harmony, in balance with his body and his world. Diet, exercise, work, rest, family, and other relations—all must be harmonious, or else the body is susceptible to a worsening of disease or new disorders. Even emotions may influence health. Treatment for the chronic patient must harmonize all these things. But treatment is hard. I mean, treating a patient with a chronic problem is never easy. You must look into the patient's condition deeply, as deeply as you gaze into his disorder. Treating the disorder alone is insufficient. In traditional Chinese medicine, every treatment is individualized, because though the disease may be the same the persons differ. You must make the treatment individual, too.

I don't really know much about Western medicine, but in Chinese medicine we are taught to educate the patient to become a doctor for his own health. That is not easy. You need to learn how to talk to patients and to listen to them. You must not criticize them too strongly, or they will not listen or even return. But you must not be silent, either, or they cannot benefit. You must search for contradictions in their bodies and in their lives. That is dialectical practice. These contradictions must be resolved so that natural harmony is restored, and the way to health is opened.

You saw that last patient with me. She suffers from an insufficiency in *yin* and an imbalance in the relationship between heart and spleen. But she also is a difficult personality. She angers her husband and children. They, they have no compassion for her; the family's harmony is broken. She has no balance in her emotions. This is all part of the contradiction in her body. To treat her we must treat each of these problems, though diet, tonics, and herbal medicine are most important. It is not easy. It takes a long time. This patient certainly is difficult. The result is still uncertain.

The doctor must believe in the treatment in order to convince the patient to persist and not to give up hope. We try to convince the patient to change. Even after treating more than ten thousand patients, I feel the difficulty of treating this woman successfully. She is convinced she is ill and cannot become better. That is dangerous. She is making the problem worse. I must educate her better about the condition of her illness and health. She must struggle for balance. I am not at all satisfied with my treatment for her problem.

When I was a student, I thought practice would be easy once I had mastered the medical classics. But I find practice is always difficult. The more I experience, the more I see that it is difficult to be a good doctor and give effective treatment. Nothing in chronic illness is clear. It takes all one's skill and knowledge to avoid error. The work of the doctor is a struggle to apply the ideas of our practice to experiences that are always different. This, too, is the dialectic of medicine.

Medicine for us is more than a profession. It is a way of living; it is a wisdom about life; it is knowledge and action, concepts and experience combined. It takes an entire lifetime to understand how to treat patients. When the treatment is right, you can feel it is so. You know it from experience. There is a natural method to treatment. You heal the patient. But where the treatment is right, you feel it yourself, in your body, in your emotions, in your relation with the patient. When the treatment goes badly, it is not just the patient who feels blocked but the doctor, too. Her illness, her failure to improve affects me. Is this not your experience? I will tell you, in old China, Chinese doctors claimed to have "secret knowledge" of herbs and ancient family remedies. For me the secret knowledge is knowledge of the patient and his relationship with you and others.

Interpretation

For Paul Samuels, Hiram Bender, Helen McNaughton, and Gu Fangwen medical practice is more than the professional job it is for Andy Spier. Healing is the center of gravity of Dr. Samuels's life. He tells us that becoming a healer resolved a key tension in his adolescent development and adult personality. Anthropologists studying healers in non-Western societies often elicit similar accounts (Kleinman 1980). Not infrequently a powerful illness experience leads a patient into the healer's role. (For example, Hadley Eliot, in chapter 9, had a serious brush with death in a car accident, after which he began his hospice work.) Paul Samuels's chronic illness sensitizes him to the experience of suffering. He also feels a need to be effective. There is a deeply personal basis to this need. His personality is part of his therapeutic work. Thousands of miles away, in a radically different culture and society, Gu Fangwen reports a therapeutic sensibility that is also anchored in personal experience, though its sources and conception are rather different. Hiram Bender's words suggest that this experiential core of doctoring is a moral domain that is not reducible to the now-dominant technical and economic metaphors used to model therapeutic relationships. For Dr. Bender each patient is a life story, and treatment means entering that peculiar life world. Helen McNaughton is deeply troubled by the constraints placed on her therapeutic skills by the institution in which she practices psychiatry. She laments the transformation of the healer's art into mere technique, the crude seduction of care into a money-making commodity.

Dr. Gu Fangwen, expressing himself in the cultural idioms and tropes of an entirely different civilization, says something similar to Hiram Bender. Both practitioners see themselves as students of human nature, teachers of moral wisdom.* They do not deny the importance of the technical tradecraft and theory of their professions. But they see their craft's moral aspects as equally central.

*I think the notion of clinical wisdom that Drs. Bender and Gu allude to is what Isaiah Berlin describes as the "ability to allow for the . . . unalterable medium in which we act . . . and to discount, less or more consciously, the 'inevitable trends,' the 'imponderables,' the 'way things are going.' It is not scientific knowledge, but a special sensitiveness to the contours of the circumstances in which we happen to be placed" (1978, 72). It is not wisdom primarily about the tradecraft of medicine; rather, it is an insight into lived experience and its meanings.

This is not Andy Spier's vision. For him, private practice is an almost intolerable burden. He wants to get out. He fears that if he continues in practice he will not merely burn out but become a danger to his patients and himself. His chief interests are concerned with the biology of disease; the psychosocial aspects of care are an intolerable intrusion into the scientific approach that he finds both personally preferable and professionally appropriate. One suspects that Andy Spier's patients (like Dr. Richards's patient Mrs. Flowers and Dr. Jones's patient Mrs. Lawler in chapter 7) would tell different stories about their care than would Paul Samuels's. Most practitioners in my experience are neither Andy Spiers nor Paul Samuels. Rather, they fall somewhere in between on this continuum which has as one end overriding concern for the science of treating disease and as the other a central interest in the art of healing illness. Effective care requires both skills, but relative inattention to the latter is particularly problematic in the care of the chronically ill.

Benjamin Winterhouse's and Helen McNaughton's disturbing experiences illustrate how the social transformation of American medicine has created bureaucratic and legal constraints that convert the role of healer into that of technician, functionary, even adversary. That Drs. Samuels, Bender, McNaughton have persevered as healers in spite of these changes indicates that there are other, more personal reasons for Dr. Winterhouse's predicament than sociopolitical and socioeconomic determinants.

How does Beaseley Will's student idealism become transformed into Benjamin Winterhouse's corrosive cynicism? Can this process be prevented? Embarrassing as it is to say, as a medical educator I have come to suspect that something in the system of training health professionals contributes to this undesirable value change. Benjamin Winterhouse, when he was twenty-three, may very well have spoken like Beaseley Will, who in turn may yet come to see patients and doctors much as Dr. Winterhouse sees them. Yet Helen McNaughton avoids this self-defeating cynicism, in spite of powerful institutional pressures to the contrary, and fashions her criticisms into a personal quest for a professional setting more conducive to humane care; her story is a heartening reminder that Benjamin Winterhouse's is not an inevitable trajectory.

Lenore Light has reached a political position far removed from Benjamin Winterhouse's upper middle class alienation. Having been exposed to the social origins of human misery and having become aware of how inadequate care for the poor and powerless has contributed to the prevalence of preventable morbidity and mortality, this young black physician has been radicalized. Too narrow a focus on healing may blind the practitioner to the crucial public health component of care as effectively as exclusively financial interests or a nihilistic vision of the purpose of medicine. Lenore Light's experience should convince us that medicine is inseparable from society, that the doctor is rooted in particular social circumstances, which, as much as professional culture and personal values, mold her vision.

What would it be like to visit these different healers for care? Expressions of personal convictions and professional values don't necessarily predict therapeutic behavior, though they indicate the kinds of concerns we should have about potential problems in care. We all want a Paul Samuels to be our physician in time of need; few of us end up with such a healer. As the words of these physicians indicate, the societal forces in our health care and medical education system make it ever less likely we will turn out or maintain in practice a Paul Samuels. Can we model what Paul Samuels, Hiram Bender, Helen McNaughton, and Gu Fangwen know and do so that we can teach it to others? Can we do something about medical education and practice to keep practitioners from becoming Any Spiers or James Blanchards (chapter 7)? Are Benjamin Winterhouse's attitude and Helen McNaughton's clinic detrimental to effective care? Can the health care delivery system be altered to protect against the negative effects on patients, families, practitioners of burn-out and cynicism and commoditization of care? Can Lenore Light's political commitment and Beaseley Will's idealism be harnessed to remake our medical system into one with less inequality and more humane care? In the final two chapters, I turn to address these questions.

Before closing this discussion, I want to emphasize that care of the chronically ill is difficult and burdensome for even the most attentive and gifted of healers. As Slaby and Glicksman write:

We all want physicians to be sensitive, warm human beings. We also want them to be professional; they must function in spite of the realities of our tragedies. We cannot expect them to be both to their fullest. Professionalism is, to a degree, a mask. In professionalism's finest form, physicians who don the mask are forever aware that they are wearing it. They may hold it with tremulous hands, but they know its necessity. They must weigh data objectively, make rapid decisions, and confront problems in a manner inspiring confidence during our most dreaded crises . . . and even our moments of death (1987, 165).

Professional training, in principle then, should make it feasible for practitioners to deliver care that is both technically competent and humane whether or not they are personally motivated toward a particular patient or work under threatening conditions. Certain aspects of professional training seem to disable practitioners. The professional mask may protect the individual practitioner from feelings of being overwhelmed by patients' demands; but it also may cut him off from the human experience of illness. Even where the education of the physician inculcates the right attitudes, the organization of the delivery system may undermine those values, replacing them with ones that complicate care and contribute to chronicity.

Why is care of the chronically ill so difficult? Perhaps it is the continuous cycling from damping to amplification of symptoms, from marginal functioning to disablement. The frustration of trying multiple treatment plans without obtaining the desired results tires the practitioner as much as the patient. The very sense of compulsive responsibility essential to the care of acute illness and the emergency exacerbation of chronic disorder may, over the long course, create chronic irritability and numbing exhaustion. Repeated treatment failure tests the physician's sense of competence, until over time and with enough cases his sense of confidence is menaced. Uncertainty, inconstancy, fear, loss, anger—all take their toll. The cases in this book illustrate the problems that assault the healer. If the match between practitioner and patient or between practitioner and family is unsuitable, or is rendered so by the institutional setting, trouble is compounded. It takes courage to extract from Hiram Bender's fearsome night thoughts personal wisdom, not professional intimations of failure and defeat. The practitioner's defenses may lead to a self-corrosive negativism or an iron cage of professional distance from which neither himself nor his family is liberated. "Burn-out" is a recent term for an old phenomenon: the physician loses interest and commitment, and eventually mastery. Gu Fangwen's sentiments indicate that the difficulties of caring for the chronically ill cross even the immense divide between Western and non-Western civilizations. But Paul Samuels's, Hiram Bender's, Helen McNaughton's, and Gu Fangwen's successes show that effective, sensitive care is possible and not uncommon. What is important is to lay out the anatomy of successful healing so that it can be understood, taught, acquired, and more routinely practiced.

15

A Method for the Care
of the Chronically Ill

We must work harder at being human, all of us: those who are
disabled, those who are normal, those who are professional
helpers.

—A severely disabled patient
with multiple congenital deformities

A doctor does more by the moral effect of his presence on the
patient and family than anything else.

—WILLIAM JAMES
(quoted in Myers 1986, 373)

There is a long tradition in medicine for master clinicians to write
books of insights into the care of patients. Sir William Osler, the
immensely influential North American physician of the early twentieth century, wrote clinical aphorisms which are still quoted with
approval by teachers of medicine. Although this tradition has
thinned out in the second half of this century, there are still exceptional examples of epistles to the neophyte practitioner, gleanings
of careers devoted to humane practice (see, for instance, Lipkin
1974; Cassell 1976; Leigh and Reiser 1980; Reiser and Rosen 1984).
But within the profession, this genre of writing has increasingly
been labeled "the art of medicine," a term of ambivalence and even
disparagement in a profession for which the preferred self-image is
decidedly that of science. I offer this chapter from a different perspective but with a similar objective of encouraging humane care.

The first two chapters of this book lay out a theory of the experience of illness based on my analysis of the meanings of illness narratives. Now I wish to return to the matters discussed in those chapters to develop a rationale for a practical clinical methodology in the care of the chronically ill. The essence of that methodology is captured by the words *empathic listening, translation,* and *interpretation,* which I take to be the craft of the clinician who treats illness, not just disease. The problems for the practitioner are abundantly illustrated in the preceding chapters.

Several cautions are in order. This clinical methodology is meant to complement and balance, not replace, the standard biomedical approach to the treatment of disease processes. (Indeed, the care of illness is feasible only when everything possible is done to maximize the technical control of disordered physiology.) Nor do I intend the approach to be seen as a panacea for the management of illness problems. There can be no such thing, as I hope I have already made clear. Rather, this is a framework for assuring that the uniqueness of illness as human experience, in all its many social and personal manifestations, becomes the center of the healer's gaze. John Hewitt (from Heaney 1980, 210) captured the healer's experience:

> Hand over hand eagerly I crawl
> back to uncertainty.

Uncertainty must be as central to the experience of the practitioner as it is to the patient. Attempts to formulate complete psychosocial systems of care that claim to answer wholesale each and every one of the serious dilemmas faced by patients, families, and clinicians (and in a standardized manner, yet!) contain a dangerous hubris which falsifies the existential experience of illness as much as that of healing. It is no wonder physicians are wary of such systems, be they psychoanalytic, behavioral, or other. Human sciences applied to sick persons must respect this innate uncertainty; they must recognize that human problems cannot be reduced to simplistic formulas and stereotyped manipulations that treat patients and their families as if they were overly rational mannequins. Nonetheless, it is possible to craft a clinical method that is neither reductionistic nor mechanistic.

Unlike care of the acutely ill, moreover, such a method need not be so seriously hedged in by the constraints of time that it is unlikely to be practicable. The practitioner and his chronically ill patients interact over many occasions, often over long blocks of time. There is time enough to carry out a variety of clinical tasks. If not this week, then next week or next month, the various components of the method outlined below can be fitted into the routine of care—as long as the physician stays with the patient (physically and existentially) over the long course.

Patients and family members might compare these suggested strategies with those actually used by their care givers. Practitioners, in turn, can compare them with the methods to which they have grown accustomed. I hope that such comparisons will lead to fruitful discussions of a collaborative kind; in and of themselves, the talks can be the source of more successful therapeutic relationships. One objective of this clinical methodology is to encourage patient (family)–doctor relationships that are in fact collaborations.

We must begin with the premise that chronic disease by definition cannot be cured, that indeed the quest for cure is a dangerous myth that serves patient and practitioner poorly. It distracts their attention from step-by-step behaviors that lessen suffering, even if they do not magically heal the disease. Patient and practitioner both need to accept that the primary goal of treatment is the reduction of disablement in the ongoing experience of an illness. To the extent possible, the goal should be to reduce the frequency and the severity of exacerbations in the course of chronic illness. A patient may always have asthma as measured by spirometry. But if that asthma creates only minimal difficulties in his life, treatment can be said to be a true success. The family as well as the patient must learn to accept this treatment objective. In order to convince them of its importance to care, the practitioner must relinquish the myth of cure. He must try to accept even modest improvement in the illness experience as an acceptable outcome. Agreement between the principals that the patient has a chronic illness should not mean confirmation of unavoidable disability, however. Indeed, the practitioner must seek to prevent the undesirable social and psychological consequences of chronicity.*

*Of course, I am not recommending that the healer educate his clients to be pessimistic. There is some evidence from the cross-cultural study of schizophrenia that overly negative Western expectations about its chronic course actually contribute to the chronicity (Waxler 1977). Although there is no convincing evidence this is true of chronic medical disorder, it

The Mini-ethnography

An ethnography is a description by an anthropologist of the lives and world of the members of a society, usually one different from his own. Traditionally, the ethnographer visited a foreign culture, learned the language, and then systematically described the social environment, the changing contexts of experience and interactions. The ethnographer observes the ecological setting; he translates cultural myths; and he interprets the systems of kinship, religion, economics, politics, even medicine. The ethnographer, first, tries to get things right from the native's point of view. To accomplish this, he practices an intensive, systematic, and imaginative empathy with the experiences and modes of thought of persons who may be foreign to him but whose foreignness he comes to appreciate and to humanely engage. The ethnographer does not seek to go native— to become a Masai warrior, a Kung Bushman gatherer, a Mbuti Pygmy hunter, or a Yanomamo shaman—but rather he struggles to learn to see things the way natives do, to enter into their experiential world.

Observation is a key ethnographic task, as is the establishment of relationships of trust and collaboration in which observation can be conducted. The tools of the ethnographer's craft are interviews, participant-observation in both everyday and special activities, and collection of available data sources (census, household, financial, family tree, life history, and so forth). After describing the native point of view, the anthropologist places it in the context of changing political, economic, and social worlds. He translates the local customs into technical terms that enable comparisons across different cultures.

The product of this work is the ethnography: a written record that interprets his findings in light of major social and psychological themes. The ethnography draws on knowledge of the context to make sense of behavior. It tells a story of sorts about the people

---

is plausible to suspect that the effect does occur. But in chronic medical disorder, a much more common event is that the biomedical ideal of a magic bullet and the popular expectation that all disease can be cured create great frustration for patient, family, and care giver. Hence the myth of cure is a large problem indeed, with expectably negative economic, personal, and clinical outcomes.

studied—disclosing myths, rituals, daily activities, and problems. The validity of an ethnography comes from the accuracy of observations and the appropriateness of the ethnographer's interpretations. The interpretation benefits from the ethnographer's having one foot in the culture he is studying and one foot outside it. As a foreigner, he can see aspects of social structure and personal experience that are taken for granted by the natives, but which reveal to his eyes deep cultural principles and disguised sociopolitical influences. Thus, his interpretation also aims to be a cultural deconstruction—a decoding—that his native subjects will find different from their conventional common sense. In fact, the ethnographer's interpretation frequently challenges common-sense understandings. By making explicit the process of interpretation, the ethnography is open to challenge, refinement, and correction by other students of the same culture. Because interpretation can be strongly influenced by the conceptual commitments and professional biases of the ethnographer, a good ethnography clarifies these concerns through a kind of self-criticism of the ethnographer's own point of view. That is to say, the ethnographer ends up juxtaposing different perspectives on the same events to work out a more valid understanding.

This *perspectivism* is one of the strengths of the anthropological approach: the ethnographer is deeply respectful of alternative interpretations—especially those of his informants—and he does not exempt his interpretation from the criticism to which he exposes the others. But neither does he expect that the most valid interpretation is one that his informants would share. He is aware that knowledge of local social reality can be hidden to those who dwell in that reality—though often it isn't.

Master ethnographers and clinicians, though their work is quite different, nonetheless tend to share a sensibility. They both believe in the primacy of experience. They are more like observational scientists than experimentalists. Like the poet and the painter, they are strongly drawn to the details of perception. They struggle with the precision of communication to render percepts authentic, but they also have firsthand experience of the hiddenness of intimate meanings and of the disguising of experience that comes from social convention and personal defenses. The core truth of semiotics—namely, that everything can be a sign and that the relationships among signs are codes of broader and deeper meanings—is as available to the seasoned practitioner as it is to the anthropologist. The anchoring of the individual's attitudes in the local politics and economics of social relations is a given for both.

Ethnographers are, of course, more interested in cross-cultural differences, clinicians more concerned with human universals. The ethnographer is supposed to see himself as a kind of professional stranger wandering dispassionately unattached through a foreign world, but in fact his practical and ethical responsibilities in the local community and to his informants are unavoidable and sensitize him to action. The clinician, supposedly in contrast, has a therapeutic mandate demanding that he must choose and act in behalf of his patients. Yet the practitioner also sees himself as an applied scientist, an onlooker who is aware of the significance of patterns and relationships. These insights become the stuff of his clinical experience and serve to inform theories, generate research reports, and stimulate a robust extraprofessional genre of essays and fiction. Both practitioner and anthropologist, furthermore, are students of the hierarchies of practical relevance that concentrate people's lives: the exigency of life difficulties that makes living "one damn thing after another," as several of the patients in this book have commented.

In spite of all the other professional differences, this affinity between the work of doctoring and the craft of ethnography implies that something useful may be gained from drawing the analogy more fully. I would not defend this likeness as complete; but I have found that for at least one aspect of clinical work it is useful to think of the care of chronic illness as involving a kind of ethnographic practice.

The purpose of conducting the mini-ethnography is for the clinician to place himself in the lived experience of the patient's illness. To the extent possible, the doctor tries to understand (and even imaginatively perceive and feel) the illness experience as the patient understands, perceives, and feels it. What is it like to have the illness experience of Alice Alcott, Rudolph Kristiva, Helen Winthrop Bell, or William Steele? By putting himself in the position of the family members and important people in the wider social circle, the physician can also empathically witness the illness as they do. This experiential phenomenology is the entree into the world of the sick person. The other steps flow directly from the first and essential, great leap into the world of the patient. For example, to record formally the experience of pain and the detailed changes in a patient's descriptions the practitioner must get the phenomenology of the illness right. Such a recording is the basis for a more rigorous evaluation of symptom change, which itself is essential to understand the key antecedents and consequents of the course of the illness.

Beginning medical students, as we have seen, often bring a sense of awe to their auditing of the accounts of their first few patients, which encourages them to resonate genuinely with the illness narrative. Later they learn to transform this always unique experience into a clinical routine. If the beginner's approach were less nervous and transient, it would be a usable model for the frame of mind conducive to a clinical ethnography. Some elements in the seasoned clinician's experience also support this task. If cultivated, attitudes and skills already present make it more likely that clinical ethnography is both properly learned and, once mastered, routinely practiced.

This first level of the mini-ethnography reconstructs the patient's illness narrative. The interpretation of that story's four types of meanings—symptom symbols, culturally marked disorder, personal and interpersonal significance, and patient and family explanatory models—thickens the account and deepens the clinician's understanding of the experience of suffering. Analysis of the narrative's content clarifies what is at stake for the patient and family. Deconstruction of the structure of the illness account—the rhetorical devices and plot outline used by the patient to assemble particular events into a more or less integrated story line—can reveal hidden concerns that the patient has not verbalized. It also can disclose how the patient's narrative shapes the meaning that particular events hold for him. In other words, the clinician comes to recognize that the narration of the illness, in part, creates the experience because of the special concerns—cognitive, affective, moral—that patients bring to their encounters with the events and career of chronic illness.

Having felt his way into the core experience of suffering, the practitioner begins next to more systematically recognize and sort out the chief consequences of the illness in the patient's personal life and social world. Here the physician begins by eliciting information on the impact of the illness on family, work, and other important aspects of the social context. Another kind of information gathering can also be undertaken. Have any menacing life changes or breakdowns in the social support network or failures in coping contributed to the onset of the illness and, more particularly, to exacerbations? Physicians can be trained to make these assessments expeditiously and supportively. By describing the course of the illness in the patient's life, the practitioner comes to know not only the patient's (and family's) response but also something about the major continuities and changes in that life. That is to say, the practitioner can come up with a rough appreciation of the patient's local social system and the recursive influence of his illness on that context and of the context on the illness.* This information should be formally recorded in order to encourage more stringent evaluation and regular use of it.

Various interviewing skills, even the application of selected questionnaires, may help to develop the ethnographic picture of the patient's world and of the place of illness within it. I have in mind the use of impact of illness scales, social functioning questionnaires, and brief clinical scales that rate stress and social support and coping skills. Cassell (1985) describes a number of expeditious techniques the clinician can use to make valid inferences from patients' use of language in the clinical interview. There are many other technical publications that can aid the clinician in this task as well. But it is important to remember that our model is ethnography, not survey research. My experience convinces me that quantitative social assessments tend to provide fairly superficial characterizations, though their thoroughness may be at times a practical benefit. Much more valuable than the actual techniques used is the show of genuine interest on the physician's behalf and his serious concern to

---

*Here I emphasize the intimate context. But the practitioner must also be sensitive to the broader, changing political, economic, and institutional context, which as we have seen are primary constraints on experience: both his patients' and his own. His tasks of witnessing and providing practical help must be seen in that wider social world. The tension between his appreciation of that world and its intimate effects and his inability to alter such large-scale forces is a crucial source of his commitment and compassion.

work out a history of the illness and the sick person in terms of the social context. This ethnographic attitude is the crux of the method.

The next step is for the physician to record the chief current psychosocial problems associated with the illness and its treatment. These illness problems will include a wide variety of difficulties that can nonetheless be grouped into a standard list of categories such as marital and other family conflicts; work problems, which can be subclassified in a number of ways; financial burdens; school problems and examination failure; and difficulties in the negotiation of activities of daily living. Psychological responses to disability that become significant problems for patients (demoralization, anxiety, phobic avoidance, maladaptive denial) should also be entered into this listing.

Coming up with an illness problem list is not an academic exercise. Rather it is an accompaniment to the biomedical list of disease problems, and like that list should be used to more systematically implement appropriate therapies (see Katon and Kleinman 1981; Rosen and Kleinman 1984). For example, in chapter 2 I describe the impact of Alice Alcott's illness on her life. The practitioner caring for Mrs. Alcott could (and, I would urge, should) list the psychosocial concomitants of her diabetes in the medical record as a means of assessing the status of these problems over time. Alice Alcott's problem list would record her various losses (of body image, function, and ability to carry out activities), her active grieving and demoralization, her extensive denial that delayed therapy for potentially remedial complications, and the practical problems her illness created in her family life. Howie Harris's (chapter 3) illness problem list would enumerate his morbid preoccupation with his back, his passive dependent coping style, and their negative effect on his work situation and family, including serious limitations in activities, withdrawal and isolation, fear of losing his job, and alienation from his wife and children. Each of the patients whose illness experience we have described could be assessed in this manner.

Side by side with the illness problem list, the practitioner should list interventions undertaken to help the patient resolve or lessen the problems. Interventions might include short-term supportive psychotherapy, family counseling, referral for social work consultation or job counseling, formal rehabilitation for activities of daily living or more specific work tasks, and legal aid. Another type of intervention is advice on diet, exercise, and life style, as well as on how to deal with difficult treatment regimens that greatly burden life and with trying relationships in the health care system that create frustration and rage. Just as the physician follows up on and records the effects of biomedical interventions, so, too, should he record the effects of these illness interventions. Indeed, determination of overall outcome should include assessment of the effect of illness interventions as well as of disease treatments. Untoward side effects and toxicities of illness interventions should be specified in the same manner that drug toxicities are documented. Over the long course of chronic illness, this system of clinical accounting will assist the practitioner to build a more valid understanding of the course of the illness, of changes in the nature and severity of its effects on the patient and his world, and of the uses and misuses of psychosocial therapy. Inasmuch as an appropriate goal for treating the chronically ill is to reduce the disabling effects of the disorder, this accounting system would also build a more systematic measure of progress in rehabilitation.

A Brief Life History

Closely related to the working up of a mini-ethnography is the solicitation of a brief life history. This history used to be (and in some places still is) a standard part of the elaborate medical history beginning clinical clerks were asked to record in the hospital record. Here the clinician asks the patient and the family to sketch in the sick individual's life course, with a review of major continuties and changes in attitude, personality, major life goals and obstacles, and relevant earlier experiences of coping with illness and other serious conditions. Chapters 4 and 5 show that the biography of the patient need not seem immediately relevant to current illness problems in order to illumine major life themes that over time may affect the illness. In chapter 4, for example, Rudolph Kristiva's current life problems keep shifting, but his biography discloses continuities that shape the long-term form of his illness experience. Antigone Paget's illness experience (chapter 5) receives its unifying significance from aspects of her biography—her quest for and fear of personal freedom—that at first glance might strike an interviewer as not directly relevant to her neck pain. For this reason, I believe that the life history review should be as broad and unrestricted by apparent relevance as the clinician can make it.

One of the great privileges of medicine is to be given access by the patient to the intimacy of his life. Besides the practical value this privileged access holds for treatment, it has at least two other significances. First, once the patient's biography becomes part of the care, the possibility that therapy will dehumanize the patient, stripping him of what is unique to his illness experience, becomes much less likely. Second, but no less important, the experience of listening to the patient's biography maintains the physician's active interest in the case. A doctor can easily become frustrated, demoralized, and bored in the care of the chronically ill, as several of the cases in this book attest. Involvement with the biography of the sick person and interest in interpreting its relationship to the illness not infrequently will revivify the practitioner. Making contact with the patient as a moral agent remoralizes the physician.

Recording a brief version of that life story in his notes enables the practitioner to borrow skills from the biographer's and historian's craft. Precise description requires a rich vocabulary and an eye for revealing detail.* It forces the physician to be more thorough in his examination of the personal context of illness, and it reveals important continuities and discontinuities that are easily missed when the account is not written down. The very process of writing can stimulate the practitioner's critical faculties, empowering him to stand back and see relationships and patterns all too easily missed when the personal history is merely a series of fragmented vignettes inchoate in his memory. The moment that the clinician-biographer realizes a unifying form to a patient's life is a thrilling one. Even where he recognizes the destructive repetition of neurotic relation-

*Cassell (1985) lists adjectives that practitioners should command to describe the patient's pattern of speech, tone of voice, logic, and presentation of self. Similar listings have been developed to describe quality of pain and other symptoms. Personality inventories and coping scales can enrich the description of the sick person. Physicians vary so widely in descriptive skills in part because few have been trained in the techniques of systematic description.

ships, knowledge of that pattern enables the clinician (and ultimately the patient) to achieve more useful control of the illness
experience.

The patient's biography also represents a life text that the practitioner should interpret in order to gain a deeper appreciation of the
patient's emotional traits and personality configuration. Two emotional reactions to chronic illness—anxiety and depression—are so
common and their effects so powerful that watching for them must
be a routine part of the practitioner's examination. Anxiety and
depression, as symptoms or even normal reactions to chronic illness,
are part of the fluctuating psychophysiology of chronic illness. To
identify them as current clinical states, the practitioner needs to be
able to distinguish a disease state from a personality trait. Major
depressive disorder, panic disorder, and generalized anxiety disorder, diagnosed according to the DSM-III criteria, can adversely
influence the course of chronic medical disorders. They must be
discovered and treated. The practitioner can do this if his suspicion
is high and if he routinely includes questions to assess the chief
symptoms of these psychiatric diseases. Yet chronic medical conditions show some of the very symptoms that are diagnostic for these
psychiatric illnesses. For this reason psychiatric referral may be
necessary and should not be delayed (as it was in the case of William Steele in chapter 7).

Knowledge of patients' personal sources of demoralization and
fear will aid the physician to counsel and support them more effectively. Similarly, awareness of patients' particular personality styles
and coping patterns or defenses will assist the practitioner in helping them negotiate their most problematic aspects of chronic illness.
In the fields of primary care internal medicine and family medicine
it is increasingly recognized that the primary care practitioner must
possess at least some rudimentary psychiatric training to be able to
carry out such assessments; then, if the practitioner does not provide appropriate treatment himself, he can refer patients in need of
help to other professionals.

Explanatory Models and Negotiation

To fully gauge the patient's perspective and be sure about what the patient wants from the care, the practitioner must elicit the patient's (and when feasible the family's) explanatory model. In chapter 7, I described explanatory models and showed how professional and patient models often (though usually tacitly) conflict. Now I will outline several practical steps the physician can undertake to get at the patient's model and negotiate with the patient over any conflicts between the lay and biomedical models.

The first step is the elicitation of the patient's (and family's) models. In the contracted format, the practitioner simply asks: "What do you think is wrong? What caused it? What do you want me to do?" In the expanded version, questions are added about reasons for the onset of symptoms at a particular time, lay understanding of what gave rise to the symptoms, and expected course and perceived seriousness. In addition, the practitioner inquires: "What is the chief way this illness (or treatment) has affected your life? What do you fear most about this illness (or treatment)?" He may also wish to follow up these questions to canvass the patient's or family's ideas about risk, vulnerability, compliance, and satisfaction with the care received. The reader can see in chapter 2 that Alice Alcott's explanatory model indicated her fear that the course of her diabetes would lead inexorably downhill, with one major complication following another until she became an invalid or died. She recognized neither the utility of specific treatments nor, in her bleakest period, rehabilitation. Both her despair and her courage took origin from this explanation. The explanatory model expressed by Howie Harris in chapter 3 clarifies his sense of great vulnerability and specifies what he views as threats. In chapter 13, the models of Arnie Springer and Phillips Bingman express the character of danger at the very center of their illness experience. For their problems any therapy that did not begin by addressing their fears would be so off the mark as to be futile.

A word of caution is appropriate at this point. The physician must remember that explanatory models are inchoate. It is often only when a patient talks about the issues raised by the physician's questions that his model firms up from vague musings into definite statements. The statements frequently contain contradictions, and they change in content over time as different situations arise. (Therefore it is useful to reelicit explanatory models at different points in the treatment.) Explanatory models are not merely cognitive representations; they are deeply rooted in the emotional turmoil that accompanies illness. Thus, it is not at all surprising that patients and families may minimize or even dissimulate answers to the physician's questions. The practitioner must interpret nonverbal, metaphoric channels of communication in order to be sensitive to what isn't said, what is covered over, and what is fabricated. The explanatory model is an interpretation of what the practitioner *thinks* the patient thinks, not just a direct rendering of the patient's actual words. Thus, it is essential for the practitioner to refer back to the mini-ethnography if he is to appreciate the patient's and family's models.

The second step in the explanatory model technique is the presentation of the practitioner's explanatory model. No doctor is taught how to explain the biomedical account to patients. Yet this is an essential task in the work of doctoring, and one which patients, in the West at least, increasingly expect to be well handled. Presenting the biomedical model is an act of translation for the practitioner. When the presentation is well done, the physician has the great advantage of collaborating with accurately informed patients and families who can contribute to the therapeutic process. When it is poorly done, however, the stage is set for clinical communication to have serious problems, which can unsettle the therapeutic relationship and thereby undermine care. Skill in explaining correlates with the practitioner's sensitivity to the patient's level of understanding and desire to know, along with an aptitude for speaking, plain and simple, the patient's language. The masters of this tradecraft are talented in using the patient's metaphors and even his model to clarify biomedical information and render biomedical judgment convincing. There is, then, a rhetoric of explaining to patients, and physicians differ greatly in their aptitude and skill in making clinical judgments convincing to patients and their intimate social circle. Alice Alcott's physicians shared much of her explanatory model, except that they recognized that her depression complicated an already very difficult situation. They were willing to accept her denial of disability; they were also willing to deny her acceptance of tragedy. Others of the patients we have described fared better at the hands of their physicians. However, Melissa Flowers (chapter 7), along with several others, experienced a virtually total breakdown in this crucial communicative function of healing.

All physicians are faced with the necessity of translating between the enormously complex concepts and findings of medical science and their patient's practical need to know about risk and vulnerability, disorder and treatment. A patient once told me this:

> We none of us know what to make of risks anymore. We've been told too many different things. If you be just an ordinary person, how can you figure it? What do you eat? What don't you? The world looks so bloody dangerous. Who can say what caused it, my cancer? And the treatment, doc: I'm only a high school graduate, I can't even understand the simplified explanations.

This problem in translation between lay and professional cultures, at least in the short run, can only become more difficult as scientific expansion outpaces the diffusion of scientific knowledge in the general public. The media contribute to an immense cloud of misinformation that adds to confusion and fuels inappropriate expectations.* Physicians are poised at the interface between scientific and lay cultures (Williams and Wood 1986). The need to explicate scientific development and correct—even debunk—erroneous information confronts them daily. Today there is in North America a wholly unrealistic popular expectation that all diseases should be treatable and that no medical encounter should lead to a negative outcome. This inappropriate expectation creates a climate in which great pressures are placed on the practitioner, including an increasing threat of lawsuits for maloccurrence, not just malpractice.

In this setting, the practitioner cannot avoid responding to the patient's perspective on risk and vulnerability and to his expectations regarding treatment. But many physicians respond according

---

*Examples are the excessive claims played up in the media for the practical use of recent research developments in understanding the biochemistry of cancer, few of which will ever be practicable and most of which are red herrings; or the recent claim (*Newsweek*, 12 Jan. 1987) that psychiatrists will soon be able to use hormonal profiles to diagnose patients. The latter is an amazing assertion when one realizes that there is not a single pathognomonic hormonal test for any psychiatric disorder at present and that the biochemistry of mental illness is a quagmire of contradictory and unsupported claims (Barnes 1987).

to an outmoded health education approach that simply configures the problem as lack of effective knowledge. The actual dimensions of the problem are much greater: laymen possess alternative forms of knowledge, not merely insufficient scientific knowledge, as the creationism controversy ominously reveals. How many professionals can fully comprehend today's medical technology and its scientific basis in other fields? Most practitioners can be misled about a subject peripheral to their own area of competence. They, too, may harbor a mix of common sense (which is often scientifically inaccurate and commercially manipulated) and just plain misinformation.

Practitioners must first elicit lay knowledge and then present their own models in order to identify questions that require more valid understandings. Furthermore, the practitioner's model—like those of his patients—is often inchoate until it is formally expressed, and it changes over time. Here we have another source of tacit misunderstandings and conflicts. The explanatory model framework is a potentially useful one for remedying this problem. The explanatory model approach can also help the practitioner disabuse himself and his patients of idealogically oriented and commercially controlled messages aimed at manipulating him and them toward the purchase of commodities that are expensive, unneeded, and dehumanizing. But to accomplish these ends requires that physicians master communicative and interpretive skills in which most are not trained and some have no interest. I shall return to the matter of training in the next chapter.

The practitioner is now ready to engage the patient and family in a negotiation. Of all the tradecraft of the physician, nothing more effectively empowers patients. The very act of negotiation, if it is genuine and not a grudging pseudomutuality, necessitates that at the very least the health professional show respect for the patient's point of view. The real challenge is for the physician to engage in negotiation with the patient as colleagues involved in care as collaboration.* The practitioner begins this phase of care by elaborating

---

*I make much of collaboration in the care of chronic illness. It needs to be remembered that different styles of clinical interaction are appropriate at different stages of the illness and for patients of different personal and cultural orientations: a severe acute exacerbation is often better dealt with by an authoritative style; patients from traditional ethnic groups may misunderstand an egalitarian style and find it unacceptable. These are things about which the astute clinician will inquire.

an explicit comparison between the lay model and the professional biomedical model. The physician can determine points of disagreement and lacunae of information to which he can respond. He must encourage the patient and family members to respond to his model: that means he must be prepared to hear out their criticisms and—what is even more difficult, given the traditional orientation of medical training—he must actively help patient and family to negotiate about areas of conflict. As part of that negotiation, he must expose his uncertainty and the limits of his understanding, as well as his critical reactions to relevant popular and commercial images. He also should clarify where his own model has changed. The negotiation may end up in a compromise closer to the patient's position, a compromise closer to the doctor's position, or a joint lesson in demystifying professional and public discourse.

If for technical or ethical reasons the physician cannot compromise, referral can made to another practitioner. But most of the time, in my experience, the negotiation will result in an effective compromise acceptable to all parties. This happened in Alice Alcott's case in chapter 2: she stopped short of giving up and again adapted to her latest loss. In turn, her psychiatrist and physicians accommodated to her denial, which they had come to see as both useful and dysfunctional. In William Steele's case (chapter 7), his physician's refusal to initiate a compromise led to an eventual agreement forced by the patient and his wife. The tacit nature of the conflict delayed effective treatment and may well have contributed to the worsening of the patient's condition. Unwillingness to accept a compromise over the thoroughness of the medical evaluation led several of the hypochondriacal patients in chapter 13 to undergo expensive and unnecessary workups and to shop around for doctors more amenable to their demands, which in the long run deepened the frustration of them and of their care givers.

A final dimension of the explanatory model paradigm is the opportunity it presents the clinician for self-reflective interpretation of the interests, biases, and emotions that underlie his own model. As we saw in Alice Alcott's story, Dr. Torres, a Hispanic-American physician, learned to change his own ethnic biases about New England Yankees: namely, that they are cold, unfeeling, insensitive. The psychiatrist had to overcome his own tendency to insist on diagnosing a treatable psychiatric disease—in spite of evidence to the contrary—and to give Alice Alcott an antidepressant pharmacological agent that would, he fantasized, produce a cure. Dr. Torres and the surgeons dealt with confounding feelings of powerlessness and the attendant anger and sadness. In the cases of William Steele and Melissa Flowers, internists proceeded unaware of strong biases that had adverse influences on care. When the medical team learned that Gus Echeverra had created his own disorder, so enraged were they that they wanted him expelled from the hospital forthwith and refused to cooperate with the psychiatrist treating him. Their rage, while understandable, complicated the patient's treatment. Of all the responses to patients, rage is the most difficult for physicians to handle. In my experience, an effective way for the practitioner to gain purchase on this and other disturbing emotional and ethical reactions to patients is by assiduously examining his explanatory model for evidence of powerfully upsetting feelings and tacit moral judgments affecting how he thinks about the treatment.

The clinician should examine his explanatory model, then, to assess whether personal or professional biases adversely influence the treatment. This should be a routine part of clinical work. Although it usually is not, many physicians nonetheless struggle to work out models that are as clear a guide to therapeutic judgments as an uncertain situation allow. Today, through Balint groups and clinical ethics rounds, primary care physicians are trained to examine their own emotional and moral reactions to difficult patients (Balint [1957] 1973), so that they can control responses that may have a damaging impact on the therapeutic relationship and develop ones that contribute to effective support—and even to the practitioner's own personal development.

Remoralization: Toward a Medical Psychotherapy

Instilling or rekindling hope in the chronically ill patient (and often in the family, too) is an essential, though poorly charted, clinical domain. Of course, there are models of short-term psychotherapy.

But these have not been widely translated into the care of the chronically medically ill (for an exception, see Karasu and Stein-muller 1978). Most primary care physicians practice a kind of psychotherapy without being trained to do so, often without realizing that they are doing so. Care for the psychosocial needs of the chronically medically ill is a field with few markers, like those unexplored portions of the maps of ancient times that carried the ominous warning, "From here on, dragons!"

I configure these therapeutic skills as a medical psychotherapy that takes its origin from the clinician's immersion in the meanings of illness. The mini-ethnographic description, the interpretation of the life history, and the elicitation and negotiation of explanatory models are the major steps in this medical psychotherapeutic process. Each of these activities contributes to psychotherapeutic care, while recursively the psychotherapeutic concern with remoralization and support aids in the performance of these core clinical tasks. That is to say, these tasks are themselves the framework for medical psychotherapy. For example, the empathy required for making the mini-ethnography fills the important need of all patients (and families) to be understood and to share their burden with others. As William James wrote: "We long for sympathy, for a purely *personal* communication" (quoted in Myers 1986, 405).

Spiro (1986), a master physician with extensive experience in care of the chronically ill, suggests that the placebo effect—the nonspecific therapeutic effect of the doctor–patient relationship—although it is despised in medical research because it confounds a clear-cut understanding of the specificity of successful treatment, is in fact the essence of effective clinical care. It is something each clinician should work assiduously to cultivate in routine medical care. This nonspecific therapeutic effect varies tremendously in research studies (from 10 to 90 percent), and is likely to do the same in routine medical care (Moerman 1983). It is of the utmost importance that physicians achieve the highest possible placebo effect rates. To do this, doctors must establish relationships that resonate empathy and genuine concern for the well-being of their patients: relationships the patient and family come to believe in as of practical help and symbolic significance.

I am agnostic about traditional psychotherapeutic orientations:

psychoanalytic, behavioral, cognitive, existential, counseling, or family. All can be helpful. Each can also be undermined if applied in a mechanical, cookbook fashion. What matters is that the practitioner genuinely believe in what he is doing and that patient and family do, too. At some point, the therapist–patient (family) interaction must activate the patient's expectant faith, if not in the outcome then in the relationship itself. A Pollyannaish hope is not what I have in mind. Physician and patient must be realistic—at least as far as the patient indicates that he can tolerate realism. Patient and family must be empowered. The practitioner must also feel that he is personally affected by the relationship. I see medical psychotherapy, then, as a collaborative relationship within which the techniques for exploring illness meanings encourage catharsis, persuasion, practical problem solving, and other of the mechanisms of psychotherapeutic change.

Whatever else it is, psychotherapy is a deeply moral relationship. The practitioner attempts to be with the patient in the ambit of suffering. The patient actively opens his life world to their conjoint exploration. Practitioner becomes a moral witness, neither a judge nor a manipulator. Patient becomes an active colleague, not a passive recipient. Both learn and change from the experience. Think of the diverse kinds of relationships necessary to accommodate the patients, families, and practitioners canvassed in the preceding chapters. The Chinese patient described in chapter 6 would neither expect nor find acceptable an egalitarian relationship; yet for Antigone Paget an authoritarian relationship would be destructive. Think of the distinctive objectives these relationships would have. The tradecraft of psychosocial care is in the fashioning of unique relationships that meet the special demands of a particular illness story, a specific life.

When the tasks of support, attention to emotional needs, and negotiation of an authentic relationship are accomplished in a caring fashion the question of how to do medical psychotherapy vanishes. That is the psychotherapy.

A concrete example is the remoralization of a depressed and defeated patient. The patient could be Alice Alcott, William Steele, Howie Harris, Rudolph Kristiva, Antigone Paget, or another of the patients whose stories I have told: sick persons who are viewed by their care givers as problem patients. The objective differs. It might be significant reduction in disability; control over unnerving anxiety; or simply dying a good death. The mini-ethnography and the life history will suggest the specific aims and the means, so that the form taken by remoralization will differ. With one patient, say Antigone Paget, the emphasis of care may be on catharsis; with another, say Howie Harris, it may be on family counseling and behavioral modification. For Alice Alcott emotional support takes the form of existential empathy, as it did for Gordon Stuart in his final days (chapter 9). Other patients, like William Steele, require a sociotherapeutic approach in which the practitioner works to help them break out of vicious local social cycles that amplify distress. Gus Echeverra failed to respond to intensive psychoanalytically oriented psychotherapy focused on his severe personality disorder, and it is unlikely that cases as serious as his could be treated by the medical practitioner; knowing when to refer patients to mental health professionals is essential. But for most patients and families, the required steps are not nearly so difficult. The chief sources of therapeutic efficacy are the development of a successful therapeutic relationship and the rhetorical use of the practitioner's personality and communicative skills to empower the patient and persuade him toward more successful coping. The care of the chronically ill, moreover, need not be overly solemn or gloomy: there is ample place for wit and humor, a sense of irony and paradox.

Almost all patients with serious chronic illness can benefit from grief work to help them mourn their losses, which as we have seen play such a large role in care. Learning how to assist in grieving and authorizing patients' right to grieve actively in care are things anyone who treats the chronically ill should master. Short-term psychotherapeutic models of grief therapy, such as that of Horowitz et al. (1984), have been used by paraprofessionals and lay counselors. For those practitioners who are themselves uncomfortable with undertaking this specific psychotherapeutic task, timely referral to appropriately trained grief counselors might be a useful alternative. But for the practitioner who wishes to be a healer with the chronically ill, working through grief is a skill that he should acquire and practice.

The practitioner might devote five or six weekly sessions for the purpose of grieving losses. He can block out thirty to forty minutes for each session. He must select suitable patients who are experiencing significant demoralization and solicit their informed consent. In the first session, he assists the patient to recognize and express major personal losses due to his chronic illness. During the second and third sessions, he encourages the patient to talk about these losses and to describe for each the emotional experience of that loss: that is, he helps the patient to grieve. These sessions also allow the physician to work with his patient to express other emotional responses (such as anger or fear) that may interfere with grieving. The fourth session can be devoted to complete the grieving by guiding the patient to grieve for his own death or for other anticipated losses of profound significance. The final one or two sessions are arranged to move beyond grief to restitution. Termination of this series of sessions should emphasize reattachment of the patient to the ongoing patient–doctor relationship, to intimate personal ties, and to his own lived experience. A long-term relationship allows the practitioner to monitor the outcome of such intervention and, from time to time, when he feels it may be useful, to revisit the work of grieving. It is the experience of many therapists that therapy may have its effect after the therapeutic process has ended, when the patient has sufficient time to synthesize new insights and initiate change on his own. Thus the general practitioner may see remoralization occur well after such sessions have ended.

Patients should achieve, as a result of therapy, a degree of distance from their former emotional state. They should feel that they have experienced a significant catharsis. But whatever new relationship they work out with their illness cannot be prescribed, and will be as different as their situations and personalities. This kind of grief work, in my experience, is an effective means of remoralizing many patients. It can also be of use to remoralize the practitioner, or at least to rekindle his enthusiasm for treating the patient. And often that is all that is needed to keep him from giving up, to enable him thereby to sustain the often fragile hope of patient and family.

I am sure that there are different and equally useful ways to conduct the grief work (see Osterweis et al. 1984). Again, I would emphasize how important it is for the patient and practitioner to undertake the experience together. The means is not what counts.

That patient and practitioner have the authentic experience of grieving for real and symbolic losses created by chronic illness is the goal. I know of no alternative that can so powerfully reconstitute an effective, humane relationship of care. To emphasize the objective rather than its means, I like to think of the tale told by the great Chinese sage Zhuangzi. A fisherman constructs an elaborate net to catch a fish. He labors to build the net in an intricate design. He worries over it, works to improve it, and spends much time with it. But once he has caught the fish, he forgets about the net (Zhuangzi XXVI; see, for example, Legge [1891] 1959).

Chronic medical patients, as I have repeatedly noted, are thought of as problem patients by their care givers. While personality disorders and difficult life situations contribute to this label, so do the inappropriate expectations of an acute care–oriented medical system and the frustrations of the care giver. The process of remoralizing the patient can change the expectations of the system and may also shake the care giver out of a pattern of behavior that does more to maintain the problem than to solve it. The methodology I have outlined aims to do both. The kind of changes that matter in the care of the chronically ill are usually not dramatic ones: they tend to be small changes in the perception of symptoms and in the tolerance of suffering. The space between a manageable distress and a defeating despair is often narrow. (The same can be said of the practitioner's sense of confidence and his feeling of frustration: a small difference can buoy his spirits or deflate them.) What is more, care with the same patient may be successful one week, unsuccessful the next. Perhaps for most of the life problems created by chronicity and disability there are no pat answers. Care is a constant struggle to experiment and persevere—like the illness experience itself. The determination of successful outcome is an ongoing, very long term affair. A successful therapeutic relationship will withstand a bad spell; indeed, its strengths will be tested by several bad spells.

One component of the practitioner's care deserves further discussion: namely, support for the family. As we have seen, chronic illness almost always holds consequences for the family and other close personal relationships, and sometimes those consequences are very serious indeed. The disease may be localized in the tissues of a single individual; the illness incorporates his social circle. The

mini-ethnography and the elicitation of family members' explanatory models will point to the sources of support as well as to the
tensions and fissures in the social network. Demoralization and fear
rarely are limited to the patient. Chronic illness places the family
under substantial, ongoing pressure that exacerbates existing conflicts while it creates new ones. The practitioner may come to see
the entire family as the focus of care. He will want to determine
specific problems in its functioning and respond, where appropriate,
to them. The response should include regular assessment and follow-up of the family's problems along with counseling and, if necessary, referral to family therapy specialists.

The elicitation of family members' explanatory models is often a
useful way to abet the expression of tensions. It points up conflicts
not just with the biomedical model but with the patient's model,
too. It is also a useful way to promote family and patient negotiations over what role in care is most appropriate for family members.
For certain families that role may be substantial; for others it may
be marginal. The practitioner also needs to be available at points of
crisis to assist families that have exhausted their personal resources
in the quest for support of sick members. Family members, as well
as patients, benefit from the physician's willingness to hear (and
thereby authorize) their account. They may require help with practical problem-solving tasks associated with the disorder; they may
require an opportunity for catharsis and more specific kinds of
emotional support, especially for anxious feelings. Sometimes it is
the spouse even more than the patient who needs someone to sanction anger and to encourage periodic withdrawal to replenish supplies, so to speak. Grieving for losses owing to illness is also a
ubiquitous family experience to which clinicians can make a contribution. For the family as for the patient there is nothing like the
realization that the practitioner is sensitive to their needs and competent to offer help.

I am convinced that ultimately what the practitioner does best is
to organize care around the phenomenological appreciation of the
illness experience and its psychological and social consequences for
the patient. This necessitates education in attitudes, knowledge, and
skills that are rather different from those currently given priority in
the training of the physician and in the health care system. I turn

now to consider the major implications this perspective holds for modern medicine.

But I feel an unease I wish to share with the reader. Is it possible to teach a professional, as Philip Larkin wrote,

> To find words at once true and kind,
> Or not untrue and not unkind.
> (from Heaney 1980, 164)

Perhaps this is an aspect of physicianhood that is so deeply indwelling that it cannot be taught didactically, that it must be learned through the difficult experiences of the student's own pain and the pressing need to do good for others. Perhaps it is also dependent on the practitioner's current stage of adult development. Can one effectively empathize and assist another person's grief, if one has not personally experienced bereavement? Perhaps nothing short of the personal reality of illness or of doctoring can fashion this wisdom.

16

The Challenge of a Meaning-centered Model for Medical Education and Practice

> The decision to seek medical consultation is a request for interpretation. . . . Patient and doctor together reconstruct the meaning of events in a shared mythopoesis. . . . Once things fall in place; once experience and interpretation appear to coincide; once the patient has a coherent "explanation" which leaves him no longer feeling the victim of the inexplicable and the uncontrollable, the symptoms are, usually, exorcised.
>
> —Leon Eisenberg
> (1981, 245)

> I have known Jimmie now for nine years—and neuropsychologically, he has not changed in the least. He still has the severest, most devasting Korsakov's, cannot remember isolated items for more than a few seconds, and has a dense amnesia going back to 1945. But humanly, spiritually, he is at times a different man altogether—no longer fluttering, restless, bored, and lost, but deeply attentive to the beauty and soul of the world, rich in all the Kierkegaardian categories—the aesthetic, the moral, the religious, the dramatic. . . . Empirical science, empiricism, takes no account of the soul, no account of what constitutes and determines personal being. Perhaps there is a philosophical as well as a clinical lesson here: that in Korsakov's, or dementia, or other such catastrophes, however great the organic damage . . . there remains the undiminished possibility of reintegration by art, by communion, by touching the human spirit; and this can be preserved in what seems at first a hopeless state of neurological devastation.
>
> —Oliver Sacks
> ([1985] 1987, 39)

I ask the reader now to consider the question, What is the purpose of medicine? If we examine the immense health care enterprise in modern industrial societies such as the United States, it is hard to imagine that such an elemental question can be answered. It seems impertinent, a gross oversimplification of a complex social system that is so fragmented the reader may feel like answering: There are probably as many purposes as there are medical institutions: why not ask, Why medicine? That question seems equally absurd.

Yet, until we pose the question of purpose it is not possible to hold the profession or the practitioner accountable. Nor can we know what patients should ask of health care. By not asking, moreover, we acquiesce with the dominant economic clichés of our age: namely, that the doctor–patient relationship is no more and no less than any other commercial relationship between a purveyor of services and a customer, that the medical profession is a conglomerate whose purpose is to control a share of the market. No, medicine is intimately involved with economics to be sure, but it must not be reduced to that.

There is a moral core to healing in all societies that I take to be the central purpose of medicine. That structure is luminously revealed by the experience of illness and by the demands made on the patient–doctor relationship; it is clouded over by a narrow examination of the nontherapeutic aspects of healing. The accounts in this book reveal that the experience and meanings of illness are at the center of clinical practice. The purpose of medicine is both control of disease processes and care for the illness experience. Nowhere is this clearer than in the relationship of the chronically ill to their medical system: for them, the control of disease is by definition limited; care for the life problems created by disorder is the chief issue.

When viewed from the human situations of chronic illness, neither the interpretation of illness meanings nor the handling of deeply felt emotions within intimate personal relationships can be dismissed as peripheral tasks. They constitute, rather, the point of medicine. These are the activities with which the practitioner should be engaged. The failure to address these issues is a fundamental flaw in the work of doctoring. It is in this very particular sense, then, that we can say of contemporary biomedicine: in spite of remarkable progress in the control of disease, it has turned its back on the purpose of medicine. This distortion, which results from external societal forces as much as from internal professional dynamics, places a great burden on the chronically ill, their families, and the practitioners who treat them.

When we place care at the center of medicine, we are forced to rethink medical training: medical students and residents must be educated to perform the therapeutic tasks that are essential to the needs of Alice Alcott, Howie Harris, Antigone Paget, Patrick Esposito, Gordon Stuart, and the other protagonists of this volume. We must also confront the barriers in the health care delivery system and in the broader social structure that interfere with the performance of these tasks. We must come to terms with a medical research enterprise that seems to ignore the problems created by the chronic illness experience while it contributes so impressively to the control of acute disease. That is to say, when judged against medicine's central purpose in the care of the chronically ill, medical research seems irrelevant. When illness rather than disease becomes our chief interest, we are led to rethink medicine in a direction that is currently unfashionable, one that runs contrary both to internal professional interests and to the criticisms of outside observers. Medicine, viewed in this light, is part of the problem; it is also the solution.

Medical Education

Students usually enter medical school with high ideals about the kind of doctor they hope to become and the kind of help they hope to provide their patients. By the time they finish medical school, many have lost these ideals. The process of professionalization replaces, in the mind of the physician, the often overly romantic lay image of healing with the often all too cynically pragmatic professional expectations of high technology and high income. For the care of the chronically ill, medical education as it is currently organized can be disastrous. Physicians are encouraged to believe that *disease* is more important than *illness,* and that all they need is knowledge about biology, not knowledge about the psychosocial and cultural aspects of illness. They are taught that using placebo effects in the clinical setting is old-fashioned. They come to believe that psychotherapy is anachronistic and need be learned only by psychiatrists. The social science and humanities components of medical education, which are central to the ideas I have discussed in this book, are poor relations with whom few medical students feel at all comfortable associating. As I described in chapter 8, the gauntlet of residency training may even dehumanize the practitioner, and certainly does not contribute to the training of physicians committed to psychosocially sensitive care.

My conclusion is harsh. There are, of course, many physicians who break the mold. In fact, becoming a skilled primary care physician in the community may *require* a kind of liberation, through experience, from professional biases acquired in training. There are, furthermore, training programs—especially in certain of the more progressive units in family medicine, primary care internal medicine, and pediatrics—that emphasize just the kinds of concerns that I regard to be essential to the healer. And psychiatry, though marginal to the medical mainstream, has long been concerned with the biography of the patient. But on the whole, I believe my judgment, though regrettable, is correct.

To change this deplorable situation, it is necessary to make the patient's and the family's narrative of the illness experience more central in the educational process. Only then will physicians gain the appropriate attitudes, knowledge, and skills to enable them to undertake a mini-ethnography of the misery of chronic disorder or support patients in their terminal days or negotiate with the values of families from other ethnic groups. How is this change to be brought about?

The only effective reform, to my mind, would be to restructure the medical training program from bottom to top. Short of that, values and behavior will not change. Time must be devoted in the curriculum to teaching students how to interpret the illness narrative and assess the illness experience. Courses in the medical social sciences and humanities are a beginning, but we also need new ways of teaching about doctor–patient transactions and supervising the clinical experiences of medical students. The essential attitudes for the performance of the core clinical tasks reviewed in chapter 15 would be encouraged if students could see that these skills really mattered to their teachers and to clinicians generally. There must be models among their teachers of masters in the care of the chronically ill. Even medical school admissions criteria need to select preferentially students with an interest and background in psychosocial, cultural, and moral fields of inquiry.

Skill in conducting a mini-ethnography can be honed by sending students out of the lecture hall and hospital to follow up on their patients in the local community. They can observe patients at home and in their dealings with health care and social welfare agents and agencies. Not often, in my experience, will students be invited to the workplace, but they usually will have access to family, friends, and neighbors. A debriefing by a social scientist familiar with the community often helps students to assemble a more valid picture of the patient's ethnographic context. Clinical mentors should then review these accounts, not to criticize the quality of the prose, but rather to evaluate the student's ability to be an intense observer of clinically relevant detail as well as a thoughtful interpreter of that detail in light of the patient's particular social context. Proficiency in eliciting the patients' and families' explanatory models, and in explaining the biomedical model in terms lay persons can understand, comes from having frequent opportunities to perform these activities under the supervision of expert clinicians, not only in clinics and inpatient units but also in patients' homes. There is a pertinent literature on taking life histories, in which students will find various strategies to elicit patients' life narratives and to write up brief biographies. But, most important, students must be given frequent chances to interpret the chief meanings of these life accounts. Students' experiences can be enriched by reading biographical and fictional stories from the worlds of patients.

In addition, medical school faculty must explicitly support the importance of these learning experiences. For students to believe that understanding illness is a crucial part of their education, they must know that they will be tested on the acquisition of relevant skills. Failure to perform adequately or to show the appropriate attitudes or knowledge should be treated in the same way as failure to understand and examine disease processes in cardiology, surgery, or obstetrics. Students should be required to undergo remedial study and reexamination. Persistent inability to demonstrate the requisite attitudes, knowledge, and skills should lead to dismissal. Nothing would so concentrate the minds of medical students and residents as the recognition that if they perform poorly in learning how to provide psychosocial care for the chronically ill, they will not graduate as doctors.

The medical school faculty must show through their actions that they share the vision that illness is as important as disease in the training of the general doctor. This redirection will require the re-education of faculty, along with a system of academic rewards that makes clear through promotion and respect that the psychosocial domain of medicine is central to the mission of the teaching faculty. The presence of practitioners who are models of the psychosocially oriented practitioner is crucial.

The challenge for the postgraduate training of residents is even greater. Perhaps it should begin with the honest, if deeply upsetting, recognition that at present many training programs tacitly inculcate values and behaviors that are antithetical to the humane care of patients. Building psychosocially sophisticated components into existing training programs is probably going to be insufficient, because the entire structure of training militates against their effective assimilation. For example, care of the chronically ill is very largely an outpatient phenomenon in which the clinician must work together with the community's network of social service agencies. Many training programs, however, emphasize the inpatient care of acutely ill patients and deemphasize the outpatient care of the chronically ill. Programs isolate trainees from the community, and they often create the impression that the chronically ill are problem patients for their failure to improve and for their frequent need of physicians' services. Moreover, by creating a menacing ethos that exhausts interns and turns them into survivors, training programs perpetuate the very conditions that work against learning humane care (Groopman 1987). To change these conditions would require fundamental change in hospital training programs, which often are driven more by demand for cheap medical labor than by concern for the care of patients. We must stop dehumanizing young physicians if we are to stop their usually inadvertent dehumanization of patients.

Programs that teach residents to spend five to ten minutes treating each chronic patient who comes for a follow-up visit or that emphasize the use of expensive techniques over labor-intensive interview and talk therapy skills are on the wrong track. Turning them around would require both a new priority system and different guidelines for delivering care. The evaluation of patient care cannot be limited to an overly narrow quantification of cost effectiveness; it must include an assessment of how the care treats problems in the experience and meaning of illness. Ultimately, the financing of care comes to the forefront. If by passing an endoscope a clinician can earn ten times in fifteen minutes what he can make in half an hour of sensitive interviewing, there is little chance that psychosocial training will have any significant effect on health care behavior. Thus, the financing of care must include appropriate levels of funding for helping patients cope with the illness experience. Inasmuch as there is evidence that psychosocial intervention can reduce the costs of health care as well as of long-term disability, it is not impertinent to demand reform of the system of reimbursement for physicians (Mumford et al. 1984; Osterweis et al. 1987).

Without the appropriate institutional support, it is very unlikely that what would be learned in medical school and residency programs would be applied in actual practice. That is to say, the practitioner could be ready and skilled to deliver psychosocially competent care, but the delivery system would not be ready to provide the incentives to support such care—indeed, the system may even offer active disincentives. Increasingly, as Helen McNaughton reports in chapter 14, care is viewed by the managers of medical units as a commodity. In keeping with the priority system of contemporary capitalism, which has in our times come to dominate not just the institutions of medicine but its value orientation as well, money is expended to enhance this commodity so that more money can be made from it (Heilbroner 1986). Thus, what counts today is not how effective the physician is in helping the chronically ill to deal with suffering, but how much time and money are spent and how much profit is left. High quality of care may not always be cost effective, at least when cost is narrowly configured by the dominant political constraints of our time. (A different political orientation might change the nature of those constraints, enabling all of us to rethink more desirable ways of delivering care.)

The system of medical care in the United States, and in the other industrialized countries, needs to be reformed. The situation is worsening at an accelerating pace. Critics of modern medicine have identified the central issues of inequity in access to care and of injustice in who benefits from care; these problems are important in their own right (Starr 1982; Navarro 1986). But their solution would be unlikely to address the problem I have identified. That problem is perhaps best thought of as a cultural dilemma that captures the values of modern societies and the professions that have come to implement those values. The secular mythology and the professional "ritual experts" of our times serve the ill poorly. The profession may seem to be doing well, but its authorizing mission is in deep trouble, its practicing members profoundly divided, its relationship to its clients greatly disturbed. What is required is no less than a transformation in the way we think of medicine.

The Health Care System

Let us reconsider the health care system, then, as an enterprise centered on the care of illness experiences. Where is illness cared for in society? That is to say, what health care system handles illness problems?

When health planners or public health professionals draw a map of the health care system, they usually include only the facilities of the biomedical profession: namely, hospitals, clinics, nursing homes, and rehabilitation units. An anthropologist who was asked to chart health care in society would describe a much broader health care system with rather different components.

Remarkably, most care for illness is delivered not in biomedical institutions or by professional practitioners but by the family (Kleinman 1980, 179–202). This family (or popular) sector of care is where illness exacerbation is first identified and coped with.

Treatments of many kinds may be used as self- and family care, including: rest, change in diet, special foods, massage, over-the-counter medications, prescription drugs on hand, a large number of devices from humidifiers to special furniture, emotional support, and religious practices. This lay arena of care also includes advice from friends and others about what to do, when to seek professional care, where to go for it, and whether to follow the advice of current professional care givers or change to other practitioners. The neighborhood pharmacy and health food store are frequently drawn into this lay therapeutic network.

For the doctor concerned with chronically ill patients, the family arena of care is of great importance. Indeed, among certain ethnic minorities and non-Western cultures, the family, not the individual, is regarded as the locus of responsibility for making therapeutic decisions (as we saw in the instance of the Chinese patient with cancer described in chapter 9). Yet few physicians have acquired systematic knowledge about the family context of care or worked out ways to evaluate how their patients' illnesses are affected by the family. Not so for drug firms, whose advertising in the media—a major contribution to the cost of medication—is directed principally at the family as lay practitioner. The popular sector of care is a major source of expenditures, an enormous industry that bypasses physicians. Commercialization, which does have the advantage of increasing the family's access to useful treatment interventions, regrettably all too frequently has brought with it inappropriate, unnecessary, and frankly dangerous practices.

The challenge for medical reform is to develop the sensibility of the practitioner for the potentially adaptive aspects of lay care. Then he can help his patients and their families to increase their command over the knowledge and technical resources that will make self-care more effective. Physicians' willingness to encourage informed self-care should be tied to reform in the laws governing patients' access to controlled drugs deemed essential to their treatment. Patients and their families can now purchase devices to monitor blood pressure, to check the ear canals of children, and to test urine. Why shouldn't they be able to purchase without prescription and use under qualified supervision those medications essential to their conditions? The chronic patient is (or can learn to become) an expert on his illness experience; he can also develop a few technical skills for treating his disease. Videotapes and written materials can be prepared specifically for this purpose. The act of formally training patients and families as care givers is a message of empowerment that is of symbolic as well as practical significance. Viewing the patient as a colleague and therapy as a collaboration would, I believe, greatly improve the quality of the patient–doctor relationship. My impression is that we are slowly and haphazardly moving in the direction of this change. What is needed now is organized change of a more substantial kind.

Though it sounds simple, this type of medical reform is hedged in with thorny questions. It would require coordinated political, legal, and medical change—thus, it can easily be dismissed as utopian. But I think that would be a sad error. We already have a large self-help movement in North American society, the popularity of which is in part a form of resistance to perceived professional dominance and in part a valid recognition of the limits of medicine. Techniques developed in training physician assistants and other paramedical staff can be redeployed in the family sector of care. Politicians might become interested in such change because of the possibility that it would reduce health care costs and alter the increasingly adversarial stance of patients toward the medical profession. Public health planners and experts in health education might be encouraged to figure out means to rationalize care given by patients and families. Social survey and ethnographic information that more precisely maps lay decision making and treatment actions will be necessary. And it will be essential to understand better the legal, legislative, and ethical aspects of such change. But, in one form or another, the chronically ill and their families will increasingly demand—and, I believe, ultimately succeed in winning—a greater degree of control over the resources required in their care.

A step away from the family sector is the folk sector of care. Folk practitioners include a very wide variety of nonprofessionalized and usually noninstitutionalized "specialists." Folk healers range from quasi-paramedical professionals to religious healers, from a huge assortment of lay psychotherapists to semilegal and even illegal peddlers of nostrums, from traditional healers in ethnic minorities to health food advisers, massage therapists, and television performers who reach out to members of the mainstream population. There is a long history of folk healing in North American society; contrary to the expectations of many, folk healers have proliferated, not decreased, as our society has developed technologically. McGuire (1983), for instance, described more than a hundred varieties of folk healing available in a middle-class suburb of New York City. These ranged from the traditional (for example, religious) to the latest (for example, polarity therapy, iridology, co-therapy, and so forth) forms of folk healing. Doctors of traditional Chinese medicine, yogis, various Christian and Jewish spiritual healers, herbalists, experts in martial arts and other forms of exercise, and characters who could only be described as unscrupulous charlatans were active in the treatment of some of the patients described in this book.

While folk healers often are helpful, they sometimes give advice and prescribe remedies that interfere with biomedical treatment and that are, in and of themselves, dangerous (Kleinman and Gale 1982). Physicians tend to be ill informed about their patients' utilization of folk healers, even where such knowledge is relevant to understand noncompliance and poor outcome. Patients hesitate to tell physicians about nonbiomedical healers whom they reckon their doctors disdain; for their part, physicians simply tend not to think about or inquire into this aspect of care. The challenge to biomedicine is for physicians to recognize that folk healers are important not just in the Third World but in contemporary Western society, too. So ubiquitous are they and so anxious are the chronically ill to receive help of any kind that doctors should *assume* that in the course of chronic illness their patients are likely to receive folk treatments. Respect for the patient's viewpoint should include a willingness to learn about the use of so-called alternative practitioners. It should also mean that the physician tries to determine when resort to folk healers and their treatments is useful and when folk healing is potentially harmful. The physician's appraisals should be shared with patients as an integral part of the negotiation between professional and lay explanatory models.

The professional sector of care in the North American health care system is also plural. There are alternative therapeutic professions— such as chiropractic, osteopathy, and naturopathy—with their own professional organizations, licensing statutes and exams, schools, texts, and research. Ophthamologists compete with optometrists for patients who require prescriptions for eyeglasses. Psychiatrists compete with social workers and psychologists in the counseling of families. In certain places obstetricians compete with nurse-midwives for delivering babies. Biomedical institutions, though usually controlled by physicians, chiefly employ persons who are not doctors. Nurses, social workers, psychologists, physical therapists, occupational therapists, dental hygienists, respiratory and radiology technicians, physician assistants, laboratory technicians, ambulance drivers, mental health aids, translators, nutritionists, experts in the fitting of prostheses, and the large numbers of support staff in hospitals and nursing homes comprise more than 95 percent of the employees in biomedical institutions. Much of the care received by the disabled is provided by members of these other health professions. Even when the chronically ill visit their physicians, most of their time is spent with receptionists, nurses, and various paraprofessionals. Such workers tend to be undervalued by physicians. Their contribution to the patient's care is often unrecognized, as is their contribution to delays, insensitive communication, and patients' frustration with treatment.

It is my personal experience that even when physicians are sensitive to psychosocial issues their office staff and the paraprofessionals who collaborate with them may not be. Indeed, some of the most reductionistically mechanical and insensitive care givers I have come across are relatively low-level clerks and technicians who seem unaware that what they do is part of the patient's experience of care. Clearly, all members of the helping professions should be trained in a framework that respects the physician's suffering and attends humanely to the illness experience.

The professional sector's institutions are profession- rather than patient-centered. Zerubavel (1981) has shown this to be the case with the organization of time in the hospital, which is ordered to fit the work hours and needs of hospital staff more than the needs of patients and their families. And this is true of the way space is arranged, too. Movement through the professional sector of care bewilders many patients. There are few maps to make sense of the system for users. Communication between its components breaks down. Chronic patients spend such a large portion of their lives in the professional system that they know better than their doctors which structural barriers and unnecessary bureaucratic steps waste their time and energy and create frustration and bitterness. This insider's knowledge of the bureaucracy's failings is rarely taken into account to accommodate the professional system to patients' needs. The challenge is to do this.

But the professional institutions of care also frustrate practitioners, especially those interested in addressing the patient's and family's illness problems. I have already mentioned how the time constraints and reward structure of clinical practice work against the kinds of therapeutic interventions that are most useful in treating the chronically ill. Medical legal concerns are particularly mischievous here. Physicians must constantly attend to the potential legal implications of their care, which tends to dissuade innovative therapeutic approaches while it encourages care givers to cover their back and stick to the letter (not the spirit) of bureaucratic constraints. Can a physician work out empowering treatment algorithms for enhancing his patients' self-care if he fears that a mistake by a patient or family member may place the doctor at risk for a legal suit involving millions of dollars? The tendency to allow the courts to resolve ethical questions about, say, how much care must be given in the terminal phase of illness to prolong life—even when patient and family wish to terminate care—discourages practitioners, making them hesitant and suspicious at just the stage in chronic illness when their humanity is most needed. The immense profusion of bureaucratic paperwork is meant to control the practitioner's actions through a regulatory approach taken over from various governmental sectors. It ends up numbing physicians and usurping huge blocks of time better spent with patients. The bureaucratization of care arguably has worsened the problems experienced by the chronically ill in negotiating health care institutions. For bureaucratic efficiency can be (and frequently is) the enemy of high quality care. Perhaps the most difficult challenge, as several of the physicians in chapter 14 observe, is how to humanize biomedical institutions.

The recent proliferation of lay and professional "therapists" who claim special expertise in ministering to the psychological, sexual, and family aspects of chronic illness confuses patients and practitioners. Is counseling something the practitioner should relinquish to other specialists while he pursues increasingly complex techno-logical questions? If so, will such a radical split in the functions of the practitioner separate the psychosocial component of care even further from its biomedical counterpart? Will this split end up alien-ating and dehumanizing the physician? If medical psychotherapy is integrated as a core clinical task of the physician, how is its quality to be assured? How will it be funded and evaluated? Dozens of equally difficult practical questions surround the professional sector of care in contemporary society. Up to now, the health debate in North America has centered on large-scale policy questions. But I wish to argue that questions about the small-scale clinical nature of our health care system must also become the focus of debate if real medical reform is to occur.

It is crucial to integrate the care of illness with the treatment of disease. Programs that foster such integration are few and far be-tween, both because medical developments are tending to split dis-ease ever further from illness and because both professional and bureaucratic priorities have not given this objective a high standing. Ideally, health care institutions should be reinvented to build this vision into the structure of delivery of care. In the practical world, reinvention is infeasible. But reform is not. Such reform must be seen as a change in the values that underpin the health care system. At present, the system is concerned principally with financial gain, institutional efficiency, professional competition, and a very narrow disease-centered paradigm of practice. What is needed to change this value hierarchy is the societywide debate I have already recom-mended, a debate that could bring together popular and profes-sional movements for change in a politically effective manner to focus the necessary pressures on the health care system.

Medical Research

To provide intellectual support for the reform of medicine so that it is better prepared to develop paradigms of practice aimed at caring for patients' illness needs, there must be a reciprocal transformation of medical research. We need to see medicine as possessing three great sources of knowledge: biological science; clinical science; and medical social science and humanities. Heretofore, the first two disciplines of research have received substantial resources and become robust enterprises. The third research field is at present inadequately developed. Until anthropological, sociological, psychological, historical, ethical, and literary studies (the human sciences of medicine) become a substantial division of medical research, we will lack the knowledge needed to more systematically conceptualize illness experience and meanings. As long as we lack such knowledge, the development of new paradigms of practice and effective treatment strategies will be delayed and the research enterprise will remain enormously unbalanced toward disease questions.

We need centers of excellence in the medical social sciences and humanities, as part of medical schools and health care institutions, where researchers can create and codify new knowledge, criticize existing knowledge, and develop usable methodologies in clinical settings. To achieve this goal will require more research funds for social science research and more research positions for medical social scientists and humanists. Although medical humanities should not be simplistically equated with humanistic care, it is more likely that practitioners will develop the requisite attitudes, knowledge, and skills if they are trained within the framework of a social and moral approach to medicine.

Again, given the limited resources and conflicting claims on those resources of a practical world, it will take pressure from both outside and within medicine to bring about such a change. Until the academic discourse of medicine is expanded beyond the languages of molecules and drugs to include the language of experience and meanings, however, medical science will reinforce the profession's resistance to the problems of illness rather than contribute to the broadening of its vision. Research that avoids the human side of disorder places the profession and its practitioners in iron chains of restricted knowledge. So fettered, medicine and doctors are unable to address some of the most difficult yet essential questions in the care of the chronically ill; the physician is prevented from having a personal stake in the patient's condition, and medicine from applying moral knowledge to suffering.

I have written this volume with a far different image in mind. If we can say that war is too important to be left solely to generals and politics solely to politicans, then we should also say that illness and care are far too important to be left solely in the hands of medical professionals, especially those who configure these innately human issues in a framework that constricts our humanity. For what should be the work of the physician of the chronically ill, if not this: that he is there in the experiential realm of suffering together with his patient and the members of the family. He joins them in that diffi-cult experience to help where feasible with the medical manage-ment of the disease process. But also, at times when technical inter-ventions are stymied, in the worst moments, he participates in the moral equivalent of what the illness experience means for patient and family. Against the commercialized self-images of our age, which corrode altruism and convert decency into merely a profes-sional gesture, the experience of the healer can be a quest for a kind of human wisdom, a model of forbearance and courage, a form of goodness, a lesson in the essentials of humanity.

References

Alexander, L. 1981. The double-bind between dialysis patients and their health practitioners. In *The relevance of social sciences for medicine,* edited by L. Eisenberg and A. Kleinman, 307–29. Dordrecht, Holland: D. Reidel.

———. 1982. Illness maintenance and the new American sick role. In *Clinically applied anthropology,* edited by N. Chrisman and T. Maretzki, 351–67. Dordrecht, Holland: D. Reidel.

American Psychiatric Association. 1980. *Diagnostic and statistical manual of mental disorders.* 3d ed. (DSM-III). Washington, D.C.

Aries, P. 1981. *The hour of our death.* Translated by Helen Weaver. New York: Alfred A. Knopf.

Balint, M. [1957] 1973. *The doctor, his patient and the illness.* New York: International Universities Press.

Barme, G., and B. Lee, eds. and trans. 1979. *The wounded: New stories of the cultural revolution, 1977–78.* Hong Kong: Joint.

Barnes, D. M. 1987. Mystery disease at Lake Tahoe challenges virologists and clinicians. *Science* 234:541–42.

Bate, W. J. 1975. *Samuel Johnson.* New York: Harcourt Brace Jovanovich.

Beeman, W. 1985. Dimensions of dysphoria. In *Culture and depression,* edited by A. Kleinman and B. Good, 216 43. Berkeley: University of California Press.

Bellah, R., et al. 1984. *Habits of the heart.* Berkeley: University of California Press.

Benveniste, E. 1945. La doctrine medicale des indo-européens. *Revue de l'histoire des religions* 130:5–12.

Berkman, L. 1981. Physical health and the social environment. In *The relevance of social science for medicine,* edited by L. Eisenberg and A. Kleinman, 51–76. Dordrecht, Holland: D. Reidel.

Berlin, I. 1978. The hedgehog and the fox. In *Russian thinkers,* 22–81. Harmondsworth, England: Penguin.

Black, D. 1980. Inequality in health: A report. London: Department of Health and Social Security.

Bloch, M., and W. Parry, eds. 1982. *Death and the regeneration of life.* New York: Cambridge University Press.

Blumhagen, D. 1980. Hyper-tension: A folk illness with a medical name. *Culture, Medicine and Psychiatry* 4:197–227.

Bokan, J., et al. 1981. Tertiary gain in chronic pain. *Pain* 10:331–35.

Bond, M. 1986. *The psychology of the Chinese people.* Hong Kong: Oxford University Press.

Bosk, C. L. 1979. *Forgive and remember: Managing medical failure.* Chicago: University of Chicago Press.

Boswell, J. [1799] 1965. *Life of Johnson.* London: Oxford University Press.

Brandt, A. 1984. *No magic bullet.* New York: Oxford University Press.

Brice, J. A. 1987. Empathy lost. *Harvard Medical Alumni Bulletin* 60(4):28–32.

Briggs, J. 1970. *Never in anger: Portrait of an Eskimo family.* Cambridge, Mass.: Harvard University Press.

Brown, G., and T. Harris. 1978. *The social origins of depression.* New York: Free Press.

Browne, T. 1643. *Religio medici.* London: Andrew Crooke.

Burton, R. [1621] 1948. *The anatomy of melancholy.* Edited by F. Dell and P. Jordan-Smith. New York: Tudor.

Bynum, C. 1985. Disease and death in the Middle Ages. *Culture, Medicine and Psychiatry* 9:97–102.

Cassell, E. J. 1976. Disease as an "it": Conceptions of disease as revealed by patients' presentation of symptoms. *Social science and medicine* 10:143–46.

———. 1985. *Talking with patients.* Vol. 1, *The theory of doctor-patient communication.* Cambridge, Mass.: MIT Press.

Chen, J. 1978. *The execution of Mayor Yin and other stories from the great proletarian cultural revolution.* Bloomington: Indiana University Press.

Cohen, S., and L. Syme, eds. 1985. *Social support and health.* New York: Academic Press.

Conrad, J. [1915] 1957. *Victory.* Garden City, N.Y.: Doubleday Anchor Books.

Crick, B. 1980. *George Orwell: A life.* Boston: Little, Brown.

Daniel, V. 1984. *Fluid signs.* Berkeley: University of California Press.

Dressler, W. W. 1985. Psychosomatic symptoms, stress and modernization. *Culture, Medicine and Psychiatry* 9:257–94.

Drinka, G. F. 1984. *The birth of neurosis: Myth, malady and the Victorians.* New York: Simon and Schuster.

Ebigbo, P. O. 1982. Development of a culture specific (Nigeria) screening scale of somatic complaints indicating psychiatric disturbance. *Culture, Medicine and Psychiatry* 1:29–43.

Eckman, P. 1980. Biological and cultural contributions to body and facial movement in the expression of emotion. In *Explaining emotions,* edited by A. O. Rorty, 73–201. Berkeley: University of California Press.

Eisenberg, L. 1981. The physician as interpreter: Ascribing meaning to the illness experience. *Comprehensive Psychiatry* 22:239–48.

Engel, G. 1968. A life setting conducive to illness: The giving-in given-up complex. *Annals of Internal Medicine* 69:293–300.

———. 1971. Sudden and rapid death from psychological stress. *Annals of Internal Medicine* 74:771–82.

———. 1977. The need for a new medical model: A challenge for biomedicine. *Science* 196:129–36.

Enright, D. J., ed. 1983. *The Oxford book of death.* New York: Oxford University Press.

Erikson, E. 1958. *Young man Luther.* New York: W. W. Norton.

Fanon, F. 1968. *The wretched of the earth.* New York: Grove.

Favazza, A. R. 1987. *Bodies under seige: Self-mutilation in culture and psychiatry.* Baltimore: Johns Hopkins University Press.

Feinstein, H. 1984. *Becoming William James.* Ithaca, N.Y.: Cornell University Press.

Fitzpatrick, R. 1984. Lay concepts of illness. In *The experience of illness,* edited by R. Fitzpatrick et al., 11–31. London: Tavistock.

Foucault, M. 1966. *Madness and civilization.* Translated by Richard Howard. New York: Mentor Books.

Fox, R. C. 1959. *Experiment perilous: Physicians and patients facing the unknown.* New York: Free Press.

Frankenberg, R. 1986. Sickness as cultural performance: Drama, trajectory, and pilgrimage. *International Journal of Health Services* 16(4):603–26.

Freidson, E. 1986. *Professional powers: A study of the institutionalization of formal knowledge.* Chicago: University of Chicago Press.

Frolic, M. 1981. *Mao's people.* Cambridge, Mass.: Harvard University Press.

Geertz, C. 1986. Making experiences, authorizing selves. In *The anthropology of experience,* edited by V. W. Turner and E. M. Bruner, 373–80. Urbana: University of Illinois Press.

Goffman, E. 1963. *Stigma.* New York: Simon and Schuster.

Good, B. J. 1977. The heart of what's the matter: The semantics of illness in Iran. *Culture, Medicine and Psychiatry* 1:25–28.

Gottfried, R. S. 1983. *The Black Death: Natural and human disaster in medieval Europe.* New York: Free Press.

Groddeck, G. V. 1977. *The meaning of illness.* Translated by George Mander. London: Hogarth Press.

Groopman, L. 1987. Medical internship as moral education. *Culture, Medicine and Psychiatry* 11:207–28.

Hackett, T. P., and A. D. Weisman. 1960. Psychiatric management of operative syndromes. *Psychosomatic Medicine* 22(4):267–82.

Hahn, R., and A. Gaines. 1985. *Physicians of Western medicine.* Dordrecht, Holland: D. Reidel.

Hahn, R., and A. Kleinman. 1983. Biomedical practice and anthropological theory: Frameworks and directions. *Annual Review of Anthropology* 12:305–33.

Hampton, J. R., et al. 1975. Relative contributions of history taking, physical examination and laboratory investigation to diagnosis and management of medical outpatients. *British Medical Journal* 2:486–89.

Heaney, S. 1980. *Preoccupations: Selected prose 1968–78.* New York: Farrar, Straus, Giroux.

Heaney, S., and T. Hughes, eds. 1982. *The rattle bag.* London: Faber and Faber.

Heilbroner, R. 1986. *The nature and logic of capitalism.* New York: W. W. Norton.

Helman, C. 1978. "Feed a cold, starve a fever": Folk models of infection in an English suburban community. *Culture, Medicine and Psychiatry* 2:107–37.

———. 1984. *Culture, health and disease.* Boston: Wright.

———. 1985. Psyche, soma and society: The cultural construction of psychosomatic disease. *Culture, Medicine and Psychiatry* 9:1–26.

———. 1987. Heart disease and the cultural construction of time. *Social Science and Medicine* 24:969–79.

Horowitz, M. J., et al. 1984. Brief psychotherapy of bereavement reactions. *Archives of General Psychiatry* 41(5):438–48.

Hsu, F. 1971. Psychosocial homeostasis and *jen:* Conceptual tools for advancing psychological anthropology. *American Anthropologist* 73:23–44.

James, W. [1890] 1981. *The principles of psychology,* vol. 1. Cambridge, Mass.: Harvard University Press.

———. [1899] 1958. *Talks to teachers.* New York: W. W. Norton.

Janzen, J. 1978. *The quest for therapy in Lower Zaire.* Berkeley: University of California Press.

Johnson, T. H., ed. 1970. *The complete poems of Emily Dickinson.* London: Faber and Faber.

Kafka, F. [1919] 1971. A country doctor. In *The collected stories,* edited by N. N. Glatzer. New York: Schocken.

Karasu, T. B., and R. I. Steinmuller, eds. 1978. *Psychotherapeutics in medicine.* New York: Grune and Stratton.

Katon, W., and A. Kleinman. 1981. Doctor–patient negotiation. In *The relevance of social science for medicine,* edited by L. Eisenberg and A. Kleinman, 253–79. Dordrecht, Holland: D. Reidel.

Katon, W., et al. 1982. Depression and somatization, parts 1 and 2. *American Journal of Medicine* 72:127–35, 241–47.

Kaufert, J. M., and W. W. Coolage. 1984. Role conflict among "culture brokers": The experience of native American medical interpreters. *Social Science and Medicine* 18(3):283–86.

Kaufert, P., and P. Gilbert. 1986. Women, menopause and medicalization. *Culture, Medicine and Psychiatry* 10:7–22.

Keyes, C. 1985. The interpretative basis of depression. In *Culture and depression,* edited by A. Kleinman and B. Good, 153–74. Berkeley: University of California Press.

Kleinman, A. 1980. *Patients and healers in the context of culture.* Berkeley: University of California Press.

———. 1982. Neurasthenia and depression: A study of somatization and culture in China. *Culture, Medicine and Psychiatry* 6:117–89.

———. 1986. *Social origins of distress and disease: Depression, neurasthenia and pain in modern China.* New Haven: Yale University Press.

Kleinman, A., and J. Gale. 1982. Patients treated by physicians and folk healers in Taiwan: A comparative outcome study. *Culture, Medicine and Psychiatry* 6:405–23.

Kleinman, A., and B. Good, eds. 1985. *Culture and depression.* Berkeley: University of California Press.

Kleinman, A., and J. Kleinman. 1985. Somatization. In *Culture and depression,* edited by A. Kleinman and B. Good, 429–90. Berkeley: University of California Press.

Kleinman, A., and T. Y. Lin, eds. 1982. *Normal and abnormal behavior in Chinese culture.* Dordrecht, Holland: D. Reidel.

Langness, L. L., and G. Frank. 1984. *Lives: An anthropological approach to biography.* Novato, Calif.: Chandler and Sharp.

Lasch, C. 1977. *Haven in a heartless world: The family besieged.* New York: Basic Books.

———. 1979. *The culture of narcissism: American life in an age of diminishing expectations.* New York: W. W. Norton.

Lazare, A. 1987. Shame and humiliation in the medical encounter. *Archives of Internal Medicine* 147:1653–58.

Legge, J., trans. [1891] 1959. *The texts of Taoism.* New York: Julian Press.

Leigh, H., and M. Reiser. 1980. *The patient: Biological, psychosocial and social dimensions of medical practice.* New York: Plenum.

Levy, R. 1973. *Tahitians: Mind and experience in the Society Islands.* Berkeley: University of California Press.

Lewis, G. 1975. *Knowledge of illness in a Sepik society.* London: Athlone.

———. 1977. Fear of sorcery and the problem of death by suggestion. In *The anthropology of the body,* edited by J. Blacking, 111–44. New York: Academic Press.

Lewis, I. M. 1971. *Ecstatic religion: An anthropological study of spirit possession and shamanism.* Harmondsworth, England: Penguin.

Li, Y. Y., and K. S. Yang, eds. 1974. *Zhongguo ren de xingge (The character of the Chinese).* Taipei, Taiwan: Academia Sinica.

Liang, H., and J. Shapiro. 1983. *Son of the revolution.* New York: Alfred A. Knopf.

Lin, T. Y., and L. Eisenberg, eds. 1985. *Mental health planning for one billion people.* Vancouver: University of British Columbia Press.

Lin, T. Y., and M. C. Lin. 1982. Love, denial and rejection: Responses of Chinese families to mental illness. In *Normal and abnormal behavior in Chinese culture,* edited by A. Kleinman and T. Y. Lin, 387–401. Dordrecht, Holland: D. Reidel.

Link, P. 1983. *Stubborn weeds: Popular and controversial Chinese literature after the Cultural Revolution.* Bloomington: University of Indiana Press.

Lipkin, M. 1974. *The care of patients: Concepts and tactics.* New York: Oxford University Press.

Lipowski, Z. J. 1968. Review of consultation psychiatry and psychosomatic medicine. *Psychosomatic Medicine* 30:395–405.

———. 1969. Psychosocial aspects of disease. *Annals of Internal Medicine* 71:1197–1206.

Littlewood, R., and M. Lipsedge. 1987. The butterfly and the serpent: Culture, psychopathology and biomedicine. *Culture, Medicine and Psychiatry* 11:337–56.

Longhoffer, J. 1980. Dying or living? The double bind. *Culture, Medicine and Psychiatry* 4:119–36.

Lown, B., et al. 1980. Psychophysiological factors in cardiac sudden death. *American Journal of Psychiatry* 137(11):1325–35.

Lu Xun. 1981. A madman's diary. In *The collected stories of Lu Xun,* translated by Yang Xianyi and G. Yang, 26–38. Bloomington: University of Indiana Press.

McGuire, M. B. 1983. Words of power: Personal empowerment and healing. *Culture, Medicine and Psychiatry* 7:221–40.

McHugh, S., and T. M. Vallis, eds. 1986. *Illness behavior.* New York: Plenum.

MacIntyre, A. 1981. *After virtue.* South Bend, Ind.: University of Notre Dame Press.

McKinlay, S., and J. McKinlay. 1985. *Health status and health care utilization by menopausal women.* New York: Plenum.

Madan, T. N. 1987. Living and dying. In *Non-renunciation themes and interpretations of Hindu culture,* edited by T. N. Madan, 118–41. New Delhi: Oxford University Press.

Mayr, R. 1982. *The growth of biological thought, diversity, evolution and inheritance.* Cambridge, Mass.: Harvard University Press.

Mechanic, D. 1986. Role of social factors in health and well being. *Integrative Psychiatry* 4:2–11.

Metzger, T. 1982. Selfhood and authority in neo-Confucian China. In *Normal and abnormal behavior in Chinese culture,* edited by A. Kleinman and T. Y. Lin, 7–28. Dordrecht, Holland: D. Reidel.

Mishler, E. 1984. *The discourse of medicine: Dialectics of medical interviews.* Norwood, N.J.: Ablex.

Mitchell, W. E. 1977. Changing others: The anthropological study of therapeutic systems. *Medical Anthropology Newsletter* 8(3):15–20.

Moerman, D. E. 1983. Anthropology of symbolic healing. *Current Anthropology* 20(1):59–80.

Mumford, E., et al. 1984. A new look at evidence about reduced cost of medical utilization following mental health treatment. *American Journal of Psychiatry* 141:1145–58.

Munn, N. D. 1973. *Walbiri iconography.* Ithaca, N.Y.: Cornell University Press.

Myers, G. E. 1986. *William James: His life and thought.* New Haven: Yale University Press.

Nations, M., et al. 1985. "Hidden" popular illnesses in primary care: Residents' recognition and clinical implications. *Culture, Medicine and Psychiatry* 9:223–40.

Navarro, V. 1986. *Crisis, health and medicine.* London: Tavistock.

Needham, R. 1972. *Belief, language and experience.* Chicago: University of Chicago Press.

———, ed. 1973 *Right and left: Essays on dual symbolic classification.* Chicago: University of Chicago Press.

Nichter, M. 1982. Idioms of distress. *Culture, Medicine and Psychiatry* 5:379–408.

Noll, P. 1984. *Diktate über Sterben und Tod.* Zurich: Pendo Verlag.

Oakeshott, M. [1933] 1978. *Experience and its modes.* Cambridge: Cambridge University Press.
Obeyesekere, G. 1985. Depression, Buddhism and the work of culture in Sri Lanka. In *Culture and depression,* edited by A. Kleinman and B. Good, 134–52. Berkeley: University of California Press.
Osterweis, M., et al. 1984. *Bereavement.* Washington, D.C.: National Academy Press.
Osterweis, M., et al. 1987. *Pain and disability: A report of the Institute of Medicine, National Academy of Sciences.* Washington, D.C.: National Academy Press.
Parish, W., and M. K. Whyte. 1978. *Village and family in contemporary China.* Chicago: University of Chicago Press.
Plessner, H. 1970. *Laughing and crying: A study of the limits of human behavior.* Evanston, Ill.: Northwestern University Press.
Porkert, M. 1974. *The theoretical foundations of Chinese medicine: Systems of correspondence.* Cambridge, Mass.: MIT Press.
Potter, J. 1970. Wind, water, bones and souls: The religious world of the Cantonese peasant. *Journal of Oriental Studies* (Hong Kong University) 8:139–53.
Ratushinskaya, I. 1987. Two poems from prison, translated by F. P. Brent and C. Avins. *New York Review of Books,* May 7, 19.
Reid, J., and N. Williams. 1985. Voodoo death in East Arnhem Land: Whose reality? *American Anthropologist* 96(1):121–33.
Reiser, D., and D. Rosen. 1985. *Medicine as a human experience.* Rockville, Md.: Aspen.
Reiser, S. J. 1978. *Medicine and the reign of technology.* Cambridge: Cambridge University Press.
Rieff, P. 1966. *The triumph of the therapeutic.* New York: Harper and Row.
Roethke, T. 1982. *The collected poems.* Seattle: University of Washington Press.
Rosaldo, M. 1980. *Knowledge and passion: Ilongot notions of self and social life.* Cambridge: Cambridge University Press.
Rosen, G., and A. Kleinman. 1984. Social science in the clinic: Applied contributions from anthropology to medical teaching and patient care. In *Behavioral science and the practice of medicine,* edited by J. Carr and H. Dengerink, 85–104. New York: Elsevier.
Rosenberg, C. 1986. Disease and social order in America. *Milbank Memorial Quarterly* 64(Suppl. 1):34–5.
Rycroft, C. 1986. *Psychoanalysis and beyond.* Chicago: University of Chicago Press.
Sacks, O. [1985] 1987. *The man who mistook his wife for a hat.* New York: Harper and Row.
Sandner, D. 1979. *Navaho symbols of healing.* New York: Harcourt Brace Jovanovich.
Scarry, E. 1985. *The body in pain.* New York: Oxford University Press.
Schieffelin, E. 1976. *The sorrow of the lonely and the burning of the dancers.* New York: St. Martin's Press.
———. 1985. The cultural analysis of depressive affect: An example from New Guinea. In *Culture and depression,* edited by A. Kleinman and B. Good, 101–33. Berkeley: University of California Press.
Schutz, A. 1968. *On phenomenlogy and social relations.* Chicago: University of Chicago Press.
Showalter, E. 1985. *The female malady: Women, madness, and English culture, 1830–1980.* New York: Penguin.
Shweder, R. 1985. Menstrual pollution, soul loss and the comparative study of emotions. In *Culture and depression,* edited by A. Kleinman and B. Good, 82–215. Berkeley: University of California Press.
Sicherman, B. 1977. The uses of diagnosis: Doctors, patients and neurasthenics. *Journal of the History of Medicine and Allied Sciences* 32(1):33–54.
Simons, R., and C. Hughes, eds. 1985. *Culture bound syndromes.* Dordrecht, Holland: D. Reidel.
Slaby, A. E., and A. S. Glicksman. 1987. Adaptation of physicians to managing life threatening illness. *Integrative Psychiatry* 4:162–72.
Spiro, H. 1986. *Doctors, patients and placebos.* New Haven: Yale University Press.
Starr, P. 1982. *The social transformation of American medicine.* New York: Basic Books.
Stjernsward, J., et al. 1986. Quality of life in cancer patients: Goals and objectives. In *Assessment of quality of life and cancer treatment,* edited by V. Ventafridda et al., 1–8. Amsterdam: Excerpta Medica.
Stone, D. 1984. *The disabled state.* Philadelphia: Temple University Press.

Strauss, A., et al. 1985. *Social organization of medical work*. Chicago: University of Chicago Press.

Taussig, M. 1980. *The devil and commodity fetishism in South America*. Chapel Hill: University of North Carolina Press.

————. 1986. Reification and the consciousness of the patient. *Social Science and Medicine* 14B:3–13.

Thurston, A. F. 1987. *Enemies of the people: The ordeals of the intellectuals in China's great cultural revolution*. New York: Alfred A. Knopf.

Tiger, L. 1980. *Optimism: A biology of hope*. New York: Alfred A. Knopf.

Tseng, W. S., and J. Hsu. 1969. Chinese culture, personality formation and mental illness. *International Journal of Social Psychiatry* 16:5–14.

Tseng, W. S., and D. Wu., eds. 1985. *Chinese culture and mental health*. New York: Academic Press.

Turner, B. 1985. *The body and society*. Oxford: Basil Blackwell.

Turner, J. A., and C. R. Chapman. 1982. Psychological interventions for chronic pain: A critical review, parts 1 and 2. *Pain* 12:1–21, 23–26.

Turner, V. 1967. *The forest of symbols*. Ithaca, N.Y.: Cornell University Press.

Unschuld, P. 1985. *Medicine in China: A history of ideas*. Berkeley: University of California Press.

Veatch, R. M. 1977. *Case studies in medical ethics*. Cambridge, Mass.: Harvard University Press.

Wagner, R. 1986. *Symbols that stand for themselves*. Chicago: University of Chicago Press.

Warner, W. L. [1937] 1958. *A black civilization: A social study of an Australian tribe*, revised edition. New York: Harper and Brothers.

Watson, J. L. in press a. Funeral specialists in Cantonese society: Pollution, performance and social hierarchy. In *Death ritual in late imperial and modern China*, edited by J. L. Watson and E. Rausch. Berkeley: University of California Press.

————. in press b. The structure of Chinese funerary rites: Elementary forms. In *Death ritual in late imperial and modern China*, edited by J. L. Watson and E. Rausch. Berkeley: University of California Press.

Waxler, N. 1977. Is mental illness cured in traditional societies? *Culture, Medicine and Psychiatry* 1:233–53.

————. 1981. Learning to be a leper. In *Social contexts of health, illness and patient care*, edited by E. Michler et al., 169–94. Cambridge: Cambridge University Press.

Weisman, A. D., and T. P. Hackett. 1961. Predilection to death. *Psychosomatic Medicine* 23(3):232–56.

Williams, G. H., and P. Wood. 1986. Common sense beliefs about illness. *Lancet*, Dec. 20–27, 1435–37.

Witherspoon, G. 1975. The central concepts of Navajo world view. In *Linguistics and anthropology: In honor of C. F. Voegelin*, edited by D. Kinkade et al., 701–20. Lisse, Belgium: Peter de Ridder.

Wolf, M. 1972. *Women and the family in rural Taiwan*. Stanford, Calif.: Stanford University Press.

Zborowski, M. 1969. *People in pain*. San Francisco: Jossey-Bass.

Zerubavel, E. 1981. *Patterns of time in hospital life*. Chicago: University of Chicago Press.

Zola, I. K. 1966. Culture and symptoms: An analysis of patients' presenting complaints. *American Sociological Review* 3:615–30.

————. 1982. *Missing pieces: A chronicle of living with a disability*. Philadelphia: Temple University Press.

Index